Art and the Arab Spring

The revolutions that began to sweep across countries in North Africa and the Middle East in December 2010 – like other revolutions in diverse modern historical contexts – have often been articulated, internally and externally, in black-and-white terms of success or failure, liberation or constraint, for or against, friend or enemy. These internal and external clichés are perpetuated by what Jellel Gasteli has called 'icons of revolutionary exoticism'. Paying particular attention to works from the Tunisian revolution of 2011, this book examines a diverse body of art including photography, sculpture, graffiti, performance, video and installation by over twenty-five artists. Examining how art can evoke the idea of revolution, *Art and the Arab Spring* reveals a new way of understanding these revolutions, their profound cultural impact and the meaning of the term 'revolution' itself.

SIOBHÁN SHILTON is Professor of French Studies and the Visual Arts at the University of Bristol. She has published on art and the 'Arab Uprisings', cultural encounters (particularly between France and the Maghreb) in late-twentieth- and twenty-first-century photography, video, graffiti, graphic novels, installation and performance art, and twentieth-century travel literature in French. Her research has been supported by grant awards from the Arts and Humanities Research Council.

The Global Middle East

General Editors
Arshin Adib-Moghaddam, *SOAS, University of London*
Ali Mirsepassi, *New York University*

Editorial Advisory Board
Faisal Devji, *University of Oxford*
John Hobson, *University of Sheffield*
Firoozeh Kashani-Sabet, *University of Pennsylvania*
Madawi Al-Rasheed, *London School of Economics and Political Science*
David Ryan, *University College Cork, Ireland*

The Global Middle East series seeks to broaden and deconstruct the geographical boundaries of the 'Middle East' as a concept to include North Africa, Central and South Asia, and diaspora communities in Western Europe and North America. The series features fresh scholarship that employs theoretically rigorous and innovative methodological frameworks resonating across relevant disciplines in the humanities and the social sciences. In particular, the general editors welcome approaches that focus on mobility, the erosion of nation-state structures, travelling ideas and theories, transcendental techno-politics, the decentralisation of grand narratives, and the dislocation of ideologies inspired by popular movements. The series will also consider translations of works by authors in these regions whose ideas are salient to global scholarly trends but have yet to be introduced to the Anglophone academy.

Other books in the series:

1. *Transnationalism in Iranian Political Thought: The Life and Times of Ahmad Fardid,* Ali Mirsepassi
2. *Psycho-nationalism: Global Thought, Iranian Imaginations,* Arshin Adib-Moghaddam
3. *Iranian Cosmopolitanism: A Cinematic History,* Golbarg Rekabtalaei
4. *Money, Markets and Monarchies: The Gulf Cooperation Council and the Political Economy of the Contemporary Middle East,* Adam Hanieh

5. *Iran's Troubled Modernity: Debating Ahmad Fardid's Legacy*, Ali Mirsepassi
6. *Foreign Policy As Nation Making: Turkey and Egypt in the Cold War*, Reem Abou-El-Fadl
7. *Revolution and Its Discontents: Political Thought and Reform in Iran*, Eskandar Sadeghi-Boroujerdi
8. *Creating the Modern Iranian Woman: Popular Culture between Two Revolutions*, Liora Hendelman-Baavur
9. *Iran's Quiet Revolution: The Downfall of the Pahlavi State*, Ali Mirsepassi
10. *Reversing the Colonial Gaze: Persian Travelers Abroad*, Hamid Dabashi
11. *Israel's Jewish Identity Crisis: State and Politics in the Middle East*, Yaacov Yadgar
12. *Temporary Marriage in Iran: Gender and Body Politics in Modern Persian Film and Literature*, Claudia Yaghoobi
13. *Cosmopolitan Radicalism: The Visual Politics of Beirut's Global Sixties*, Zeina Maasri
14. *Anticolonial Afterlives in Egypt: The Politics of Hegemony*, Sara Salem
15. *What Is Iran? Domestic Politics and International Relations*, Arshin Adib-Moghaddam
16. *Art and the Arab Spring: Aesthetics of Revolution and Resistance in Tunisia and Beyond*, Siobhán Shilton

Art and the Arab Spring

Aesthetics of Revolution and Resistance in Tunisia and Beyond

SIOBHÁN SHILTON
University of Bristol

CAMBRIDGE
UNIVERSITY PRESS

CAMBRIDGE
UNIVERSITY PRESS

University Printing House, Cambridge CB2 8BS, United Kingdom

One Liberty Plaza, 20th Floor, New York, NY 10006, USA

477 Williamstown Road, Port Melbourne, VIC 3207, Australia

314–321, 3rd Floor, Plot 3, Splendor Forum, Jasola District Centre, New Delhi – 110025, India

79 Anson Road, #06–04/06, Singapore 079906

Cambridge University Press is part of the University of Cambridge.

It furthers the University's mission by disseminating knowledge in the pursuit of education, learning and research at the highest international levels of excellence.

www.cambridge.org
Information on this title: www.cambridge.org/9781108842525
DOI: 10.1017/9781108909778

© Siobhán Shilton 2021

This publication is in copyright. Subject to statutory exception and to the provisions of relevant collective licensing agreements, no reproduction of any part may take place without the written permission of Cambridge University Press.

First published 2021

A catalogue record for this publication is available from the British Library.

ISBN 978-1-108-84252-5 Hardback

Cambridge University Press has no responsibility for the persistence or accuracy of URLs for external or third-party internet websites referred to in this publication and does not guarantee that any content on such websites is, or will remain, accurate or appropriate.

Contents

List of Figures	*page* ix
Acknowledgements	x
Introduction: Exceeding Icons of Revolution in North Africa and the Eastern Mediterranean	1
New Approaches to Aesthetics of Revolution	21
Chapter Summaries	31
1 Aesthetics of Revolution and Infra-thin Critique	36
Transnationalising the Infra-thin: Revolutionary Arabesques and *Le Printemps arabe*	43
'Poetics of Absence': Commemoration and Resistance from Tunisia to Syria	53
Infra-thin Critique and Transnational Criticism	71
2 Contingency and Resistance: Exceeding Icons through Matter and Motion	74
Forms of Revolution and Revolutionary Formlessness	82
Revolutions in the Peripatetic Mode: Micro-visions and -voices of Tunis	98
Conclusion	115
3 Contingent Encounters: Artists, Artisans and Amateurs	117
Artists and Artisans: Textiles and Transnational Resistance from Ramallah to Sidi Bouzid	124
Performing Encounters, Weaving Spaces: Tunis/Sfax/Sejnane	130
Faces and Spaces of Resistance: Contingent Icons of Tunis, Egypt and Syria	142
Participating across Borders: From Textiles to Virtual 'Stitching'	157
Conclusion	164

4	Corporeal Resistance and Aesthetics of the Interface	166
	Concealing and Revealing: Beyond Revolutionary Exoticism?	172
	Performing Revolution: Constraint and Liberation in Tunisia, Libya and Syria	186
	Digitising Street Encounters: Tunisia in Graffiti, Photography and Dance	202
	Conclusion	220

Conclusion. Art and Revolution: Aesthetics and Approaches   222

References   229

Index   245

Figures

0.1 Nicène Kossentini, *Heaven or Hell* (2012)	page 12
0.2 Hela Lamine, *Nous ne mangerons plus de ce pain-là* (2011)	13
0.3 Majd Abdel Hamid, *Mohammad Bouazizi* (2011)	14
1.1 Safaa Erruas, *Les Drapeaux* (2011–12)	37
1.2 Sonia Kallel, *Which Dress for Tomorrow?* (2011)	37
1.3 Aïcha Filali, *L'Angle mort* (2012–13)	38
1.4 Shada Safadi, *Promises* (2012)	39
2.1 Aïcha Filali, *Bourgeons en palabres* and *Bourgeons d'i(n)vers* (2011)	75
2.2 Meriem Bouderbala, *Flag Nymphéas* (2012)	75
3.1 Selma and Sofiane Ouissi, *Laaroussa* (2011)	118
3.2 Collectif Wanda, *Le Ciel est par-dessus le toit* (2012–13; exterior view)	118
3.3 Collectif Wanda, *Le Ciel est par-dessus le toit* (2012–13; interior view)	119
3.4 Mouna Jemal Siala and Wadi Mhiri, *Parti Facelook / Parti Facelike* (2012–13)	119
3.5 Sonia Kallel, *Tisser la médina* (2012–13)	120
4.1 Mouna Karray, *Noir* (2013)	171

Acknowledgements

This project began during a period of research leave funded by the Arts and Humanities Research Council in the UK and was completed during a University of Bristol Research Fellowship. I am very grateful for their generous support.

An earlier version of parts of Chapters 1 and 2 first appeared in *French Cultural Studies* as 'Art and the Arab Spring: Aesthetics of Revolution in Contemporary Tunisia' (February 2013, 24, pp. 129–45), and an earlier version of parts of Chapter 1 first appeared in *Paragraph* as 'Alterity in Art: Towards a Theory and Practice of Infra-thin Critique' (first published October 2014, 37.3, pp. 356–71). These sections are reproduced with kind permission of the journal editors.

Very special thanks go to the artists of the inspiring works I have presented in this book for answering my questions and reading drafts, when possible: Nicène Kossentini, Mounir Fatmi, Safaa Erruas, Sonia Kallel, Aïcha Filali, Shada Safadi, Hela Lamine, Meriem Bouderbala, Lara Favaretto, Nadia Kaabi-Linke, Mouna Karray, Ismaïl Bahri, Majd Abdel Hamid, Selma and Sofiane Ouissi, Collectif Wanda, Febrik, Mouna Jemal Siala and Wadi Mhiri, Lalla Essaydi, Majida Khattari, Naziha Arebi, Philip Horani, Ahl Al Kahf and Ridha Tlili, JR and Alistair Siddons, El Seed and El Madinati, and Art Solution. It has been a real pleasure and an honour to work with them. For allowing me to reproduce images of works, I sincerely thank Nicène Kossentini, Safaa Erruas, Sonia Kallel, Aïcha Filali, Shada Safadi, Hela Lamine, Meriem Bouderbala, Mouna Karray, Majd Abdel Hamid, Selma and Sofiane Ouissi, and Mouna Jemal Siala.

I am extremely grateful to Charles Burdett, Andreas Schönle, Ruth Bush, Edward King, Susan Harrow and Bradley Stephens for reading parts of my manuscript and for their invaluable comments. I am also very grateful to the anonymous reviewers of this book, and to the excellent team at Cambridge University Press – particularly Maria

Marsh, Dan Brown, Atifa Jiwa, Thomas Haynes, Ken Moxham and Vinithan Sedumadhavan – for all their support and extremely helpful recommendations. It is a pleasure to thank all those who made it possible for me to present earlier versions of this research at conferences or seminars: Sandra Daroczi, Kaya Davies Hayon, Julia Dobson, Gemma Edney, Joe Ford, Jane Hiddleston, Nicki Hitchcott, Claire Launchbury, Charles Mansfield, Wen-Chin Ouyang, Mathilde Poizat-Amar, Maria Scott, Katherine Shingler and Seán Williams. I am very grateful to Jane Hiddleston, Françoise Lionnet and Emma Wilson for all their support and encouragement, and to Dora Latiri and Anna Rocca for their very helpful comments on my work. I am also grateful to the School of Modern Languages at the University of Bristol for funding many of my Arabic lessons, and to my Arabic teacher, Maryam Almohammad, for her wonderful classes and her friendship.

For their constant support, encouragement and kindness, I would like to thank my family, Seán Shilton, Bev Shilton, Michael Shilton, Katie Hill and Gloria Shilton, and my friends, especially Debbie Thomas, Coral Huxley, Sasha Daly, Lorna Fox, Ruth Glynn, Steffan Davies and Vicky Higman-Davies.

Introduction
Exceeding Icons of Revolution in North Africa and the Eastern Mediterranean

The revolutionary wave of demonstrations and protests that began to sweep across numerous countries in North Africa and the Middle East in December 2010 shocked the world. The significance of the uneven phenomenon which has often been named the 'Arab Spring' is still not fully understood. What is certain is that the events triggered partly by the self-immolation of the Tunisian fruit-stall owner Mohammed Bouazizi have changed this diverse region irrevocably, leading to the explosion of enduring political frameworks or – in Syria – to civil war and mass exodus. These revolutions – like other revolutions in diverse modern historical contexts – have often tended to be articulated, internally and externally, in black-and-white terms of success or failure, liberation or constraint, for or against, friend or enemy. The complex range of perspectives in Tunisia has, for example, at times, been reduced to binary perceptions of secularism and religion or, more extremely, a 'Western' notion of democracy and a radical version of Islamism.[1] The metaphor of an 'Arab Spring' was swiftly replaced, in both journalism and scholarship, by that – equally reductive – of an 'Islamist Winter'. The revolutions came often to be presented as a closed chapter. Yet, art engaging with this phenomenon frequently contributes an alternative perspective. A striking range of art evokes, and encourages, a more nuanced understanding of these revolutions, and of the idea of 'revolution', more widely. In this book I ask how such work – in photography, sculpture, graffiti, performance, video and installation – forges a way between internal and external clichés. How does this art evoke the idea of revolution? How does it invent

---

[1] An example of scholarship that questions the Islamist/secular divide can be found in Andrea Khalil's indication of the common goals for women in Tunisia, at least in urban contexts (Khalil, 2011). On political Islamism in Tunisia and the long tradition of reflections on the compatibility of Islam and democracy, see, for example, Marzouki (2013). For more on external essentialising visions of Tunisia, see Dakhlia (2011).

new aesthetics? How do these works call for alternative critical approaches?

The expression 'Arab Spring' is frequently used by artists and critics. Some critics have argued that it is more common in Arabic than the term 'Arab Uprisings' (Brownlee et al., 2015: 5, n. 5). Yet, Imed Ben Labidi has highlighted the tendency of Arab media to use terms such as 'revolutions' (*thawrat*), 'uprising' (*intifada*), 'awakening' (*sahwa*) and 'renaissance' (*nahda*) (Ben Labidi, 2019: 459, citing Rami G. Khouri, 2011).[2] The seasonal metaphor, 'Arab Spring', is a foreign invention which obscures the diversity and uniqueness of the multiple forms, trajectories and experiences of the revolts that unfolded in different countries (the term 'Arab' itself, of course, conceals the heterogeneity and specificity of cultures in the Middle East and North African (MENA) region) (Al-Sumait et al., 2014: 16–17).[3] The use of horticultural terms, such as 'Arab Spring' and 'Jasmine Revolution' (to refer to the Tunisian revolution), essentialises these cultures and maintains uneven power relations, as Ben Labidi argues persuasively: 'Nature talk imposes a clear rupture between Arabs and their struggle for democracy ... as if the events were not about free will, empowerment, and human agency'; '[it] places these revolutions outside history and sets up Arabs as apolitical; it dictates a certain way of thinking which dislodges real and existing diversity among the various countries, cultural differences, political experiences, and distinct underpinnings and conditions for each revolutionary uprising' (2019: 459). The term 'Uprisings', '[a]lbeit still imperfect', more adequately captures their complex and transitional nature, as Fahed Al-Sumait, Nele Lenze and Michael C. Hudson argue (Al-Sumait et al., 2014: 20).[4]

---

[2] When using transliteration in this book, I have used the same system as the author cited. For names of artists and authors, I have adopted the spelling they use.

[3] As Al-Sumait et al. state, 'Arab' 'is not the single supra-identity for everyone who took part in the events we are describing – though arguably it is among the most salient denominators. However, to change this word as well would both broaden a lens we are trying to narrow and depart too far from the common terminology for practical purposes' (2014: 36, n. 5).

[4] The term 'Uprisings', as Al-Sumait et al. indicate, reflects the plurality of the events it seeks to describe; it also refers specifically to the demonstrations and revolts: 'This restricts its meaning slightly, while still maintaining the flexibility to accommodate a broad range of occurrences across countries – plus the possibility of more to come' (2014: 17). Following Al-Sumait et al., I use the capitalised term 'Uprisings' to refer to the collective revolts across countries, and 'uprisings' (lower case) to refer to the demonstrations that occurred within a single country (2014: 36, n. 5).

The uprisings in Tunisia, Egypt, Yemen and Libya in each case led to the removal of an autocrat and a change in regime, yet with contrasting outcomes. The revolutions in Tunisia and Egypt led to multi-party elections. Tunisia's former president Zine el Abedine Ben Ali was deposed on 14 January 2011, leading, in October that year, to a coalition dominated by the moderate Islamist Ennahda party. The 2014 elections were won by the centrist secular party Nidaa Tounes led by Beji Caid Essebsi, who had served in the governments of Ben Ali and, previously, Habib Bourguiba. The Egyptian revolution of 25 January 2011 resulted in the resignation of Hosni Mubarak and the election of the Muslim Brotherhood in June 2012, which was overthrown by the army the following month.[5] In Yemen, by contrast, the uprising against Ali Abdullah Saleh, which began on 27 January 2011, led to the election, in February 2011, of Abd Rabbuh Mansur al-Hadi, his vice president and the only candidate on the ballot. This government was taken over by the Houthi armed movement in March 2015, leading to a civil war. Libya has experienced a regime change since Gaddafi was captured and killed on 20 October 2011, but the first elected governments have been constrained by local militias and the country 'shares much with the more doleful cases of Bahrain and Syria' (Brownlee et al., 2015: 4). In Bahrain and Syria the peaceful uprisings, which began respectively in February and March 2011, were rapidly repressed by the state. Revolt and repression led in Bahrain to low-key civil activism, but in Syria, under the regime of Bashar Al Assad, they intensified, developing into a full-scale war and the displacement of at least half of the population.[6] In terms of citizens' demands, too, the 'revolutions' (I will return to this term) have been diverse. While, as journalist Rami G. Khouri asserts, they have tended comparably to combine material rights and intangible political rights, 'there is no single, unifying theme to the Arab Uprisings' (Khouri, 2014: 9).

---

[5] Mubarak resigned on 11 February. The presidential election of June 2012 was narrowly won by the Muslim Brotherhood; former president Morsi was overthrown by the army in July 2013. Former army chief Abdul Fatah El-Sisi won the presidential election of May 2014.

[6] My presentation of these events draws on the work of Al-Sumait et al, eds. (2014) and Brownlee et al. (2015).

The 'Spring' suggests, also, a sudden emergence, 'as if by an act of nature' (Ben Labidi, 2019: 459). Yet, the Uprisings can be seen to have begun decades earlier. Critics and commentators such as Khouri take a 'long view', which perceives the Uprisings to have started with the first wave of Islamist movements in the 1970s (2014: 6–14; see also, on 'The Third Arab Spring', Brownlee et al., 2015: 1–14). Nouri Gana highlights a long history, since the 1970s, of activist and political engagement, in the specific context of Tunisia, by groups such as the labour union (the UGTT), the illegal Tunisian Communist Workers Party, Islamist student groups and the women's movement (Gana, 2013: 10–14). Crucially, Gana's edited collection on the 'making of' the Tunisian revolution – often called, in Tunisia, *Thawrat al-Karama* (the Dignity Revolution) or *Thawrat al-Shabab* (the Youth Revolution) (Jaouad, 2011) – conveys the intertwined genealogies of political and cultural dissent that contributed to the people's mobilisation. It expands our understanding of dissent to include both explicit and implicit forms by a range of actors: 'everyday Tunisians, journalists, novelists, playwrights, filmmakers, intellectuals, lawyers, high school teachers as well as university professors. Even soccer players, singers, and other popular figures have at times embraced and passed on the tradition of dissent in the Tunisian public sphere whether through explicit or encoded means and intents' (Gana, 2013: 15). 'Everyday' Tunisians might be taken to include the cyberactivists who have, over the years, fought against internet censorship (Kahlaoui, 2013). Gana traces the tradition of cultural critique in Tunisia back at least to the opposition to French colonialism in the 1930s and 1940s and the formation of the intellectual collective 'Jama'at tahta al-sur' (Against the Wall Group). He draws attention to the latent or indirect critique in the Arabic literature of figures such as Tunisia's foremost national poet Abou Al-Kasem Chebbi and playwright Mahmoud Al-Messadi, and in the post-independence work of writers such as Bashir Khrayyif, Mohamed Laroussi el-Metoui and Muhammad Salih Al-Jabiri and filmmakers including Nouri Bouzid, Moufida Tlatli and Mohamed Zran, as well as playwrights, stand-up comedians, and musicians. He comments on the increasingly direct critique of Ben Ali in the months prior to the revolution, in the online videos of hip hop musicians and rappers, such as El Général's renowned *Raïs El Bled* (Head of State; 2010) (Gana, 2013: 15–20).⁷

To his corpus we might add the work of visual artists (beyond filmmakers) since the 1990s, including, for example, the work of Mohamed Ali Belkadhi ('Dali') who, in 1998, presented his *Boisson pour faire la révolution* (Drink to Make a Revolution), a series of sixty cans each printed with the face of Che Guevara; the photographic or installation work of artists such as Aïcha Filali, Wassim Ghozlani, Halim Karabibene, Nicène Kossentini and Patricia Triki; painting by Medhi Bouanani and Mohamed Ben Slama; or the work of Selma and Sofiane Ouissi (dancers, choreographers, video artists and directors of multidimensional participatory projects and the Dream City festival) (see Ben Soltane, 2011, 2012; Machghoul, 2013). But we might also include ancient traditions of satire in the public space, as I discuss below (see Bruckbauer and Triki, 2016).⁸

Protesters in 2011 in Tunisia – and then Egypt, Yemen, Libya and Syria – resurrected the opening couplet from Chebbi's poem 'The Will to Life' (1933), an appropriation which, as Gana asserts, should be understood as 'an evocation of the inextricable relationship between fighting both foreign and indigenous forms of oppression' (Gana, 2013: 16): 'Once a people assert their will to life / Destiny must answer their call / Their darkness will have to vanish / and their chains to break and fall' (Chebbi, 1966: 5, translated from Arabic by Gana, 2013: 16).⁹ Gana resists the idea that there could be a master narrative of the Tunisian revolution, showing that it emerges, rather, 'as a complex chain of dispersed endeavors and micronarratives whose chapters have been (and are being) written in concert between different peoples in

---

⁷ See also Gana's chapter on postcolonial Tunisian film and song (2013: 181–203).
⁸ As Patricia Triki has stated, 'Faire de l'art politique était, il me semble, impossible', though she suggests that indirect treatment of issues was possible: 'Il fallait utiliser des moyens détournés pour exprimer certaines problématiques de notre société' ('Making political art was, it seemed to me, impossible'; 'you had to use subtle means to express certain issues in our society') (Bruckbauer and Triki, 2012: 26). Nicène Kossentini states that she attempted to convey the rigid political context in an abstract way through videos, such as her installation *Myopie* (Myopia) (2008; see Cohen Hadria, 2013). Aurélie Machghoul refers to the use of metaphors to circumvent political censorship (and to the choice of some artists, given these pre-revolutionary constraints, to develop apolitical art); she also suggests that self-censorship continues to occur to some extent (Machghoul, 2012a: 131), as I discuss below. See also Ounaina (2012) and Ben Soltane (2012).
⁹ On the use of this poem, see also Salah-Omri (2012).

different times and locations' (2013: 2). It was, he states, the eventual outcome of what Asef Bayat has called 'the collective actions of non-collective actors' (Bayat, 2010: 14, cited in Gana, 2013: 2). My use of the term 'revolution' (without a capital) in this book draws on Gana's definition of the Tunisian revolution as a 'historic event *and a historical process that has been years in the making and is not over yet.* It is the crowning moment of decades of collective endeavors, fragmented engagements, transversal tactics, small-scale or micro-rebellions, and *social, political, literary, and cultural practices of insurrection and revolt*' (2013: 22; my emphasis).

The 'Arab Spring' metaphor, in addition to obscuring the 'long view', seems to impose an impossibly short time frame on the Uprisings, which are, inevitably, still ongoing, as Gana suggests here of the Tunisian revolution (see also Al-Sumait et al., 2014: 17). Artist and curator Mohamed Ben Soltane also distinguishes between the revolution that ended with the first free, plural and democratic elections in Tunisia on 23 October 2011 and that which remains 'une lutte continue pour un pays (et un monde) plus juste, plus libre, plus équitable et plus humain …' ('an ongoing battle for a country (and a world) that is fairer, freer, more equal and more human …') (Ben Soltane, 2012: 217).[10] As Khouri continues,

The hard fact is that we do not know fully and clearly the precise balance among socioeconomic, political, rule-of-law, and security priorities that citizens speak about in different countries, because we have only been experiencing structured transformations for a short period, in erratic conditions, and in only three countries, essentially, with much more change to come. (Khouri, 2014: 10)

He emphasises the time it will take in each individual case for people 'to define what it means to be an Arab, what it means to be a citizen of the state, and what it means to be sovereign. This process will take time – not hundreds of years, but certainly dozens of years' (2014: 13–14). He argues, therefore, for humility and patience in attempting to understand the complex Uprisings, warning against 'the false syndrome of definitive instant analysis via television or blogging' (2014: 14). By contrast with certain instantaneous media responses, art can

---

[10] All translations are my own, unless otherwise stated. Ben Soltane elects to refer to the historical event with a small 'r' and to the ongoing resistance with a capital 'R'.

Introduction: Exceeding Icons of Revolution

create a space and a moment in time for reflection on specific local experiences of revolt or on the wider complex phenomenon of the Uprisings. Artists have, at times, employed the 'Arab Spring' metaphor, while their work tends to move beyond the simple, unifying narratives that it conjures, encouraging the patience and humility for which Khouri calls.

The media played a major role in historicising the Uprisings and constructing iconic stories, such as that of the death of Mohammad Bouazizi, as argued by Adel Iskandar (2014). The process of iconising Bouazizi's story made it appear unanimous and unambiguous, erasing inconsistencies: '[a]s the media actively move toward rendering these accounts into narratives – all of which are to varying degrees fictionalized – they attempt to ossify perspectives on these Uprisings. These narratives become increasingly rigid interpretations of events and actors' (Iskandar, 2014: 136–37). The same point can be made regarding visual iconic images of revolution, such as the portraits of Mohammad Bouazizi which circulated widely online via news and social media platforms. Such images can function as a shorthand for those unifying and rigid narratives of the Tunisian revolution and the subsequent uprisings. Iconic images convey the revolution – like the literal meaning of the word 'revolution' – as a completed cycle. They communicate an absolute rupture with the past and portray a people as ideologically unified in their vision of their country's future. The immediate recognisability and legibility of iconic visual images aids in their communication of 'revolution' as void of ambiguities, inconsistencies, complex histories and unresolved competing agendas. Iconic images obscure the non-collective and non-linear genealogies of dissent highlighted by Gana; Bouazizi's self-immolation, though a major catalyst of the uprisings in Tunisia, built on decades of subtle and overt resistance to authoritarianism.

In the Tunisian context, photographer Jellel Gasteli has pointed to the need to avoid what he calls '[des] icônes de l'exotisme révolutionnaire' ('icons of revolutionary exoticism') (2012).[11] Certain

---

[11] This expression appeared in the artist's statement beside his work at 'Dégagements... La Tunisie un an après', Institut du Monde Arabe, Paris, 2012. The curator of this exhibition, Michket Krifa, also used the expression 'revolutionary exoticism' when discussing her reservations regarding the word 'Dégagements' for the title ('Dégage!' ('Out!') was shouted by Tunisians at the protests against Ben Ali in January 2011): 'We have not been in the ousting stage

visual representations of the Tunisian revolution of 2011 reuse iconic visions from other, earlier revolutionary contexts, such as Delacroix's painting *La Liberté guidant le peuple* (Liberty Leading the People) (1830).[12] Revolutionary icons could also be seen in visual images that accompanied political demonstrations, such as that of Che Guevara within the Tunisian flag (reminiscent of Belkadhi's *Boisson pour faire la révolution* of 1998). Many artists, by contrast, seek to avoid such iconic language. Scholars of communication and culture, Robert Hariman and John Louis Lucaites, have signalled the icon's power to reproduce ideology, even while it can contain within it dominant and resistant responses to social authority: 'the iconic image's combination of mainstream recognition, wide circulation, and emotional impact is a proven formula for reproducing a society's social order' (2007: 9). Yet, there is a further crucial reason for eschewing, specifically, icons of revolution – distinct from the icons of US public culture analysed by Hariman and Lucaites – in countries with a history of dictatorship and colonialism. This is particularly the case when employing the iconic language that is associated with the French Revolution, which would run the risk of providing support for neo-colonial identifications of Tunisia in 2011 with France in 1789. An iconic language of this type was, in addition, employed to encapsulate the national myths of 'revolution' perpetuated by the government of Ben Ali, whose ubiquitous portrait dominated key sites of Tunis before 2011. The same can be said of the images and statues of his predecessor, Habib Bourguiba, the founder and first president of the Republic of Tunisia following independence from France in 1956. Portraits of the leaders of countries including Egypt, Libya and Syria have similarly been used to centralise and personalise regimes, while legitimising their authority, as Lina

for some time, but rather in the "engaging" stage. Maybe, as a Tunisian, the perception that we have of this title is very different from that of westerners; we've had enough of the ousting and we want to move on to something else. For them, this word represents the force of the Tunisian revolution' (Krifa, in interview with Wafa Gabsi, 2012). As Krifa states, discussing her intentions for the exhibition, 'I wanted to show that the revolution wasn't just about Bouazizi's immolation and cries of *"dégage, dégage!" ("out, out!")*. It's also a thought process, a series of values and choices made by society, and artists are conscious of all of this' (Krifa, in interview with Gabsi, 2012).

[12] Delacroix's pyramidal composition for *La Liberté guidant le peuple* is reappropriated to render Tunisian protesters in Omar Bey's metal sculpture, exhibited at 'Art Paris Tunis: Art Contemporain en Tunisie' (Musée du Montparnasse, Paris, 2011).

Khatib has shown in her study of the growing importance of the role of the visual in political culture in the Middle East (2013: 183, 186).

Gasteli's use of the term 'exotisme' calls to mind the tendency, shared by images of revolution in diverse contexts, to romanticise the rupture with a tyrannical regime and to present an ideal, stable and cohesive image of a nation united in its understanding of the meaning of 'revolution'. At the same time, it conjures persistent essentialising visions of Tunisia. Tunisia has long been caught between conflicting images. As historian Jocelyne Dakhlia states, Ben Ali's regime, like that of Bourguiba, was seen as constituting a progressive step in an evolution towards democracy (perceived as a 'Western' notion), particularly given the façade presented in relation to *laïcité* (secularism), literacy, class diversity, and especially women's rights (Dakhlia, 2011). Views from France and Europe tended paradoxically, as Dakhlia argues, either to perpetuate Tunisia's official image of national unity, harmony and political stability or (unofficially) to portray the country as an unchanging dictatorship (2011: 13).[13] Tunisia was, therefore, already subject to internal and external reductive visions:

> C'est en somme l'essentialisation par la dictature qui était insupportable et le caractère totalitaire de cette lecture politique elle-même. Alors que la société tunisienne, comme toutes les sociétés arabes, se concevait elle-même dans une histoire politique faite de tensions, de petites victoires internes et de progrès, comme de régressions et d'échecs, elle se voyait enfermée sans nuances dans l'image d'une société intemporellement sous contrôle, sans pensée ni penseurs. (2011: 14)

> (To summarise, it is the essentialisation by the dictatorship which was intolerable and the totalitarian nature of this political interpretation itself. While Tunisian society, like all Arab societies, conceived of itself within a political history constituted by tensions, small internal triumphs and markers of progress, as well as regressions and failures, it saw itself enclosed without nuances within the image of an eternally dominated society, lacking in thought or thinkers.)

Paradoxical views of the country continued, beyond the revolution of 2011, either to assimilate Tunisia within a linear narrative of 'progress'

---

[13] Regarding the Franco-Tunisian networks that supported Ben Ali's regime, see Bredoux and Magnaudeix (2012). On the support of other Western countries for Ben Ali's regime, and particularly on USA–Tunisian relations, see Ben Rejeb (2013).

towards (a Western notion of) democracy or to convey a fear that the former dictatorship would be replaced by a (radical) Islamist state.[14] Emphasising 'sameness' or 'difference', from within or beyond Tunisia, these visions are reminiscent of colonial exoticism in presenting a culture as monolithic and timeless (discourses of assimilation and differentiation coexisted, moreover, in certain French colonial exoticist imagery).[15] Iconic images run the risk of simply reinforcing external and internal clichés.

Iconic – and iconoclastic – interventions in photography and graffiti have received particular attention from the scholars and journalists who have addressed the role of the visual in the Arab revolutions.[16] Some have focused on what Marwan Kraidy calls 'spectacular body acts' in *The Naked Blogger of Cairo: Creative Insurgency in the Arab World* (2016). Kraidy focuses on the human body as a medium of political expression, and particularly on 'nude activism' and self-immolation, as well as street art commemorating the heroic bodies of martyrs. Examples include the online nude activist selfies of Egyptian Aliaa Al Mahdy and those of Tunisian Amina Sboui, as well as the media image of the demonstrator killed in Tahrir Square who came to be known as 'The Girl in a Blue Bra'. Such images – whether created independently or by the media – are iconic in combining 'mainstream recognition, wide circulation, and emotional impact' (to reprise

---

[14] On the absence of foundation for persistent conflations of Islamism and Islamic fundamentalism, see Roy (2012) and Piot (2011: 129–31).

[15] Such ambivalence could be found, for example, in the architecture of the Exposition Coloniale Internationale (Paris, 1931). Patricia Morton (2000) has explored the 'hybrid modernities' of this exhibition.

[16] See, for example, Hafez (2014), Labidi (2014a, whose chapter examines the nude activism of Tunisian Amina Sboui alongside the work of female Tunisian artists working in a range of visual media), Khatib (2013; see especially 117–67) and Georgeon (2012). Further short essays on visual art (other than film) that responds to different manifestations of the Uprisings can be found in catalogues related to exhibitions including 'The Changing Room', 'Dégagements ... La Tunisie un an après', 'Rosige Zukunft', 'ComeTogether#' (part of 'Edge of Arabia'), 'The Turn: Art Practices in Post-Spring Societies' and 'Creative Dissent: Arts of the Arab World Uprisings' (see also the related special issue with essays on Bahrain, Egypt, Libya and Syria, ed. Gruber, 2018), as well as a collection on new media from North Africa and the Middle East (ed. Downey, 2014; see chapters by Downey, Kaabi-Linke and Kholeif). Charles Tripp (2013, final chapter) provides a broad historical consideration of the role of art in resistance (primarily in Palestine, Lebanon, Iraq, Iran and Algeria).

Introduction: Exceeding Icons of Revolution

Hariman and Lucaites's definition, cited above). They can be reappropriated to affirm binary visions of a revolution from different, yet equally rigid, ideological perspectives. Indeed, some perceived the naked, sexually provocative body of Al Mahdy as heroic and revolutionary, while many saw it as traitorous, anti-revolutionary and anti-Egyptian, as I elaborate in Chapter 4 (see Hafez, 2014; Kraidy, 2016). The response to the Tunisian Amina Sboui's naked selfies was similarly fractured (see Kraidy, 2016). National flags can, similarly, be reappropriated. The Tunisian flag was used to indicate a singular revolutionary affiliation, uniting diverse subjectivities, or violently rejected, exposing historical divisions, but then reclaimed to reimpose an essentialist vision of the nation, as Joachim Ben Yakoub has demonstrated (2017).

My focus, by contrast, is on art that negotiates a way *between* a range of icons, including these revolutionary (or anti-revolutionary) bodies or objects; that is, art that reveals the unsaid, the unheard or the unseen of 'revolution'. This art – crossing a range of media – tends to interact ironically or ambiguously with iconic objects, structures, faces or spaces – from portraits of leaders or revolutionary figures, or the national flags brandished at demonstrations, to monuments or sites that have similarly come to embody the values of a regime or a people's resistance to it.[17] Or it creates an alternative to iconic imagery, alluding indirectly to the discourses that it reinforces, by presenting or performing habitually marginalised spaces or bodies in ways that resist their easy reuse for ideological purposes. At the same time, it moves beyond straightforward iconoclasm, as well as reappropriations of the icon in ways that replace it with another, as exemplified by the reworking of 'The Girl in a Blue Bra' into a 'strategy of dissent' (see Hafez, 2014: 182).[18] This artwork tends to refer to apparently stable visual forms

[17] The word 'icon', and the adjective 'iconic', are usually used, in the context of representation, to refer to 'a very famous person or thing considered as representing a set of beliefs or way of life' (as defined in the Cambridge English dictionary). I am extending this definition to include sites and architectural landmarks, which have been considered similarly. I use the term in relation to flags, which are symbols: unlike icons, symbols do not resemble what they stand for, but flags function like icons in representing a nation and a set of beliefs about that nation. I do not usually use the term 'icon' in its religious sense, in this book, though I will show how some artists have drawn on religious iconography in representations of the Arab Uprisings. 'Iconic' is often also employed to refer to images on a surface, but I use the word in relation to representations across a range of media.

[18] See also Khatib on 'the floating image' (2013: 11–12).

Figure 0.1 Nicène Kossentini, *Heaven or Hell* (2012), Sabrina Amrani Gallery, photographer Juan Cruz Ibañez, courtesy of Nicène Kossentini

and languages, while exceeding them by using disjunctive sensorial, often contingent elements.

It is through this central dynamic between stability and *in*stability, I argue, that such art creates a space for alternative voices and visions. Nicène Kossentini's video for her installation *Heaven or Hell* (2012, 6′), for example, displays a rotating arabesque, alluding ironically to French artist Marcel Duchamp's kinetic sculptures at the same time as Islamic art (Figure 0.1). Both visual languages are exceeded when this stable form spins and gradually explodes to evoke liberation – but also fragility – in Tunisia and the wider region. Icons are frequently contested by using organic, perishable elements: Hela Lamine highlights the decline of Ben Ali by portraying him in a decaying mixture of bread

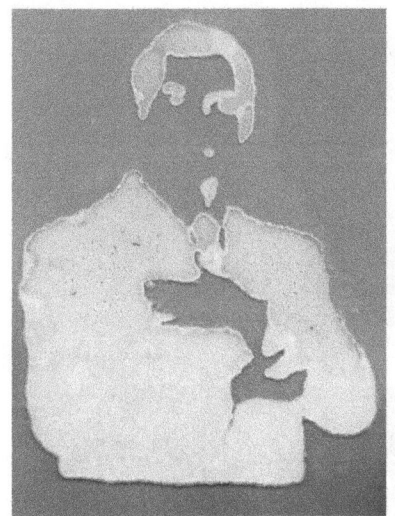 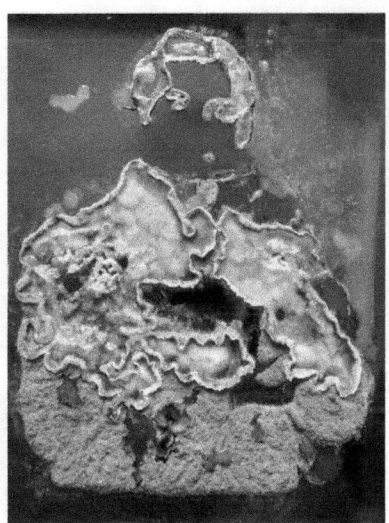

7 NOVEMBRE 1987   14 JANVIER 2011

Figure 0.2 Hela Lamine, *Nous ne mangerons plus de ce pain-là* (2011; photographs 1 and 7 of seven: '7 novembre 1987' and '14 janvier 2011'), courtesy of the artist

and water (*Nous ne mangerons plus de ce pain-là* (We Will Not Eat That Bread Anymore), 2011; Figure 0.2). Mouna Karray reworks the city of Tunis by filming in the peripatetic mode. In her video installation, iconic propagandist images of Ben Ali are accompanied by the conversation between a taxi driver and his passenger as they observe changes on the streets of the capital (*Live*, 2012). Other artists allow their work to be determined in part by artisans, amateurs or members of the public. Majd Abdel Hamid commissioned eight women from the West Bank village of Farkha each to weave a portrait of Tunisian martyr Mohammad Bouazizi and wove the ninth portrait himself (*Mohammad Bouazizi*, 2011; Figure 0.3). Selma and Sofiane Ouissi's project with female ceramicists from Sejnane in northwest Tunisia led to a range of co-produced work in sculpture, mixed media, video and performance (*Laaroussa*, 2011). Spectators create their own parodic icons of Tunisia in photo/voting booths animated by Mouna Jemal Siala and Wadi Mhiri (*Parti Facelook / Parti Facelike*, 2012). Instability is also generated through the moving bodies of dancers, passers-by and cameramen in online videos of interventions in the

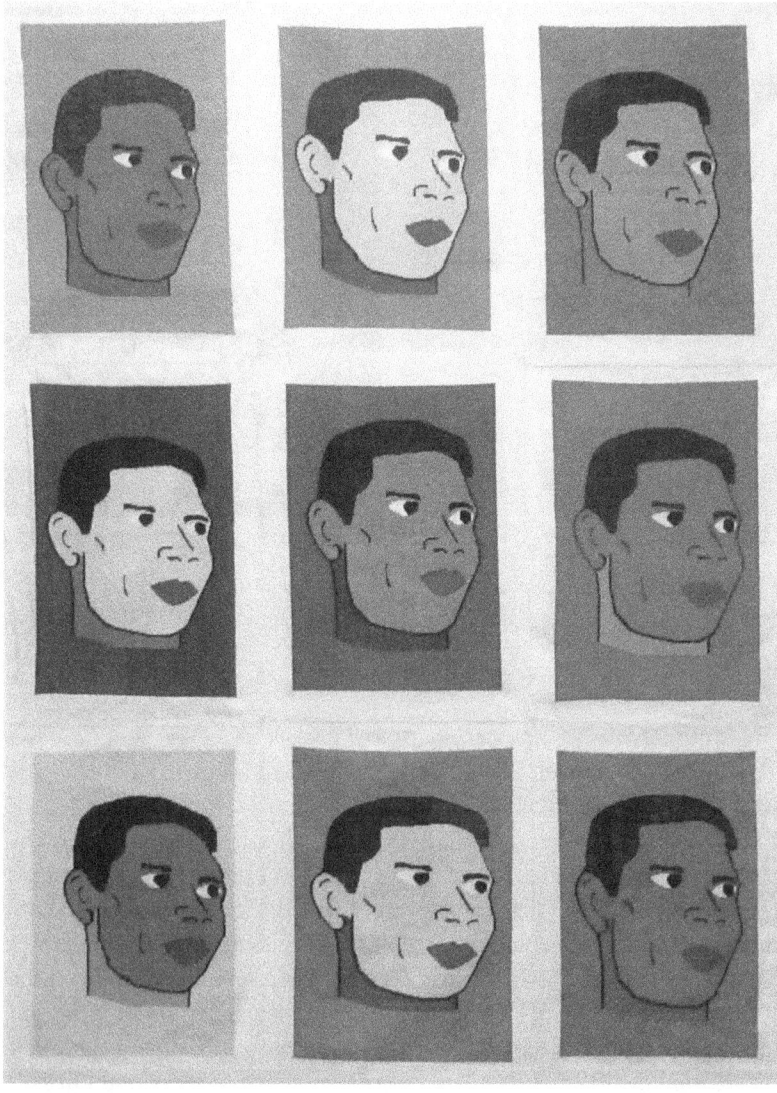

Figure 0.3 Majd Abdel Hamid, *Mohammad Bouazizi* (2011), courtesy of the artist

streets of Tunis by the dance collective Art Solution (*Je danserai malgré tout* (I'll Dance Despite Everything)), 2011; see www.youtube.com/watch?v=4OfWQ2GaVHg). From such art, 'revolution' comes to signify not simply liberation but also fragility and uncertainty. It moves

Introduction: Exceeding Icons of Revolution 15

beyond binary understandings which perceive a clear distinction between enemy and friend, past and present to allow for diverse perspectives, for transition and negotiation. This art contributes to the enduring non-collective revolutionary actions addressed by Gana in relation to literature, theatre, comedy and music. At the same time, it enables spectators to develop a greater consciousness – mediated through their senses as well as through their intellect – of the meaning of the term 'revolution'.

These examples reflect the wide range of work to be explored here, in terms of medium, material, practice, format and curatorial context – in galleries, in the street or online. The artists of the work I analyse in this book are not members of a cohesive group or a particular movement. They are not usually very familiar with the work of other artists exploring the Uprisings, except for the artists who have presented or performed their work at the biannual Dream City festival (in Tunis, Sfax and, in 2012–13, Marseilles) directed by Selma and Sofiane Ouissi, including Mouna Jemal Siala, Sonia Kallel, Wadi Mhiri, Collectif Wanda and the Ouissis.[19] They do not all share the same location. Many live and work in Tunis, such as Aïcha Filali, Mouna Jemal Siala, Sonia Kallel, Nicène Kossentini, Hela Lamine, Wadi Mhiri, the dance group Art Solution and the graffiti artists Ahl Al Kahf. Others are based at different sites in North Africa or the Middle East: Ramallah (Majd Abdel Hamid), Tetouan (Safaa Erruas) and Majdal Shams (Shada Safadi), for example. Others work in Europe or the United States or, more often, between locations, such as Selma and Sofiane Ouissi between Paris and Tunis, or Mounir Fatmi between Paris and Tangiers. Many artists use a pseudonym to preserve their anonymity in the Syrian context, as is the case for 'Philip Horani'.[20] These works are produced, exhibited and received by diverse spectators locally and/or transnationally. Some are shown abroad (in addition, often, to being exhibited locally), reflecting the artist's access to international art circuits. Others, uncommissioned

---

[19] I know this from my exchanges with the artists represented in this book (most of whom I have been able to contact). Sonia Kallel also contributed to the Ouissis' project *Laaroussa*, which I discuss in Chapter 3.

[20] An exception can be found in the work for the Facebook page 'Art and Freedom', established by artist Youssef Abdelki, who asked artists to sign their work as an act of solidarity with the victims and prisoners of the Syrian revolution (Halasa, 2012).

and unsanctioned, are uploaded directly to virtual platforms, such as YouTube, Vimeo or Facebook. Some work exists in more than one format, as is the case for ephemeral street interventions that become – and are most often experienced as – online videos or photographic collections.[21] Such digital work has frequently been transposed to gallery contexts, while videos and images of works or exhibitions in galleries are circulated on social media. The boundaries between the spaces conventionally associated with art and activism have, thus, become blurred.

In certain cases works are recreated and adapted to new sites, which can produce alternative effects for their shifting audiences – and, indeed, have implications for critical interpretation.[22] I write with awareness, moreover, that there are multiple possible experiences of these works, regardless of site, which depend on diverse factors, such as the spectator's physical viewpoint and, importantly, their cultural locatedness and histories of travel. My own interpretation is contingent on my position as a white woman of British nationality in a UK university and a French Department (with a training in French and History of Art also in the UK). My perspective on these works, which often include local or regional cultural references and/or written Arabic, is greatly influenced by the long periods I spent as a child/adolescent in countries such as Morocco and Dubai, and by learning Arabic at school in Dubai and later as a young adult in Egypt. For the purposes of this book I developed my knowledge of Modern Standard Arabic, which enabled me to read the text that is incorporated into some of the artwork – or to understand the degree to which it is designed to be legible (the production of writing between legibility and illegibility can be seen in the work of artists such as El Seed,

---

[21] I give a particular place in this book to such digital versions of the work – as well as work that originated as online video art – since, I suggest, they involve a rearrangement of space which can encourage alternative interpretations of the revolutions and their aftermaths. A further reason was my desire to include uncommissioned and unsanctioned work, though online videos or collections have frequently been 'recuperated' and transposed to gallery contexts.

[22] Travel from the UK to the sites of revolution was restricted during the years in which this corpus was produced. Therefore, in the case of installation works by Sonia Kallel, Collectif Wanda and Mouna Jemal Siala / Wadi Mhiri, exhibited at three iterations of the 'Dream City' festival in 2012–13 in Tunis, Sfax and L'Estaque, near Marseilles, I use a combination of first-hand experience of the works at L'Estaque, conversations with the artist, and/or reviews and other documentation, to highlight the process of 'loss' and 'gain' in which such adaptations result (see Chapter 3).

Essaydi and Fatmi). My perspective, though unconventional, is nonetheless inevitably 'Western'. Critics such as Walter Mignolo have written powerfully about the necessity of remaining conscious of the subjectivity of knowledge and of one's situatedness in relation to the colonial history of knowledge-making, cautioning against the enduring tendency to present knowledge from the West as disembodied, unlocated and universal (Mignolo, 2011).

I have sought to balance my perspective as far as possible by drawing on the views of the artists, who have kindly answered my questions and commented on the parts of this book related to their work. The secondary sources I engage with include many by critics and curators who are based in or originate from countries in the MENA region and are literate in Arabic, even while they tend to write about this art exploring the revolutions predominantly in French or English.[23] The artists themselves (who can, in most cases, speak Arabic) tend to create with both local and international audiences in mind and, therefore, often to comment on their work in French or English. I have, though, used certain texts which appear both in French/English and Arabic, as in multilingual exhibition catalogues or festival documentation or online magazines such as *Jadaliyya*. Of course, 'local' perspectives, regardless of the language in which they are articulated, are multiple. For Tunisian art historian Rachida Triki, Tunisian art is itself 'transcultural', as I discuss below. These works reflect what critics such as Paul Jay have shown to be the inevitable 'contamination' (though not erasure) of the local (Jay, 2011); they are 'rooted' but also 'routed' (as James Clifford has said of 'culture' (1997)).

I have attempted to bring together different perspectives, as well as various types of knowledge and understanding, by drawing on a range of sources, from articles and exhibition catalogues to artists' statements and emails and spectators' online responses, in addition to the art itself, created in diverse media. The multisensorial works presented in this book, which incorporate a range of cultural references and, at times, languages (Arabic, English and/or French), embody the spectators, encouraging them to be conscious of their locatedness. They also transmit types of knowledge that move beyond the intellect via corporeality, materiality or music, for example. Although Mignolo does not

---

[23] Tunisian art historian Ridha Moumni comments on the tendency of art historians in Tunisia to write in French (see Laggoune-Aklouche et al., 2017).

refer to art, these works exemplify what he has called 'other [we might simply say "various"] ways of knowing and sensing', which have been hidden by 'zero point epistemology' (the belief that there is a transparent and universal knowledge) (Mignolo, 2011: 80).

I address primarily art exploring the Tunisian revolution and works evoking the wider, uneven phenomenon of the Arab Uprisings, while I also highlight the similarities in art engaging with distinct contexts – the revolutions in Egypt and Libya, and particularly that in Syria. As my project developed, I found it natural to bring together works engaging with local struggles for democracy and those addressing wider regional tensions, since both are frequently evoked within individual works. Kossentini's *Le Printemps arabe* (2011), which I mentioned above, is a case in point. Some works allude to more than one distinct local context. An example can be found in Febrik's *Watchtower of Happiness* (2012), which responds to the differences between photographs of demonstrations in Tunis, Cairo and Damascus. I was also struck by the fact that some works, addressing radically divergent revolutionary circumstances and trajectories to those of Tunisia, reveal comparable means of creating a space for alternative voices and visions. The Syrian 'revolution' is frequently perceived as the polar opposite of that in Tunisia, which is the reason for the attention I give to art exploring Syria. This art tends, indeed, to focus distinctively on conflict, commemoration, displacement and/or exile. Yet, despite crucial differences, this art often demonstrates remarkably comparable practices and means of avoiding iconic visual language. I address converging aesthetics of revolution. How are transparent screens and light employed to create a space for ordinary Tunisians in Aïcha Filali's *L'Angle mort* (2012–13) or to mourn the loss of thousands of civilians in Syria in Shada Safadi's *Promises* (2012–13)? How is the uncertain future of Tunisia, Syria or Libya explored through the reworking of the national flag by Meriem Bouderbala (2012, photography), Philip Horani (2012, painting-performance) and Naziha Arebi (2012, video)? How is unedited or found footage mobilised to produce non-iconic perspectives on revolutionary demonstrations in Mouna Karray's auditory journey around Tunis in *Live* (2012), Khaled Hafez's three-screen *Video Diaries* exploring Cairo (2011) or Dia Batal's *Mourning Hall*, which commemorates victims of the Syrian conflict through the use of audio footage in an installation at Leighton House, London (2012)? What differences

Introduction: Exceeding Icons of Revolution 19

and similarities can be discerned between art engaging with urban sites or rural localities and 'marginal' communities within or between countries – the participatory textile projects which took place in a village in the West Bank (Majd Abdel Hamid, 2011) and at a refugee camp on the Syria–Turkey border (Hazar Bakbachi-Henriot, 2012), for example?

This art is often produced in distinct contexts of revolution and different conditions of censorship. At times, as we will see, work responding to the Tunisian revolution indicates freedom from decades of censorship, but also hints at the new constraints that have emerged for the production and exhibition of art. Freedom from the censorship experienced under the former regime in Tunisia is evident, for example, in the more explicitly revolutionary work shown at the biannual Dream City festival, and in post-2010 events such as the almost annual festival *Jaou*.[24] New forms of constraint, though, are reflected by incidents such as the attack on the 'Printemps des Arts 2012' exhibition at the Palais Abdellia in La Marsa, Tunis (June 2012), which showed works deemed by some Salafists to be religiously offensive.[25] Alternatively, the artist's practice reveals the dangerous and, therefore, clandestine conditions in which they work, particularly in Syria, where the intense conflict continues, at the time of writing, under Bashar Al Assad's regime. Philip Horani's online video (2011) displays the artist's performing, yet partially concealed, body, for example, while Azza Hamwi's *A Day and a Button* (2015) films her journey on foot through Damascus from a hidden camera. As Leila Al-Shami has stated, while numerous artists opposed to the regime have fled Syria, those who have stayed face insults and danger to their lives; they are also deprived of

---

[24] The Dream City festival (held in Tunis, Sfax and, in 2013, Marseille) was launched by Selma and Sofiane Ouissi in 2007 (see www.dreamcity.tn, and, for more on the Ouissis' Association l'Art Rue, see https://lartrue.com; last accessed March 2019). The Jaou festival is held in Tunis and was founded in 2013 by Lina Lazaar (see jaou.art; last accessed March 2019).

[25] Ongoing restrictions on freedom of expression are also the subject of more recent works of art, including the installation *La Chronologie* (Patricia Triki and Christine Bruckbauer, in progress, begun 2011), which encourages spectators to move along a timeline indicating details of censorship and repression, including instances of imprisonment and assassination. This work was exhibited on the Avenue de la Démocratie in Tunis and at the exhibition 'Effervescence' (Institut des Cultures d'Islam, Paris, 2016). For more on the post-revolutionary art scene in Tunisia, see especially the work of Triki (2012a, 2012b).

the financial means to produce their work and the opportunities to exhibit it (see Leila Al-Shami – in particular, her citation of the writer Khaled Khalifa (2016)). This explains the abundance of online platforms and virtual galleries particularly for Syrian art (see Stonock, 2016).[26] At the same time, online fora provide a means for artists to bypass self-censorship (Halasa, 2012).[27]

This book does not produce an overview of work exploring the revolutions in North Africa and the Eastern Mediterranean. Nor does it explore art or artists from one particular locality. Rather, it addresses a selection of works which demonstrate new directions in aesthetics of revolution – aesthetics that evoke, and encourage, an understanding of 'revolution' as uncertain, contingent, subject to evolution, and open to perspectives beyond essentialising internal or external visions.

This wide-ranging corpus converges in exploring revolutions between politics and poetics. The type of direct political critique exemplified by El Général's rap track *'Raïs El Bled'* (Head of State) (2010), or the slogans, chants and graffiti writing that Gana views as inspired by Chebbi's poetry (Gana, 2013: 16), can be found in art other than the iconic or iconoclastic interventions to which I referred above. Examples include the popular Tunisian satirical cartoon series *Willis from Tunis* by Nadia Khiari (which began in 2011) and, in the context of the ongoing war in Syria, the highly subversive puppet shows, *Top Goon* (which also began in 2011). The art in this book, however, is not activist in the conventional sense of communicating a straightforward political message. This art cannot be extracted from its political context, but it is distinctive in lending itself to different interpretations and in conveying aspects of the lived experiences of revolution during or beyond protest. Drawing on the work of Jacques Rancière, Anthony Downey asserts that '[a]rtistic practice opens up a horizon of future

---

[26] Stonock (2016) also provides details of organisations that have been established, directed and supported by Syrian artists, facilitators and producers – both in and beyond Syria – though their location and the names of the founders and artists are not always known. These artists are beset, in addition, by practical difficulties, including only intermittently functioning electricity and internet connection (see Halasa, 2012, quoting Aleppo-based artist Issa Touma).

[27] Leila Al-Shami (2012) indicates that art in Syria was popularised and democratised when the revolution began in 2011, and that, despite the ensuing violent conflict, there is a 'profound and ongoing cultural revolution'. For more on art as a means of resistance in the Syrian context (crossing a range of visual and verbal forms), see Halasa et al., eds. (2014).

possibility within which civic imagination can flourish. Indeed, art as a practice contributes to the forms that civic space assumes whilst also engaging with public space through various modalities of engagement and resistance' (Downey, 2014: 66). 'This is not', though, as Downey states, 'about art as a form of political protest (an all too easily co-opted cultural paradigm), nor is this to confuse the artist as protestor (or vice versa)' (2014: 66). The works I explore in this book are not simply forms of political protest. Yet, nor is the political in them limited to Rancière's sense of '[re-]distributing the sensible' (2004: 12–13 [2000]) (that is, challenging the established framework of perception, or 'police order', through aesthetics).[28] Certain art does resonate with Rancière's work in (literally) privileging senses other than the visual – which is central to icons – or in 'reordering' space, challenging sites of power through elements such as framing, camerawork, editing and corporeal movement. This art, though, tends to be 'anchored' more explicitly in relation to a specific cultural space – local or regional – and a particular historical moment. This art explores diverse relationships between art and activism, frequently crossing the imagined boundaries dividing not only their spaces but also their languages, practices and audiences. This art, I argue, creates a shifting space between politics and poetics, as it engages with the revolutions while encouraging spectators to reshape their memories of them and to imagine alternative futures for countries from Tunisia to Syria.

New Approaches to Aesthetics of Revolution

Precedents for such aesthetics, as we will see, can frequently be discerned in earlier art examining Maghrebi spaces or communities, even while new combinations or strategies have emerged in response to

[28] Indeed, Downey's comment on 'various modalities' of engagement and resistance with public space can be taken to allow for art that is more explicitly political (Rancière's examples include novels such as Flaubert's *Madame Bovary* (1857)). Downey's focus, here, is not on the nature of such aesthetics but rather on 'the potential of art as a practice to open up horizons of possibility for civic imaginations to emerge, and be thereafter supported within a community-based network of social relations that remain independent of the diktats of politics, the edicts of religion and the deterministic, often divisive, rationale of the market' (Downey, 2014: 66). His chapter focuses on the post-revolutionary situation in Tunisia 'where civil society is precisely that which is most under threat after what for many must have appeared an interminable hibernation' (2014: 66).

revolutionary contexts. Such art – particularly since the mid-1990s – has sought to negotiate an alternative to Orientalist clichés and to monolithic visions emerging from countries in the Maghreb. When critics have drawn on theory in relation to art that renegotiates Orientalist clichés, in various contexts, they have often tended to use postcolonial concepts developed in relation to literature or anthropology.[29] This art resonates at times, to some extent, with certain postcolonial theories; for example, Khatibi's 'double critique' of essentialising tendencies in both Western and (in his case) Islamic traditions (Khatibi, 1983).[30] This theory, which is not usually cited in analyses of art, involves opposing totalising ideologies formulated in either French or Arabic by thinking 'otherwise, in *multilingual* ways, listening to any utterance – wherever it may be coming from' (Khatibi, 1983: 63; my translation; emphasis in original).[31] Such art tends increasingly to evoke an increasingly complex *multi*directional critique, engaging with, and contesting, various alternative extremisms from external and internal sources, as I have demonstrated elsewhere.[32] I use the term 'multidirectional' specifically to characterise such a critique – explicit or implicit – of multiple translatable essentialising visions, which allows alternative, untranslated or 'untranslatable' voices or visions to emerge (distinct from Michael Rothberg's use of this term).[33] This is frequently the case for art exploring the

---

[29] In art history and visual studies, critics have explored 'Arab art', and its renegotiation of Orientalism, since the mid-1990s; see, for example, Lloyd (1999); Lloyd, ed. (2001); Bailey and Tawadros, eds. (2003); O'Brien and Prochaska (2004). Studies of aesthetics of resistance to (neo-)colonial views can be found in the work of Enwezor and Okeke-Agulu (for example, 2009), Mercer (for example, 2008) and Shohat and Stam (1994).

[30] As Françoise Lionnet has stated, 'Khatibi's insights, in 1970, already herald Gayatri Spivak's now classic formulation "Can the Subaltern Speak?" (1988), while also anticipating responses to her work regarding the need for the dominant to learn to "listen"' (Lionnet, 2011: 387–407, 400).

[31] Regarding postcolonial art criticism, analyses have tended to draw on concepts such as Homi Bhabha's 'hybridity' or Edward Said's 'counterpoint'. See Bhabha (1994) and Said (1994 [1993]). An example of art criticism drawing on these, among other, postcolonial concepts can be found in Crinson (2006).

[32] My study of Franco-Maghrebi crossings in contemporary art demonstrated means of negotiating a way between clichés of 'otherness' and images of integration (understood as a one-way process), in relation to postcolonial concepts (Shilton, 2013a).

[33] The term 'multidirectional' has been employed, in conjunction with 'memory', by Michael Rothberg in his exploration of Black Atlantic and Franco-Algerian

revolutions. It evokes such a critique, often, by combining images, symbols, styles and media, or art practices and techniques, associated with, for example, local artisanal traditions, European or American art movements, or regional (highly diverse) Arabic modernist tendencies, such as the incorporation of writing (on the use of writing in Tunisian modern art, see Nakhli, 2017).[34] This work frequently involves lateral or 'minor transnational' connections, as evoked, for example, by Hamid's commissioning of Palestinian weavers to create portraits of a Tunisian martyr.[35] Comparable literary experiments can be found in Lina Ben Mhenni's blog in Arabic, French and English. Published as a book in French, with a trilingual title, *Tunisian Girl* (2011) continues to incorporate Arabic and English words. It also includes both verbal and visual references to online formats (a grey bar with red, orange and green buttons, along the top of the cover, mimics the frame of a webpage, for example).[36] But visual artwork exposes discursive gaps in ways that are particular to its multisensorial forms.

Such artwork moves beyond stable, discursive, 'readable' forms and languages.[37] It presents different cultures or communities and views of

'contact zones', which he reads across and through diasporic Jewish history (see Rothberg, 2009). The multidirectional process that is frequently a characteristic of postcolonial and recent post-revolutionary art resonates, in addition, with the term 'intervisuality', as used by Hafid Gafaïti in relation to literature by Franco-Algerian writer Rachid Boudjedra, and Nicholas Mirzoeff with regard to 'diaspora art' in African and Jewish contexts (see Gafaïti, ed., 1999; Mirzoeff, 2000).

[34] Some scholars have argued that the incorporation of Arabic writing comes mainly from a desire to 'Arabise' modern art; Alia Nakhli cites, for example, Afif Bahnasî (1984), Silvia Naef (1992) and Charbel Dagher (1990). Nakhli, however, focusing on Tunisia (1960–2015), demonstrates that this modernist practice varies between and within countries, historical contexts and the work of individual artists (Nakhli, 2017).

[35] On this notion, see Lionnet and Shih (2005). In tending to suggest both vertical and lateral connections between diverse sub- and supranational spaces, such artwork is also reminiscent of work in the field of anthropology, including Jonathan Xavier Inda and Renato Rosaldo's conceptualisation of a 'dislocated cultural space' (see Inda and Rosaldo, 2008).

[36] See also Dora Latiri's *Un amour de tn. Carnet photographique d'un retour au pays natal après la Révolution* (2013), which switches between French, English and Arabic (both written standard Arabic and transliterated Tunisian *Darija*), formal and informal (sms) modes and different fonts, in addition to incorporating text and photographs.

[37] Art critic Jean Fisher warns against reducing works of art to cultural products, highlighting the importance of their *affective* impact (Fisher, 2005 [1996]: 234; emphasis in original).

'difference' in ways that avoid constructing a hierarchy between them and, at the other extreme, reductively unifying them (for example, via the neo-colonial discourse of 'democracy' as a 'Western' ideal). It does so specifically by simultaneously bringing together, or evoking, different languages, states or identities, and holding them in tension. These works often point in alternative directions while rendering perceptible the separation between, or beyond, them through haptic, auditory, olfactory, kinetic or kinaesthetic elements. Apparent polar opposites are questioned through an emphasis on instability and are frequently shown to coexist interdependently, in a reciprocal, relational dynamic that allows alternative visions to emerge. Other works question and exceed one particular constraining vision. In numerous works of art, I argue, it is precisely the dynamic between stability and instability, control and contingency, the discursive and the non-discursive, which encourages spectators to adopt a more nuanced view of specific cultures in the MENA region and, latterly, of the Arab revolutions.

Rather than analyse these multisensorial works via postcolonial concepts, I explore this central dynamic through three alternative ideas, which are inspired by the works themselves and particularly by their tendency to combine diversely transnational elements through their practices and materials as a means to resist essentialising views. Two years before the demonstrations that led to the deposition of Ben Ali, Tunisian art historian and curator Rachida Triki examined what she perceived in the work of the latest generation of artists from the Maghreb, and particularly Tunisia, as 'résistance transculturelle' (Triki, 2009). She saw creating *between* the internal and the external – '[c]réer dans l'entre-deux de l'endogène et de l'exogène' ('creating in the gap between the endogenous and the exogenous') – as a potential means to resist 'à la fois à l'uniformisation du goût opérée par le marché mondialisé de l'art, et au traditionalisme à visée identitaire' (resist 'simultaneously the uniformisation of taste undertaken by the globalised art market and a traditionalism motivated by a concern with national identity') (2009: 58, 54). This tendency continues, as I have suggested above, in many examples of aesthetics of revolution in and beyond Tunisia, though this artwork is increasingly complex. Resonating with Triki's earlier observation, Mohamed Ben Soltane points to the need, since the revolution, to create the necessary structures to support the production and dissemination of art from Tunisia, 'un art dans lequel une grande partie des Tunisiens pourront se reconnaître et tout en étant ouvert sur l'extérieur et sur l'universel' ('an art in which a large portion of Tunisian society will be able to recognise itself while remaining open to the external and the universal') (Ben Soltane, 2012: 227; see also Triki, 2017). He signals the difficulties for artists in relation to the hegemonic international art system in which those whose work appears to conform to stereotypes (depicting subjects such as the Islamic veil, Islamist terrorism, and war) more easily gain international visibility (Ben Soltane, 2011; his comic strip, 'The Artist and the Emigrant', 2010, critiques this issue directly).[38] He also states that the very notion of 'contemporary art' is directly related to a Western history of art from which the 'south' has been marginalised (Ben Soltane, 2012: 217). As he asserts, citing Tunisian thinker Mondher Kilani (whose words anticipate Mignolo's argument), '[L]'art est bien sûr universel, mais ... "L'histoire universaliste du monde prouve qu'elle n'est qu'une version particulière de l'histoire"' ('[A]rt is, of course, universal, but ... "the universalist history of the world proves that it is merely one particular version of history"') (2012: 219; Kilani, 2002: 89). While the term 'transnational' could potentially be associated with the hegemonic recuperation and decontextualisation of such art, or with the 'uniformisation of taste' to which Triki refers, these works communicate an alternative understanding of the transnational.

Transnational flows, as critics such as Appadurai (1996) and Jay (2011) have argued, lead to increasing interconnectedness, but not to the erasure of local particularities. Jay warns, though, against the fetishising of the local as pure and static, insisting that the local is already a product of cross-cultural contact, appropriation and transformation (2011: 49, 70; see also Drewal, 2013). The history of Tunisian art exemplifies such a process. Tunisian art historian Hocine Tlili details its complex evolution 'entre Orient et Occident' ('between East and West'), beginning with the development of the artisanal tradition of painting under glass via the influence of Turkish and Italian figurative conventions, which it combined with certain Islamic aesthetics as well as themes from Muslim historiography (Tlili, 2012).[39] We must be equally critical, Jay indicates, in our use

---

[38] Ben Soltane also refers to Paris-based Moroccan artist Mounir Fatmi's reference to a 'commande cachée' when alluding to the expectations of some who commission his work (Ben Soltane, 2011).
[39] This tradition, Tlili states, '[s]ans renier l'esthétique de l'art musulman' ('without rejecting the aesthetic of Islamic art') (maintaining its calligraphic or decorative,

of the term 'global', for 'there are no global forms that are not made up of particulars from this culture and that' (Jay, 2011: 70). The emphasis, he says, 'ought to be on the multidirectionality of cultural flows, on the appropriation and transformation of globalized cultural forms wherever they settle in, with close attention to how those forms are reshaped and sent off again to undergo further transformations elsewhere' (2011: 71). In balancing a range of internal and external elements, the works of art I analyse in this book are often 'transnational' in a sense that coheres with what critics have shown to be the shifting complexity and heterogeneity in which multidirectional and often transversal global flows have resulted (see, for example, Appadurai, 1996; Lionnet and Shih, 2005; Inda and Rosaldo, 2008; Jay, 2011; Drewal, 2013). They involve both metaphorical and literal crossings, which evolve as the work itself shifts; indeed, these works are also transnational through the literal journeys they undergo during the process of their production, adaptation (in many cases), exhibition and reception. At the same time, the expectations and clichés they must negotiate at each stage of this process reveal the unevenness and diversity within transnational flows, countering celebratory and simplistic narratives of harmony.[40] Simplistic definitions, and celebratory perceptions, of the transnational can also be seen to be resisted by these works, as we will see, when certain external art practices or critical terms are employed in relation to local contexts.

My critical approach to this art aims, itself, to be diversely transnational in the sense of drawing inspiration from 'local', regional or other cross-cultural art practices, artists' statements and emails, and public responses to the works, as well as academic criticism. This multidirectional crossing of theory and practice, of different disciplinary fields and of divergent genres of writing, is only one possible approach, but it is perhaps appropriate in this context. It aims to allow for a multiplicity of converging, and sometimes conflicting, voices and

---

floral or geometric traditions), began, from the end of the eighteenth century to draw on themes from Muslim historiography (Tlili, 2012: 163). Tlili also details the shifts undergone by Tunisian art in relation, particularly, to Orientalist painting, the École de Tunis (formed in 1949–50) and, from the 1970s, modernised Arabo-Muslim art, combining the traditions of calligraphy or the arabesque with abstraction (Tlili, 2012).

[40] Jay refers to the criticism that authors such as Appadurai have received in relation to this subject (Jay, 2011: 33, 60).

viewpoints in analysing these emerging aesthetics and their shifting relationships to evolving revolutionary circumstances. The three interconnected concepts I develop below involve, variously, (1) 'transnationalising' (which includes 'localising') ideas and practices most often associated with 'Western' modernism – these are transformed in relation to specific contexts (in ways that demonstrate that this is only one variant of modernism); (2) highlighting the *already* transnational, specific and enduring nature of certain 'modern' practices and examining how they are developed or lead to new aesthetics in contexts of revolution; and (3) engaging with, but also contesting, ideas developed differently by academics and artist-curators in local and external locations. In each case, while this art might be seen to resonate with enduring ideas and practices – and, at times, engages directly with them – it invents new combinations or strategies in response to specific contexts of revolution, thus requiring alternative concepts.

I develop, first, the concept of 'infra-thin critique'. I show how certain art allows a reworking of the 'Western' modernist notion and practice of the infra-thin by drawing on, and developing, enduring or more recent local or transnational practices and anchoring these in relation to specific contexts of revolution. The infra-thin (developed by French artist Marcel Duchamp) refers playfully to the almost imperceptible separation, and passage, between two things. Among the examples provided are the warmth of a seat that has just been left, the reflection from a mirror or glass, and tobacco smoke when it smells also of the mouth that exhales it. The idea emerges in his practice through the use of elements such as moulds and casts (between presence and absence). Inspired by works that engage directly and ironically with Duchamp's practices, or with those of his successors, I examine such works and others that resonate with the dynamics of the infra-thin. My intention is not to suggest that this art is simply derivative, or indeed that criticism should 'turn back' to this variant of modernism to seek tools for analysis. Infra-thin dynamics – which can be discerned in numerous contemporary works by artists from Yves Klein to Roman Ondak, Kader Attia or Mounir Fatmi – are, in this art of resistance to clichés and extremisms, anchored in relation to specific cultures or communities for the purposes of resistance. While this work resonates with the dynamics of the infra-thin, moreover, it draws on, and adapts, diverse practices, including certain Arabic modernist uses of Islamic art, or the incorporation of local or regional artisanal traditions – the traces of weaving or the motifs of Islamic arabesques. This work can be seen to hold in tension dominant visual languages (including those of European/American and Arabic modernisms) while making way for an alternative. By viewing such works through the lens of the infra-thin, this concept becomes a form of transnational critique. These works resonate with the words of critics such as Gitti Salami and Monica Blackmun Visonà, who affirm, in their chapter on 'Writing African Modernism into Art History', that 'Modernism, modernity's expressive aspect, has as many local and regional variants as modernity itself' (Salami and Blackmun Visonà, 2013: 3). 'The flows and currents of the modern', moreover, as Drewal states, 'are rarely unidirectional'; 'Modernity is not a European invention'; and it is not particular to one period: 'Everywhere, and in every era, modernity is the result of trade-offs with tradition and vice-versa: both combine incessantly, reach compromises with each other, negotiate their respective places' (Drewal, 2013: 23). The art I analyse in this book continues a process of transformation and exchange that has long been transcultural.[41]

Secondly, I explore 'contingent encounters of resistance', which, I argue, are rooted in transnational aesthetics of contingency. The dynamic between stability and instability in this art is produced via the contingent encounter between stable and unstable forms or substances (ink, bread and water, or jasmine, for example), parameters and processes (including local practices of weaving or ceramics), or artists and participants (artisans, amateurs or spectators). The contingent processes employed in some works are reminiscent, to an extent, of European modernist aesthetics, including formlessness, which is most often associated with Georges Bataille, and the peripatetic mode (filming or photographing while travelling), which might call to mind Guy Debord's notion of the *dérive* (1956). But these works reveal distinctive practices, distancing them from such figures. Contingency, I argue, comes to be associated with resistance and this is precisely because of its emergence together with icons; that is, with apparently stable and instantly identifiable forms. The aesthetic resistance to form

---

[41] I employ the term 'transcultural' to refer to the reciprocal, relational, non-hierarchical processes of exchange suggested by Mary Louise Pratt's use of the word 'transculturation' (1992).

in these works evokes political resistance to authoritarianism. This diverse artwork, similarly to that conveying an infra-thin critique, adapts existing practices, or develops new means of balancing control and contingency, to communicate an ongoing 'revolution' between constraint and liberation, certainty and uncertainty. One way in which such art develops aesthetics of contingency, moreover, is by engaging with local and regional practices, including weaving, ceramic production and calligraphy. At times, this art draws directly on such enduring practices and deliberately uses the effects of their contingent processes to exceed iconic visions.

Works of art that generate contingency for the purposes of resistance develop practices that diverge from, and contribute to advancing debates surrounding, conventional understandings of chance aesthetics or participatory art. A proliferation of participatory art has appeared in Tunisia since the revolutionary events of 2011. As Tunis-based curators Christine Bruckbauer and Patricia Triki state, 'the idea of public space as a site for artistic presentations is ... rooted in the history of the Maghreb region' (2016). They refer to the traditions of public storytelling, dancing and music, as well as satirical shadow puppet theatre (which can be traced back to fourth-century Tunisia). Participation, though, they say, is new in Tunisian art, and significant in this context in which space was formerly monopolised by former heads of state through statues or posters of them, or streets named after them (see also Karoui, 2012). Certain work, though, I would add, involves *artisans* and their practices – practices which have long involved participation. Scholarship on participation in art frequently examines works that are ephemeral, consisting of a set of instructions for the spectators, for example, or of an exchange that takes place beyond the gallery and that can only be understood through documents. Certain critics and curators have favoured participatory art over what they see as 'autonomous' and 'exclusive' objects (see, for example, Kester (2004) and Bourriaud (1998)). I argue that works exploring the revolution or ongoing resistance often do produce a tangible art object – from wall hangings to video art or photographic collections. In works involving artisanal practices this is particularly important as a means to preserve a struggling tradition *and* to develop an aesthetic that is appropriate for communicating experiences and perceptions of Tunisia since 2010. These objects *do* tend to be inclusive, though they cohere with the view shared by Claire Bishop and Hal

Foster that participatory art is not inherently 'good' and has 'no intrinsic or fixed political affiliation' (Bishop, ed., 2006; Foster, 2006 [2004]: 195; Bishop, 2012).[42] I attend to formal and affective aspects of collectively made objects, while considering the ethical risks, but also the potential benefits, of various participatory methods in this political context. I examine works involving artisans or spectators at the stage of the work's production, exhibition or reception and show how participants are included directly or indirectly, knowingly or unknowingly, in fabricating an art object. I argue that such art exploring the revolutions spurs a rethinking of definitions of participatory art in developing new ways of involving others as a means to create contingent counterpoints to iconic faces or spaces.

In relation to the third concept I develop, my transnational approach involves engaging with the statements of a Tunis-based Franco-Tunisian artist and curator regarding the 'interface', and a North American art historian on the space between self and image generated by representations of the body. I develop the alternative idea of the 'multi-layered interface' as that which interpolates yet distances diversely located (and travelled) spectators to convey ongoing revolutions between constraint and resistance. Meriem Bouderbala comments on the 'interface' as 'that which separates the body from that which offers it to the gaze: skin, coverings and fabrics' (2012; my translation). She relates this interface to Islamic tradition, in which marks on the skin or folds of fabric both beautify and hide the body. I assess alternative practices and purposes of concealing and revealing, while expanding this trope to encompass images of performance between work of art and *hors champ* (that which lies beyond the frame), clandestine act and public intervention, and between spaces: physical and virtual, local and transnational. I show how the 'layers' created by presenting the performance on screen – and, frequently, online – contribute to the ambivalent interface between the spectators and what is presented. In maintaining a gap and point of tension between object and subject these works also resonate, to some extent, with Amelia Jones's argument that certain images of the body immerse the spectator but 'retain rather than attempting to resolve or disavow

---

[42] Claire Bishop comments on the false polarity of 'bad' singular authorship and 'good' collective authorship in discourse on participatory art (2012: 8). She also argues against the tendency to evaluate such art from a sociological perspective, which judges a work solely in terms of its demonstrable outcomes (2012: 13).

[the] tension between the subjective and objective world' (Jones, 2013 [2006]: 370). In this way, she suggests, such works break with enduring Euro-American perceptions of self and image that conflate them or see them as radically opposed. Works exploring the revolutions similarly present alternative perceptions, but they do so partly by drawing on local or regional corporeal practices, which they similarly contest and develop. They interpolate the spectators through sensorial elements, resonating with Jones's argument. Yet, these works, which tend to show the body interacting with visual icons, verbal languages or specific sites, produce an ambivalent, multi-layered interface specifically by partially obscuring, distorting or reworking the bodies and icons or iconic spaces they display through material, medial or cultural elements.

These three concepts are interconnected, and their related practices can sometimes be found in the same work. This art engaging with the revolutions can familiarise and alienate internal and external spectators in ways that depend on their location and knowledge. In these works, the gap between object and subject can be heightened not only through material, medial or cultural elements but also through contingent substances, the peripatetic mode, the involvement of others, or the dialectic between presence and absence. Such means can be seen to protect *opacité* (opacity), in Edouard Glissant's sense of irreducible 'otherness' in which the self is always implicated (Glissant, 1990: 203–09). 'Otherness', though, depends on who is looking and from where. This work – which, as I have suggested above, shifts as it is adapted or recreated in different formats or sites – is experienced by a diverse and evolving audience.

Chapter Summaries

Each chapter develops my argument that these works between art and activism engage spectators in ways that encourage them to think beyond binary perceptions of the revolutions, and allow, more widely, for an understanding of 'revolution' that accommodates transition, negotiation and diversity. Chapter 1 shows how this occurs in art that explores the relationship between visibility and invisibility for the purposes of resisting essentialising perspectives of specific revolutions or the wider, problematic idea of the 'Arab Spring'. I develop the theory and practice of 'infra-thin critique' in relation to works that resonate with the dynamics of the infra-thin or that engage directly and ironically with Duchamp's practices, or with those of his successors. This chapter addresses two particularly recurrent means of exceeding the iconic. Ambivalence between sensorial and dimensional elements is analysed with reference to Nicène Kossentini's video, *Le Printemps arabe* (The Arab Spring) (2011), and her later version of this work, a video and sound installation entitled *Himmel oder hölle* (*Heaven or Hell*, 2012), as well as Mounir Fatmi's *Les Temps modernes, une histoire de la machine – la chute* (Modern Times: A History of the Machine – The Fall) (2012). Alternative means of evoking the revolutions emerge in diverse manifestations of a 'poetics of absence'. I examine the contrasting ways in which an infra-thin critique emerges through: a practice of layering white on white in an installation by Safaa Erruas (*Drapeaux* (Flags), 2011–12); evocations of corporeal absence through the use of sculptural 'casts' resembling skin, in Sonia Kallel's *Which Dress for Tomorrow?* (2011); and the use of transparent materials: Aïcha Filali's *L'Angle mort* (Blind Spot) (2012–13) presents photographs on windows, and Shada Safadi's *Promises* (2012–13) uses multiple clear plastic screens to display distorted human forms. I argue that certain art allows a reworking of the 'Western' modernist notion and practice of the infra-thin by drawing on, and developing, local or transnational practices and anchoring these in relation to specific contexts of revolution. I develop my point that these works of art call for a critical approach that is inspired by art theory and practice and that is transnational, as well as transhistorical and multidirectional.

In the second and third chapters, I show how a comparable dynamic between stability and instability is produced through 'contingent encounters of resistance'. Contingency, I argue, comes to be associated with resistance through its convergence with icons. In the first section of Chapter 2, I analyse works that incorporate contingent processes and materials: Aïcha Filali's pair of sculptures – *Bourgeons en palabres* (Buds in Discussion) and *Bourgeons d'i(n)vers* (Opposing Buds) (2011) – is formed of twisted branches which bud with incongruous sculpted or ready-made objects indicative of diverse political voices. Hela Lamine presents distorted portraits of Ben Ali made in a decomposing mixture of bread and water in *Nous ne mangerons plus de ce pain-là* (2011). Meriem Bouderbala's *Flag Nymphéas* (Waterlily Flags) (2012) depicts a Tunisian flag sinking gradually into water. Lara

Favaretto's *As If a Ruin* (2012) consists of a cube made of brown confetti, which shifts, falls and scatters around the base of the sculpture as the spectator breathes on it and walks around it. Nadia Kaabi-Linke's installation, *Smell* (2012), reworks the black Salafist flag by embroidering the usually white calligraphic Shahada (Muslim confession of faith) with real jasmine, which wilts and loses its scent during the course of its exhibition. In the second section, I examine video work produced in the peripatetic mode: Mouna Karray's *Live* (2012) projects static images of Ben Ali together with the unedited soundtrack of a conversation between a taxi driver and a passenger who comment freely on the transitional government as they journey through Tunis. I examine a precedent in Ismaïl Bahri's *Orientations* (2010), which focuses on the evolving reflections in a cup of ink held by the artist as he walks within the streets of the capital. I consider how this work anticipates the more extreme limitations placed on vision in Bahri's videos *Foyer* (Home) (2016) and *Film à blanc* (Blank Film) (2013–14), for which he fixes a blank sheet of paper in front of the lens. Comparative reference is made to works such as Azza Hamwi's visually poetic tour around Damascus in *A Day and a Button* (2015).

Chapter 3 develops the idea that contingent encounters are rooted in diversely transnational aesthetics of contingency, but also that this art invents new combinations or strategies specifically to exceed iconic visions. It focuses on work that generates contingency by involving local or regional traditions of weaving and ceramics, as well as artisans themselves. This chapter also addresses art that engages spectators through recent transnational practices, including interactions characteristic of uses of social media. I show that this work diverges from conventional understandings of chance aesthetics and participatory art. I also argue that participatory works exhibited in physical and virtual public spaces, as well as in galleries, blur the boundaries between sites which are conventionally viewed as separate and as associated with either art or activism. The first section of this chapter explores contrasting means of evoking encounters between artist and artisans. I focus, first, on Ramallah-based Majd Abdel Hamid's *Mohammed Bouazizi* (2011), for which he commissioned female weavers from the Palestinian village of Farkha each to fabricate a portrait of the Tunisian martyr and wove the ninth portrait himself. I compare Hamid's work to a video performance by Selma and Sofiane Ouissi (*Laaroussa*, 2011), which was inspired by the gestures and sounds of female ceramicists at work in Sejnane, as part of a project to encourage development in this rural region of Tunisia. I show how Sonia Kallel involves artisans and their practices in comparable indirect ways in *Tisser la medina* (Weaving the Medina), an audio tour and video installation exploring the endangered profession of silk weaving in the medinas of Tunis and Sfax. The Ouissis and Kallel can be seen to invent new forms of participatory art by allowing the sounds, voices, images or gestures of artisans engaged in a local process in some measure to shape the work. The second part of the chapter addresses art that involves spectators in 'reordering space' or in making alternative 'icons' of Tunisia today or of the revolutions in Tunis, Cairo and Damascus. It gives particular attention to three installations: Collectif Wanda's *Le Ciel est par-dessus le toit* (The Sky Is over the Roof) (2012–13), Febrik's *The Watchtower of Happiness* (2012) and Mouna Jemal Siala and Wadi Mhiri's *Parti Facelook / Parti Facelike* (2012–13).

Finally, Chapter 4 explores the relationship between the work of art and its diverse spectators by developing the idea of the 'multi-layered interface'. I argue that this work engages spectators in ways that move beyond previous theory and practice examining images of the body. I focus on performance in photography and video, exhibited in galleries or disseminated online. This art negotiates a way between a complex web of icons, from Samuel Aranda's photograph of a fully veiled Yemeni woman holding her injured son to the controversial naked selfies posted on social media by certain women from Tunisia and Egypt in 2011. This chapter begins by addressing Lalla Essaydi's *Bullets* and *Bullets Revisited* (2012) and Majida Khattari's *Liberté, j'écrirai ton nom* (Freedom, I Will Write Your Name) (2012). I examine their development of a complex interface through the use of Arabic writing, photography and a range of French, other European, or Arabic and Persian imagery, in interaction with the performing body. I consider the extent to which these artists' adaptations and developments of the counter-Orientalist aesthetics they had practised since the 1990s question 'icons of revolutionary exoticism'. The chapter contrasts these works, produced in diaspora contexts, to local performances of revolution in Tunisia, Libya and Syria. I analyse new means of concealing and revealing the body to evoke revolutionary dynamics of constraint and liberation but also fragility and uncertainty. This section gives particular attention to a photographic series displaying the artist's body shrouded in white (Mouna Karray: *Noir* (Dark), 2013) and two videos in which a flag is reworked through corporeal gestures and voice or music tracks and found footage: Naziha Arebi's *Granny's Flags* (2012) and Philip Horani's online painting-performance, *Liberté* (2011). In the final section I focus on online videos of graffiti by Ahl Al Kahf and El Seed, a photographic street project by JR (*InsideOut*, 'Part 1 –Tunis', 2011), and street dance by Art Solution (*Je danserai malgré tout*, 2011). I show how these online videos of street art and dance at public sites in Tunisia ambivalently interpolate their diverse global audience in ways that compare with Horani's creation of a multi-layered multisensorial interface, while extending the work in time and space.

While the first two chapters give particular attention to works exhibited in galleries, and address primarily art exploring the Tunisian revolution, Chapters 3 and 4 compare works across a wider range of media, formats and contexts. The Conclusion reflects on the idea of the 'multi-layered interface' as central to works across this corpus, whether they address a potentially iconic body, object or space. It returns, in addition, to the approach adopted in the book, considering how these works of art allow for a reassessment of existing concepts and practices, as well as a movement beyond them.

1 Aesthetics of Revolution and Infra-thin Critique

One way in which art encourages an understanding of the revolutions that exceeds perceptions of them in simplistic binary terms of success or failure is by exploring the space between or beyond things or states. Some works, for example, examine the relationship between presence and absence. Safaa Erruas explores the Uprisings across North Africa and the Middle East by embroidering the flags of the twenty-two member states of the Arab League in tiny white pearls on white cotton paper in her installation *Les Drapeaux* (2011–12; Figure 1.1). Sonia Kallel uses an alternative colourless organic material – jute fibre – to evoke corporeal absence in her response to the Tunisian revolution, *Which Dress for Tomorrow?* (2011; Figure 1.2). Transparent screens or windows are employed by Aïcha Filali to support photographic cut-outs of ordinary Tunisians in *L'Angle mort* (2012–13, a work she began before the Tunisian uprising, in 2010; Figure 1.3). Shada Safadi also uses multiple clear plastic screens, but for etching distorted human forms commemorating the loss of numerous Syrian civilians in *Promises* (2012; Figure 1.4). Other works might be seen to explore the space between dimensions through, for example, two-dimensional discs which evoke three-dimensionality when in motion. Videos of spinning arabesques are employed in contrasting ways to reflect on the Tunisian revolution and/or the wider 'Arab Spring' in Kossentini's *Le Printemps arabe* (2011) and *Heaven or Hell* (2012; Figure 0.1) and Mounir Fatmi's *Les Temps modernes, une histoire de la machine – la chute* (2012). This range of gallery-based works exemplifies the more poetic responses to the revolutions. These works are, nonetheless, clearly anchored in relation to specific contexts through visual or verbal elements. Indeed, the space they create allows for alternative voices and visions of revolution between or beyond tangible or clearly legible, but static and reductive, icons. These works contrast notably with some of the more explicitly political – and, at times, controversial – participatory art in public spaces that I analyse in

1 Aesthetics of Revolution and Infra-thin Critique

Figure 1.1 Safaa Erruas, *Les Drapeaux* (2011–12), Institut du Monde Arabe, courtesy of the artist

Figure 1.2 Sonia Kallel, *Which Dress for Tomorrow?* (2011), Centre National d'Art Vivant de Tunis, courtesy of the artist

Figure 1.3 Aïcha Filali, *L'Angle mort* (2012–13), IFA Gallery Berlin, courtesy of the artist

Chapters 3 and 4.[1] Yet, they similarly evoke a dynamic between stability and instability and, often, control and contingency.

In this chapter I analyse this central dynamic through the concept and practice of 'infra-thin critique'. I show how certain art exploring the revolutions resonates, to some extent, with French artist Marcel Duchamp's notion of the 'inframince' ('infra-thin'), which he developed in the 1930s. Duchamp (1887–1968) is often viewed by art historians as the most radically original artist of the twentieth century. His pioneering approach to thinking about art and the art process – particularly in relation to the use of replication, appropriation, chance and ambivalence – has had a profound influence on artists across the world (see, for example, Ades et al., 1999;

---

[1] The works I analyse in this chapter have not triggered any negative responses, to my knowledge. The various critiques they entail are more subtle than those evoked in some of the work I discuss in subsequent chapters. Mounir Fatmi has not been able to exhibit his installation, *Les Temps modernes, une histoire de la machine – la chute* (which includes calligraphy associated with sacred inscriptions), in the Maghreb, as he told me in our email exchange of December 2019. One of Fatmi's earlier pieces, *Technologia* (2010), to which I refer briefly, was misinterpreted as blasphemous when displayed on the ground of the Pont-Neuf in Toulouse (2012). This was due partly to the accidental projection of the work without a sign to deter people from walking on it, and partly to the tense context in which it was exhibited (see Le Bars, 2012).

Figure 1.4 Shada Safadi, *Promises* (2012), The Young Artist of the Year Award (YAYA 2012) exhibition, A. M. Qattan Foundation, Ramallah, © photography Rula Halawani, courtesy of the artist

Naumann, 1999; Cros, 2006). My intention, as I indicated in the Introduction, is not to suggest that this art is simply derivative, or that criticism should 'turn back' to European modernism to seek tools for analysis. These artists do not draw intentionally on the infra-thin, though some do engage directly, and ironically, with Duchamp's work, and it is their work that inspired my critical approach.[2] I argue, rather, that such art resonates with the *dynamics* of the infra-thin, while it adapts a range of transnational (particularly Arabic and/or European) modernist or enduring local practices, or develops *new* practices, for the purposes of resistance. It continues what critics have shown to be the transcultural process of transformation and exchange which has long been central to variants of modernism in different locations and times, including early twentieth-century European modernism (Drewal, 2013; Salami and Blackmun Visonà, 2013). Holding onto the term 'infra-thin' serves to highlight not only the, at times, striking resonances of these works with this notion but also their differences from it, given their engagement with local or diversely regional practices and specific contexts of revolution.

Marcel Duchamp's notion of the infra-thin refers playfully – often humorously – to the almost imperceptible separation, and passage, between two things. Among the examples provided by the artist are: the warmth of a seat that has just been left, the reflection from a mirror or glass, people who pass through the metro gates at the very last moment, the sound made by felt trousers as the legs rub together when walking, tobacco smoke when it smells also of the mouth that exhales it, or the passage between dimensions (Duchamp, 1999 [1945]: 19–36). The recurrent emphasis, in Duchamp's notes, on sensorial elements other than the visual is in keeping with his resistance to both academic and avant-garde art – especially painting – and the privileged status it gave to the ocular. Duchamp's notion of the infra-thin emerges in his practice through the use of elements such as moulds and casts (between presence and absence), the portraits of the artist as his female alter ego, Rrose Sélavy, or his ready-mades (between functional object and work of art).[3] The infra-thin refers not only to the interval or nuance that separates material objects or dimensions, but also concepts, such as sameness and similarity, or signifier and signified.[4]

---

[2] On the evolution of the infra-thin in the work of Duchamp, his successors and indeed his predecessors (exclusively in Western contexts), see Davila (2010).

[3] On Duchamp's notion of the infra-thin and his manipulation of the boundaries of sexual difference through his portraits of Rrose Sélavy, see Amelia Jones (1994; particularly 142–45, 156 and 159). Jones highlights the interdependence of self and other, masculine and feminine, which is indicated by the notion of the infra-thin.

[4] This chapter necessarily draws on a selection of the numerous instances of the infra-thin that emerge both in Duchamp's forty-six notes and in diverse examples of his practice.

1 Aesthetics of Revolution and Infra-thin Critique

Art exploring the revolutions, as I indicated in the Introduction, avoids constructing a hierarchy between cultures and communities and, at the other extreme, reductively unifying them (for example, via the neo-colonial discourse of 'democracy' as a 'Western' ideal). It does so by simultaneously bringing together, or evoking, different languages, states or identities, and holding them in tension. Duchamp is not known to have thought about the infra-thin in relation to encounters between cultures or communities. Yet, this notion offers a means of thinking about such encounters in ways that avoid the extremes of hierarchisation and reductive unification. This is because numerous instances of the infra-thin point in alternative directions while also materialising the 'hinge' that connects them.[5] Specific states or identities are brought together, or simultaneously evoked, and are held in tension, rather than being fused to produce a synthesis or hybrid 'third' entity.[6] The infra-thin renders perceptible the separation between or beyond such states or identities to allow the singular to emerge.[7] Such a dynamic can frequently be discerned in art exploring the revolutions. At the same time, in such works, this dynamic is 'anchored' in relation to a particular context and specifically creates an alternative to iconic visual languages of revolution. It brings to mind Rami G. Khouri's call for humility and patience in attempting to understand the complex

---

[5] Duchamp's infra-thin resists absolute definition. While numerous instances of this notion evoke or materialise the space between *two* things or ideas, certain examples render perceptible the infra-thin space beyond *one* thing. For example, 'Les buées – sur surfaces polies (verre, cuivre / infra mince)' ('Condensation – on polished surfaces (glass, copper / infra-thin)') (note 36, 33).

[6] The notion of 'hybridity' is most frequently associated with Homi Bhabha, though this theorist explores the complex entanglement of cultures, as opposed to their reductive fusion. On criticism of the notion of hybridity in terms of a cultural fusion or synthesis, see, for example, the work of Fisher (2005) [1996].

[7] I use the term 'specific' to designate a sensorial or verbal component (of a work of art) that refers to an identifiable cultural space or language, and the term 'singular' to designate an element that exceeds the discursive and the culturally locatable. My use of these terms is reminiscent of the definitions given by Peter Hallward in his distinction between different modes of individuation: 'Roughly speaking, a singular mode of individuation proceeds internally, through a process that creates its own medium of existence or expansion, whereas a specific mode operates, through the active negotiation of relations and the deliberate taking of sides, choices and risks, in a domain and under constraints that are external to these takings. *The specific is relational, the singular is non-relational*' (Hallward, 2001: xii; emphasis in original). In the works of art I examine here, specific and singular elements coexist; indeed, the singular disruption, the evocation of untranslatable voices or unrepresentable perspectives, depends on allusions to the specific.

Uprisings beyond instantaneous media responses (Khouri, 2014: 14). Through what I am calling an 'infra-thin critique', the art I analyse in this chapter creates a space and a moment in time for reflection on specific local experiences of revolt or on the wider complex phenomenon of the Uprisings.

In this chapter I address two recurrent forms of infra-thin critique. Ambivalence between sensorial and dimensional elements is discussed with reference to Nicène Kossentini's video, *Le Printemps arabe* (2011), and her later version of this work, a video and sound installation, *Heaven or Hell* (2012), as well as Mounir Fatmi's *Les Temps modernes, une histoire de la machine – la chute* (2012). I argue that Kossentini's and Fatmi's works demonstrate how a multidirectional, infra-thin critique can be evoked through dimensional and sensorial shifts, and particularly through the use of kinesis. Both Kossentini and Fatmi engage directly and ironically with Duchamp's work by reappropriating his renowned spinning discs, or 'Rotoreliefs' – some of the first examples of kinetic sculpture – and combining them with Islamic cultural forms, reminiscent of Tunisian and other Arabic modernisms. I demonstrate that in contrasting ways a transcultural visual symbol is exceeded in their works, and a space for alternative voices and visions is evoked, through the use of specific aspects of the infra-thin: the passage between empty sounds and abstract referential meaning, the passage between the second and third dimension via movement, and the evocation of a fourth dimension through multidirectional outward expansion. In these ways the videos evoke both fragility and resistance to diverse essentialising views of the revolutions in a transnational context and simultaneously, in Kossentini's installations, in post-2010 Tunisia.

Such an alternative space is materialised through diverse manifestations of a 'poetics of absence'. I examine the contrasting ways in which an infra-thin critique emerges through: practices of layering white on white in Safaa Erruas's *Les Drapeaux* (2011–12); evocations of corporeal absence through the use of sculptural 'casts' resembling skin in Sonia Kallel's *Which Dress for Tomorrow?* (2011); and the use of transparent screens, combined with natural or artificial light, in Aïcha Filali's *L'Angle mort* (2012–13) and Shada Safadi's *Promises* (2012). Erruas's process of weaving in white is a form of mourning and her delicate flags evoke the fragility of nations across North Africa and the Eastern Mediterranean. Kallel's similarly colourless ball of jute suspended by metal wires (or tied with hemp string) conjures, by contrast, a constrained body and encourages reflection on Tunisia's uncertain future beyond the revolution. Yet, both can also be seen to resist essentialising perceptions of countries in the process of revolution, including clichés surrounding women. Filali, like Kallel and Kossentini, engages with the specific context of Tunisia. Her back-views of ordinary people in the street privilege the everyday over iconic images of Tunisia and the revolution. Safadi's poignant installation presents a marked divergence in its sombre tone, mourning and commemorating those lost in the civil war in Syria. I show how both installations, nonetheless, use transparent screens, human figures and light to create a space for alternative visions of 'revolution' and to engage the spectators physically and emotionally.

These works use different media, materials and techniques to convey what critics such as Fahed Al-Sumait et al. have insisted is the complex and transitional nature of the Arab Uprisings (2014a: 20). They highlight the importance of distinct states of ongoing revolution, from what scholars have shown to be the ambivalence and turbulence of nascent democracy in Tunisia (Dakhlia, 2011; Gana, 2013) to what rapidly became a complex and intractable civil war in Syria. The Syrian uprising, unfolding in more complicated circumstances, '[went] beyond its own internal dynamics to become an integral part of the region's major geopolitical conflicts', as Raed Safadi and Simon Neaime have detailed (2016: 187–8; see also Hashemi and Postel, 2013a: 6–7). At the same time, I argue, these works converge in their aesthetics and in their evocation of an 'infra-thin critique'. I consider this art, and this critical tool, in relation to wider aesthetics of resistance. This diverse corpus resonates with the infra-thin. At the same time, I argue, it innovatively combines existing transnational – including local and regional – practices, or develops alternative means of rendering visible the invisible, in ways that question reductive internal and external views of cultures, communities and revolutions.

Transnationalising the Infra-thin: Revolutionary Arabesques and *Le Printemps arabe*

One way in which the infra-thin passage between dimensions emerges in the work of Duchamp is through the use of rotating discs. His 'Rotoreliefs', though two-dimensional, give an illusion of three-dimensional relief. Early versions of these spiralling animated drawings were depicted in Duchamp's experimental film, *Anémic Cinéma* (1926). These Rotoreliefs were alternated with nine revolving discs displaying whirling alliterative puns, such as: 'Bains de gros thé pour grains de beauté sans trop de bengué', or: 'Esquivons les ecchymoses des Esquimaux aux mots exquis.' Alternative instances of the infra-thin frequently coexist in the same work. These absurd, ludic phrases can be seen in terms of a verbal instance of the infra-thin in their indication of the passage between empty sounds and abstract referential meaning, between signifier and signified. A further example can be discerned in the (partial) mirror reversal in the film's title, which is reminiscent of Duchamp's recurrent reference to mirrors, glass and reflections as generators of the infra-thin: 'Réflexion de miroir – ou de verre – plan convexe' ('Reflection of mirror – or of glass – convex surface') (note 9r, 22). He relates mirrors and reflections, moreover, to the passage between dimensions: 'Miroir et réflexion dans le miroir maximum de ce passage de la 2e à la 3e dimension' ('Mirror and reflection in the mirror maximum of this passage from the second to the third dimension') (note 46, 36). The film's opening shot can be seen to allude visually to this passage: the two capitalised words of the title seem almost to be hinged together, the 'c' of both appearing nearly to touch an imaginary mirror. This shot – like the dimensionally ambivalent discs it anticipates – evokes visually an infra-thin separation between surface and depth, which is explored verbally through Duchamp's sonorous language.

Two versions of a work by Tunis-based Nicène Kossentini – her video, *Le Printemps arabe* (2011, 6′), and her later version of this work, a video and sound installation, *Heaven or Hell* (2012, 6′) – explicitly rework Duchamp's *Anémic Cinéma* to explore the uncertainties surrounding the Tunisian revolution and the wider 'Arab Spring' (Figure 0.1). *Le Printemps arabe* (2011) displays a rotating circular arabesque which gradually loses cohesion. Patterns within the disc spin in alternative directions at different speeds, as the white border gradually shifts away and disappears, allowing the individual parts to scatter chaotically to the edges of the frame. This visual explosion resonates with Tahar Ben Jelloun's figurative image of the Arab Uprisings: 'La patience des peuples a ses limites, le vase devait finir par déborder: il s'est brisé en mille morceaux' ('There are limits to people's patience; the vase had eventually to overflow: it shattered into a thousand pieces') (Ben Jelloun, 2011: 12). This process of fragmentation communicates revolutionary liberation, but also the loss of a secure sense of social and cultural identity. Shots of the fragmenting arabesque are interspersed with others displaying rotating discs on which isolated Arabic words are written in a spiral. Each of the five discs presents a selection of disconnected words and expressions associated with hell and paradise, taken from the Qur'an (which appear translated into French or transcribed phonetically in the corner of the screen) – 'jardins, paradis, délices, faveurs, le bien, ruisseaux, Salsabil, haut placé, vive, source' ('gardens, paradise, delights, favours, the good, streams, well') (disc 1); 'subissez, jetez, carcans, bruyantes, attisé, gardiens de vergers, vignes, liqueurs, cachetées, surélevés, à leur journée, étalé, coupe, débordante' ('endure, throw away, constraints, noisy, stirred up, orchard caretakers, vines, liquors, sealed, raised, on their day, spread out, bowl, overflowing') (disc 2); 'ne leur parle pas, malédiction, Saqar, flambée, flammes ardentes' ('don't speak to them, curse, Hell, burnt, burning flames') (disc 5).[8] The images of the hypnotic rotating discs are accompanied by the similarly incessant sound of rhythmic clapping, reminiscent of a revolutionary march.

In Kossentini's work, dimensional and verbal ambivalence are combined with transcultural tension for the purposes of a multidirectional critique. In bringing together the Rotorelief and an arabesque, Kossentini produces a form that comes to represent neo-imperialism, as well as political singularity and apparent social unity within Arab countries such as Tunisia (this work can be read as evocative both of the wider Arab Uprisings and of the specific case of the Tunisian revolution, particularly given its exhibition at 'Dégagements ... La Tunisie un an après').[9] *Le Printemps arabe* evokes not only political and social upheaval and transition but also an *artistic* revolution. Kossentini perceives the alternation in *Le Printemps arabe* between rotating discs inscribed with Arabic words, or formed to resemble an arabesque pattern, 'comme une métaphore sur un "art contemporain arabe" qui oscille entre les couleurs vives des racines et les voix saturées des horizons' ('as a metaphor for a "contemporary Arab art", which oscillates between the bright colours of its past and the myriad voices

---

[8] *Saqar* and *Salsabil* are proper nouns referring to Hell and to a source of water in Paradise, respectively.
[9] Institut du Monde Arabe (IMA), Paris, 2012.

of its future') (Kossentini, 2012).[10] The explicit reappropriation of the French artist Duchamp calls for a more inclusive history of art; it critiques the persistent marginalisation of works that explore Arabic forms as 'traditional' or 'decorative' (Rachida Triki has highlighted the importance for Maghrebi art of distinguishing itself from the label 'contemporary Arab art' established by the 'northern' art market system (Triki, 2017); see also Ben Soltane, 2012).[11] This visual manoeuvre can equally be seen to critique the tendency to essentialise and exoticise Tunisia, which persisted in both French and Tunisian political rhetoric until the very end of Ben Ali's leadership; it indicates the entanglement of French and Maghrebi histories more widely. It is also reminiscent of the history of Tunisian artists' distinctive critical engagements with the regional tendency to combine modern art with enduring Arabic forms such as the arabesque and calligraphy, particularly since the 1970s (see Tlili, 2012; Nakhli, 2017).[12] Yet, the evocation of an 'art contemporain arabe' appears simultaneously to articulate liberation from the former censorship of art and culture in Tunisia, as part of the work's more general opposition to the political and social constraints associated with the former regime. Viewed in 2012, the work could also be seen to contest new forms of extremism and attempts at censorship in politics and society as well as in art. In Kossentini's work the circular form functions, like an icon, to represent political singularity and apparent social unity within Arab countries such as Tunisia, as well as forms of 'neo-imperialism' via the global art market – through its trends and its curatorial practices – and through French and European foreign policy. The circular form emerges in this

---

[10] The artist's statement appeared in the accompanying note at 'Dégagements ... La Tunisie un an après' (IMA, Paris, 2012).

[11] I referred in my introduction to this book to Mohamed Ben Soltane's observation that the very notion of 'contemporary art' is directly related to a Western history of art (Ben Soltane, 2012: 217).

[12] Kossentini's individual combination of visual forms, languages and sources, including Arabic, the arabesque and the Qur'an, also reflects her quest for the close relationship she had to Arabic during her childhood. In an interview with Nakhli, who investigates Kossentini's use of writing in works such as *Shakl*, in 2014, the artist stated: '"Dans ma culture, je n'ai pas grandi avec l'image, mais avec la poésie arabe" ... "Durant mes études, j'ai dû abandonner la langue arabe. Cela a créé une déchirure. Je pense en français et je rêve en arabe" ('"In my culture, I grew up not with the visual image but with Arabic poetry" ... "During my studies, I had to abandon the Arabic language. This created a rupture. I think in French and I dream in Arabic"') (Nakhli, 2017).

work as a visual language of domination in both 'Western' and 'Arab' cultures and, moreover, of complicity between the French government and that of Ben Ali.

In Kossentini's work, dimensional ambivalence is ironically exacerbated through fragmentation. The visual symbol of alternative 'centres' of power is exceeded through the use of kinesis in combination with a display of gradual centripetal diffusion. The disc does not actually dissolve; rather, it mutates into a formless, shifting array of multiple individual parts, which resists the organising principles of the circular form. This evolving configuration can be seen to allude to a location beyond iconic, translatable, 'complicit' visual languages. This visual process is echoed by the rotating discs of isolated verbal signifiers. Kossentini heightens the verbal ambivalence present in Duchamp's *Anémic Cinéma*. Singular and plural nouns, with or without articles, coexist with adverbs and imperatives, as well as adjectives and past participles with feminine, masculine singular or plural agreements. These words and expressions, which are disconnected from a specific object and abstracted from syntactical order – and, moreover, from a single language – coalesce to generate an impression of an ambivalent and precarious Tunisia in transition. Associations can be made within and across discs between words connotative of freedom and constraint (an impression reinforced by the proliferation of imperatives), utopia and chaos, heaven and hell. This impressionistic use of the verbal – in parallel to the visual disintegration of the cohesive circular mosaic – articulates radical, intractable diversity, which cannot be contained by a system, be it linguistic, visual or political. The impression of intractability is compounded by the visual transculturation of artistic forms – the Islamic arabesque and the Duchampian Rotorelief – as well as the verbal insistence on 'untranslatability' in the transliteration of a number of Arabic words.

In Kossentini's installation, *Heaven or Hell*, the same translatable visual symbol is exceeded not only through movement but also through additional, auditory and kinaesthetic, elements. In this alternative version of *Le Printemps arabe* (2011) the video of a fragmenting arabesque is projected onto the gallery floor. The discs displaying Arabic words are absent; instead, the same words are sung in German as part of an experimental soundtrack (the piece was first exhibited as *Himmel oder Hölle* at the IFA-Galerie in Berlin and Stuttgart, 2012). The disconnected words are accompanied by sounds that could be identified with shattering glass, multiple tumbling objects and a slowly creaking door. These contingent sounds exist beyond a musical order; that is, like the disconnected words, in the infra-thin passage between signifier and signified. In relation to the creaking door, it is tempting to recall Duchamp's photograph of his door at *11, rue Larrey* (1927), between closed and open, an ironic engagement with the French proverb, 'Il faut qu'une porte soit ouverte ou fermée' ('A door must be open or closed'). In Kossentini's work these untranslatable material processes are employed specifically to evoke an ambivalent, transitional Tunisia, between past and future, and a revolution that is ongoing.

The uninterrupted shots of the apparently arbitrary pattern of rotating and dispersing coloured fragments evoke a kaleidoscope – an impression that is enhanced by the sounds of loose, tumbling objects and shards of glass. It is suggestive of the multiple reflections produced by inward-facing mirrors – not only in a kaleidoscope but also in Duchamp's use of a hinged mirror to produce a photograph portraying him simultaneously from five different vantage points (*Portrait multiple de Marcel Duchamp*, unidentified photographer, 1917).[13] Moving beyond the idea of multifaceted personal identity that is present in Duchamp's portrait, Kossentini's emphasis on multiplicity – and competing perspectives – signals post-revolutionary uncertainty since the (re-)emergence of diverse political voices. In this installation the shattering glass – together with the disconcerting, off-key song between music and recitation – heightens the sense of fragility. But visual, verbal and auditory multiplicity in Kossentini's work equally evokes radical, intractable diversity. Duchamp's five-way portrait suggests, as Craig Adcock writes, 'the complexity, the multi-directionality, and outward expansion of the four-dimensional continuum away from normal space' (Adcock, 1987: 155). Kossentini's expanding pattern can similarly be seen to indicate metaphorically such an alternative space, while this is mobilised specifically to make way for an interpretation of the revolution in terms other than the binaries of success and failure. The words evocative of heaven and hell, in the soundtrack, could appear to interrogate the revolution in binary terms; moreover, the presentation of the literal revolutions of a disc could seem ironically

---

[13] A kaleidoscope usually functions through the use of three such mirrors positioned at 60° angles.

to question whether the revolution is a reality or merely an illusion.[14] Yet, the visual diffusion of the arabesque points to the irrevocable rupture with dictatorship. *Le Printemps arabe* communicates ambivalence and tension; but the sensorial and dimensional shifts beyond symbols and systems in this work appear to allow for the idea that instability and fragility are inherent in the necessarily gradual process of democratic transition. The visualisation of an explosion and shattering resonates as much with Ben Jelloun's characterisation of the onset of revolution as with Dakhlia's emphasis on the resultant process of nascent democracy in the proper sense of the term:

Le piège de la dictature est brisé. Quand bien même elle entrerait dans la tourmente, la société tunisienne, comme d'autres sociétés arabes, serait sortie du schème mortifère d'une histoire étale et subie, d'une stabilité illusoire et imposée. Le rapport démocratique au politique est quant à lui par nature instable, toujours réversible et fragile. (Dakhlia, 2011: 114)

(The fetters of dictatorship have been broken. Even while it might experience a period of upheaval, Tunisian society, like other Arab societies, will be free of the fatal monolithic representation of a history of weakness and subjugation, of a stability that is illusory and imposed. The relationship between democracy and the political is, by its very nature, unstable, always reversible and fragile.)

A further contingent, kinaesthetic element is introduced into this work via the spectator's physical movement through the light projection, which disrupts, and further fragments, the kaleidoscopic arabesque. We might recall, here, Duchamp's interest in 'toutes les sources de lumière' ('all the sources of light') and in the shadows they produce; as he states, 'les porteurs d'ombres travaillent dans l'infra mince' ('the carriers of shadows work in the infra-thin') (note 3, 21). The spectator's physical interaction with the work doubles the conceptual exchange between the art object and the spectator, a further instance of the infra-thin.[15] In Kossentini's work the spectator can be seen to

---

[14] At the 'Dégagements …' exhibition (IMA, 2012), Kossentini stated in the note accompanying the work: 'Le jour et nuit s'alternent et "l'histoire se répète" disait Ibn Khaldoun. Alors, "le printemps arabe" est-il illusion ou réalité?' ('Day and night alternate and "history repeats itself", as Ibn Khaldoun would say. So, is "the Arab Spring" an illusion or a reality?').

[15] In his notes Duchamp refers specifically to: 'L'échange entre ce qu'on offre aux regards … et le regard glacial du public (qui aperçoit et oublie immédiatement). Très souvent cet échange a la valeur d'une séparation infra

embody this notion as they simultaneously create shadows and provide the shifting backdrop for equally mobile fragments of the evolving pattern. In this work, multidirectional shifts between dimensional and sensorial elements combine to generate a multisensorial experience of opacity for the diverse spectators. The reciprocity between ungraspable identities that is central to Glissant's postcolonial concept is just as fundamental to Duchamp's infra-thin. In its juxtaposition of both translatable and untranslatable elements, *Heaven or Hell* encourages the spectators to rethink their perceptions of the Arab Uprisings, while highlighting their inevitable involvement in their histories and representations.

Kossentini's work resonates with the notion of the infra-thin – and Duchampian practices of the infra-thin – but, through the dynamic that it generates between stability and instability, it critiques, and holds in tension, different cultures and views of 'difference'. It conveys a sense of 'Western' and 'Arab' cultures as interconnected and porous, yet specific, while it equally evokes alternative, singular perspectives. A strikingly comparable critical adaptation of Duchamp's Rotoreliefs to communicate cultural interaction in ways that avoid, on the one hand, neo-colonial exoticism or abjection and, on the other hand, hybridisation can be found in the work of Mounir Fatmi. Fatmi (who works between Tangiers and Paris) reappropriates and adapts the Rotoreliefs specifically to critique alternative forms of global hegemony. His discs displaying Islamic calligraphic hadiths (sayings ascribed to the Prophet Muhammad) are accompanied by the jarring sounds of machinery to signal an equivalence between extremist uses of religion and the rapid technological developments characteristic of late capitalism, as well as exclusive canonical histories of art (Fatmi's discs allude ironically not only to Duchamp but also to celebrations of modernity in paintings by Fernand Léger or Robert and Sonia Delaunay). This process appears to desacralise 'Islamic' objects, while it reorientates them to inhibit reductive perceptions of 'Islam'. As in Kossentini's work, the infra-thin passage between dimensions, which is

> mince (voulant dire que plus une chose est admirée ou regardée moins il y a sépa. inf. m.?' ('The exchange between what we offer to the onlookers' gaze ... and the glacial gaze of the public (who perceives and immediately forgets). Very often, this exchange carries the value of an infra-thin separation (meaning that the more a thing is appreciated and looked at, the less there is an inf. t. sep.?') (note 10, 22). In his practice he seeks to retain this infra-thin separation.

rendered visible through kinesis, is allied to a multidirectional critique. Translatable visual languages are similarly held in tension, allowing for singular, untranslatable voices and nuanced perspectives. In Fatmi's work 'globalisation' emerges as a multidirectional process, rather than a one-way phenomenon originating in 'the West'. In video installations such as *Technologia* (2010, 15′) the spinning hadiths gather such a speed as to suggest the potential assimilation or annihilation of one culture by the other or, alternatively, their eventual fusion in a harmonious, universal, utopian space.[16] Yet, while the distinctive, translatable visual languages threaten to dissolve into a haze of whiteness, the sense of tension and irresolution between coexistent entities is maintained. Alternative cultures – symbolised by the hadiths and Rotoreliefs – remain recognisable and identifiable.

Fatmi's video installation *Les Temps modernes, une histoire de la machine – la chute* (2012) engages with diverse states of revolution in North Africa and the Middle East. This work transposes and develops the artist's earlier video installation *Les Temps modernes, une histoire de la machine* (2009–10; see https://www.youtube.com/watch?v=lgXHL91MaQg).[17] Named after Chaplin's ludic examination of the connection between industrialisation and alienation in *Modern Times* (1936), the earlier version of this work explores contemporary global forces of domination and alienation with particular reference to the rapid pace of urbanisation in the Middle East. The video – in this work and the later version – consists of a complex panoramic cluster of multiple circular hadith–machine cogs of different sizes, rotating clockwise or anticlockwise. These are combined with linear blocks reminiscent of skyscrapers within which ancient Kufik script shifts up and down, or right and left. Characteristically, manifestations of global hegemony – embodied by architecture and technology – are ambivalently aligned with religion through divine calligraphy.

Fatmi's installation foregrounds the dangerous power of 'machines' or systems, including that of language – a connection which emerges emphatically through the inclusion, on the far right-hand side, of a number of Arabic letters with a key, in Latin script, to their pronunciation. This key can be seen to allude to the translatability of systems of

---

[16] Exhibited at *#Cometogether* (Old Truman Brewery, London, 2012; part of the 'Edge of Arabia' project).
[17] This video shows the work alongside Fatmi's video *Technologia* (last accessed June 2020).

power across cultures and, moreover, the complicity of Middle Eastern centres with global forces of urbanisation and economic liberalisation. Yet, the alternative 'languages' – still identifiable – are ambiguously contested through their juxtaposition and their setting in motion. Dimensional and cultural dissonance is exacerbated by the affective scraping and, at times, high-pitched sounds of machinery. These sounds can, from one perspective, be equated with the overwhelming, assimilating power of the global machine. But, in their irregularity and their frenzy, they appear to point to the instability and the unsustainability of mutually reinforcing systems. *Les Temps modernes, une histoire de la machine* was, indeed, created in the context of the worldwide recession which, by the end of 2009, had reached Dubai. Fatmi's work resonates particularly with the situation of this Emirate which had managed, particularly through the lavish construction projects of companies such as Dubai World, to sustain an image of imperviousness to the credit crunch. In November 2009, though, this company announced that it would seek a six-month moratorium on repayments of its debt of £36.5 billion, sending shockwaves through the world markets (Teather, 2009). Viewed against this backdrop, Fatmi's work conveys resistance to 'mirages' of wealth and power. It also creates an impression of the fragility of 'East–West' relations in the context of a world on the brink of economic collapse.

Fatmi's more recent version of this video installation combines references to the economic downfall – of the Middle East and the wider world – with allusions to the fall of dictatorships in the wake of the Arab Uprisings. This multi-layered 'fall' is signalled in the extension of the title: *Les Temps modernes, une histoire de la machine – la chute*, and emerges emphatically and dramatically in the video: the same intricate panoramic arrangement eventually fragments when the multiple objects are dislodged and literally fall away to leave a black screen. This work can be seen to allude not only to the complicity of 'East' and 'West' in the perpetuation of extravagant, yet debt-fuelled, construction projects but also to the diplomatic support given by many Western governments to former dictatorial regimes (see, for example, Lofti Ben Rejeb, 2013). Reminiscent of Kossentini's installations, Fatmi's work engages with, and contests, such political (and economic) complicity through the creation and dispersal of a transcultural symbol or linguistic system of symbols. Through such a process, it similarly alludes to the 'fall' of social and cultural stability – which was founded on a myth of political cohesiveness – ambivalently raising the question as to whether those revolutions that have taken place have succeeded or failed. Exhibited in 2012, it could be seen to ask whether the uprisings that continue, in countries such as Syria, are worth the tragic loss of life they have engendered. Yet, the work resists a firm political statement, functioning rather to raise questions for further debate and to highlight what critics such as Fahed Al-Sumait et al. (2014b) have shown to be the complexity and uncertainty of diverse states of ongoing revolution. As in Kossentini's work, the process of deconstruction and destruction evokes irrevocable rupture, a necessary tabula rasa, and the inevitable turmoil of emergent (and potential) democracies.

Kossentini's and Fatmi's works demonstrate how a multidirectional, infra-thin critique can be evoked through dimensional and sensorial shifts, and particularly through the use of kinesis. They evoke both fragility and resistance to diverse essentialising views of the revolutions in a transnational context and simultaneously, in Kossentini's installations, in post-2010 Tunisia. The tension between stability and instability, the translatable and the untranslatable, that is central to such a critique can alternatively be evoked by exploring the dialectic between presence and absence.

'Poetics of Absence': Commemoration and Resistance from Tunisia to Syria

This 'poetics of absence' (to employ the expression used by artist Safaa Erruas) takes a number of forms, from the use of light and shadow or reflection to the practices of weaving in white or etching on glass (Erruas, 2012: 80). While the works of Kossentini and Fatmi allude to local and regional practices of ceramic production and calligraphy, the methods and materials employed by Erruas, Kallel, Filali and Safadi are reminiscent of a range of existing transnational or local practices. Their works resonate with the notion of the infra-thin in their suggestion of passage, nuance, instability and contingency, while they innovatively adapt and combine existing practices or develop alternative means of rendering visible the invisible. At the same time, reminiscent of Kossentini's and Fatmi's 'revolutionary arabesques', their poetics of absence comes to be associated with both fragility and resistance as they respond to regional and/or local instances of revolution.

Installations by Safaa Erruas (based in Tetouan, Morocco) and Tunis-based Sonia Kallel explore revolutionary tensions through contrasting uses of colourless organic material. Erruas's *Les Drapeaux* (2011–12) consists of the flags of the twenty-two member states of the Arab League, which are remade through the painstaking process of embroidering tiny white pearls onto white cotton paper (Figure 1.1).[18] While the use of white on white was not a practice employed by Duchamp, the attenuated flags resonate with his note regarding colours: 'Transparence "atténuant" les couleurs en infra mince' ('Transparency "attenuating" the colours in infra-thin') (note 24, 26). This practice resonates more immediately with Russian artist Kasimir Malevich's *White on White* (1918), a tilted square within a square in different tones of white. Through this non-objective Suprematist painting, produced one year after the October Revolution, Malevich sought a language that would distance art from the visible world – and from service to the state or religion – cohering with his anti-materialist, anti-utilitarian philosophy ('Suprematism' is the name Malevich gave to his abstract art characterised by basic geometric forms painted in a limited range of colours, from 1913; see Tate.org, n.d. a). In Erruas's work, by contrast, this practice is ironically adapted to depict objective, political symbols.[19] *Les Drapeaux* retains clear links to the visible world, while it avoids both the iconic language of revolution and the opposite extreme of abstraction. It forges an 'infra-thin' language between visibility and invisibility. Grouping together the multiple flags, this work signals diversity within the MENA region. It draws attention to the contrasting situations of the nations that are frequently encapsulated in the international media by expressions such as 'Arab Spring'. Draining these symbols of colour, however, the installation simultaneously questions the idea of national, or regional, cohesion. These delicate objects communicate the current fragility of diverse Arab countries.

[18] Exhibited at: '25 ans de créativité arabe' (IMA, Paris, 2012–13).
[19] A precursor for Erruas's *Les Drapeaux* can be found in Fatmi's use of white-on-white to contest iconic visual languages, despite differences in practice, context and tone. Fatmi's multiple white bas-reliefs of Arabic calligraphy sculpted with antenna cables allude ironically to ancient Islamic art, the contemporary global media and Malevich's painting. He sculpts proverbs or, in other works, religious or media icons from Michelangelo's *Pietà* to the captured, dishevelled Saddam Hussein or the Al-Jazeera logo.

Erruas's delicate colourless handmade flags are reminiscent of Brazil-based artist Mira Schendel's drawings on rice paper combined with clear acrylic, through which she pursued the idea of 'transparency'.[20] Erruas's suspension of multiple flat rectangular objects, which can be seen from both sides, is particularly comparable to Schendel's installation *Variantes* (1977).[21] A connection can also be made to a further rare installation by Schendel, which visualised invisibility as a silent means of resisting the military dictatorship in Brazil (1964–85): *Ondas Paradas de Probabilidade* (Still Waves of Probability) (1969) consisted of thin nylon threads hanging from the ceiling and gathering on the floor.[22] But Erruas, who creates all her work in white, uses the method of embroidery. She forges a visual language which resonates as much with transnational modernist aesthetics as with a method traditionally practised by communities of women in the Maghreb. Her white-on-white practice reminiscent of Malevich's geometric abstraction is combined with this delicate 'feminine' practice. Yet, it is through this 'feminine' practice that she resists essentialising views.[23] The absence articulated by this work can be seen to create a space specifically for women's voices. It draws attention to the particularly fragile and uncertain situation for women in apparently post-revolutionary

[20] Safaa Erruas mentioned the influence of Schendel on her work (as well as Richard Serra and Andy Goldsworthy) in an email exchange of May 2015. Schendel, by contrast, uses abstract forms of letters and numbers. This artist's aim to produce visual, temporal and spatial 'transparency' has been compared to the work of philosopher Jean Gebser (see 'Mira Schendel', 1 March–24 June 2014, Tate Modern, London, and Pinacoteca do Estado de São Paulo (Tate Modern, 2014: exhibition document, no author's name provided; www.serralves.pt/documentos/Roteiros/MiraSchendel_Eng.pdf).

[21] Rather than seeing the same translucent forms, as we could in Schendel's installation pursuing transparency, we view different flags on each side.

[22] See www.drosteeffectmag.com/mira-schendel-tate-modern/ (2013: exhibition document, no author's name provided). The installation was accompanied by a text from the Old Prophet of Kings. While many artists chose to boycott the 1969 São Paulo Biennial, Schendel, as the Tate Modern suggests, created these 'waves' evoking freedom together with a text alluding to crisis and the faith required to endure it (www.drosteeffectmag.com/mira-schendel-tate-modern/).

[23] Erruas's work cannot simplistically be described as 'feminine', despite her use of embroidery and frequent incorporation of the tools used by women in this practice, as Bernard Collet has suggested in relation to her earlier production: 'the forcefulness that exudes from Erruas' paintings and installations challenges this notion and we find that it balances on the fragile frontier that outlines us all, men and women and the time we are allotted in the days of our lives' (Collet, 2009).

contexts such as that of Tunisia. The work was produced in the same year as the controversy in Tunisia provoked by the draft constitution (released in August 2012) in which women's role would be 'complementary' rather than 'equal' to that of men (see, for example, Allani, 2013; Charrad and Zarrugh, 2014; Labidi, 2014b). *Les Drapeaux* diverges from other pieces by this artist, which evoke violence against the female body. It can be seen, rather, as a quietly subversive expression of female subjectivity and regional solidarity. For Erruas, her 'poetics of absence' is also a form of mourning (Erruas, 2012). In its fragility this work poses questions as to futures of nations in North Africa and the Middle East, while it simultaneously mourns the deaths of martyrs for the cause of the revolutions, and perhaps the oppression of certain communities in their aftermath. The laborious process of embroidery comes to be associated with catharsis. Reminiscent of Kossentini's work, in *Les Drapeaux* the infra-thin passage between colour and transparency, the objective and the non-objective – and, moreover, artistic practices constructed as 'masculine' and 'feminine' – can be seen to convey fragility but also to evoke a multidirectional critique. It is this dynamic that encourages an 'other' mode of thinking and viewing in Khatibi's sense. This work resonates with infra-thin tensions between opposites, while it develops a distinct and diversely transnational poetics of absence and resistance to alternative essentialising forces: neo-colonialism, dictatorship, (internal and external) patriarchal views of women, and the art historical canon.

The dynamic, in Erruas's work, between presence and absence, death and life, fragility and resistance, past and future, finds a parallel in Sonia Kallel's sculptural work *Which Dress for Tomorrow?* (2011; Figure 1.2). Kallel's minimal work, by contrast, evokes an absent body through the use of beige jute fibre, analogous – both in its colour and in its organic, porous qualities – to human skin. Kallel has employed this material in previous works, such as *Ma Robe de mariage* (My Wedding Dress) (2003), which resembles both a constrictive dress and the distorted skin 'cast' of a human body. Suspended on a wire hanger chained to the ceiling, this dress evokes a haunting apparition. In *Which Dress for Tomorrow?* The same 'cast' is compressed into a tight ball which is held together by taut metal wires and suspended by a transparent thread.[24]

---

[24] As presented at 'Rosige Zukunft' in Stuttgart (2013). As Sonia Kallel stated in our email exchange of December 2019, the work was suspended by a transparent thread, the idea being to concentrate on the subject rather than on the installation.

Through ambivalent sculptural 'casts' between presence and absence, Kallel's sculptures communicate simultaneously both incarceration and liberation:

> My coverings are an expression of experiences and conflict situations. In my works I allow body and clothing to encounter each other in a relationship of power. The desire to attach the body and subject it to extreme aggression was triggered by an immense, almost compulsive drive within me. My approach is based on compulsion and characterized by a kind of sadism towards the body: I pull my inadequate items of clothing over it, causing unpleasant, painful sensations. To an equal degree, these coverings are skins that I remove to release the body; they oscillate between dream and reality. They are independent subjects, porous surfaces that breathe and live. And they are complex skins that disclose an injury to the body and project anyone attempting to resist them into an oppressive universe. These coverings call to mind unpleasant situations and express a feeling of being imprisoned, a shortness of breath and fear. They tell of pain and suffering ... (Kallel, 2012: 91)[25]

Kallel's works convey a similar dynamic to that which is present in Erruas's work. But Kallel focuses on the antagonistic relationship between body and clothing. Her visceral practice, which exploits the contrasting qualities of jute, conveys sensorial – as well as conceptual and emotional – ambiguities, which affect and interpolate the spectator.

Ma Robe de mariage can be seen to use this ambivalent material to signal the separation and dynamic between the constructed identities imposed on women and their 'real' status as living, breathing, embodied subjects. While this work seems to point to the pain and suffering that can arise from this discrepancy for women in diverse ways across the world, it is related specifically to Tunisia, cohering with the aims of the exhibition in which it was presented: 'La Part du corps' (Palais Kheireddine, Tunis, 2010).[26] Sonia Kallel has said that the idea was to express the tension between the female body and 'une

---

[25] I use the translation provided by the catalogue.
[26] This exhibition presented the work of nineteen artists from Tunisia and Europe. The curator, Rachida Triki, wanted to demonstrate the degree to which 'l'imaginaire du corps' ('the corporeal imaginary') united artists from all places (see Belhassine, 2010). At this exhibition, Sonia Kallel's work was unambiguously entitled 'Corps étoffé / étouffé' [literally, 'Body Fleshed Out / Suffocated') (see Belhassine, 2010).

société conservatrice, oppressive et étouffante dans laquelle on vit. Une pulsion immense, presque compulsive en moi m'a poussé à traduire ce sentiment d'oppression dans cette peau-vêtement' ('a conservative, oppressive and suffocating society we live in. I was driven by an immense, almost compulsive, urge to translate this feeling of oppression into this skin-dress').[27] As the curator of this exhibition, Rachida Triki, stated: 'In an Arabo-Islamic country, it is important that artists remind [us] and highlight the importance of the body in the private, social, and cultural life' (Triki, in interview with Binder and Haupt, 2010). Kallel's skin-dress offers, though, a nuanced exploration of oppression: 'elle reflète cette identité opprimée où le port du voile n'est qu'un "chapitre" d'oppression parmi d'autres' ('it reflects this oppressed identity in which the wearing of the veil is merely one "chapter" of oppression among others').[28] Kallel's dress-sculpture can perhaps also be seen to counter the visions of women's complete liberation perpetuated by Ben Ali's regime and supported by Western governments at that time. Created eight years in advance of the revolution, this work materialises an infra-thin 'skin', contesting alternative iconic visions; it reveals enduring aesthetics of resistance. It anticipates the increasing complexity of such critiques in a post-revolutionary context in which women continue to be employed, from different perspectives, as symbols of national identity.

Kallel's *Which Dress for Tomorrow?* transposes her specific use of jute fabric to a 'post-revolutionary' context to explore uncertainties regarding Tunisian identity and the country's future, while the reuse of the material for *Ma Robe de mariage* suggests that oppression continues, despite the revolution. As Kallel has stated, '[c]ette même enveloppe, avec la révolution, s'est transformée, elle s'est enfermée sur elle-même en une sorte de boule' ('this same envelope, with the revolution, transformed itself; it closed in on itself in a kind of ball').[29] The bundle of material, comparable to a tightly compressed yet living and breathing body, appears constricted by the metal wires that suspend it. The jute, though, necessarily bulges and sags beyond the rigid wires. The irregular mass of natural, porous material evokes inevitable, organic growth despite any attempts to restrain it. On one level, this

---

[27] Sonia Kallel related this to me in our email exchange of December 2019.
[28] The artist added this in our email exchange of December 2019.
[29] This was confirmed by Sonia Kallel in our email exchange of December 2019.

sculpture can be understood to express the uncertainties facing women in the light of rising extremist forms of Islamism. The question regarding 'dress' can be interpreted literally to allude to the concerns of some Tunisians regarding the future of sartorial liberalism. This interpretation is encouraged when the sculpture is placed in close proximity to Mouna Jemal Siala's video, *Le Sort* (The Fate; 2011–12), as it was at 'Rosige Zukunft' (Rosy Futures) (Stuttgart, 2013). Jemal Siala's three-minute piece displays a shifting portrait of the artist, whose face is progressively 'veiled' using black paint as we hear Erik Satie's 'Lent et douloureux''(Slow and Painful) (Paris, 1888) (see Chapter 4). While Kallel's work engages only implicitly with debates surrounding the practice of veiling in Tunisia, via its title, both works use 'dress' to raise the wider question of national identity. Like Erruas's installation, Kallel's *Which Dress for Tomorrow?* evokes the revolution's impact on women and on wider society (indeed, the idea of oppression conjured by her earlier 'skin-dress' already exceeded the question of veiling, as indicated above). The title, looking towards the future, can be understood to be asking: what will Tunisia 'look like'? Where is the country heading? Can a way be found to allow diverse perspectives to coexist? The compressed, yet still 'living', organism evokes those voices of democracy that were suppressed during decades of dictatorship and that – even despite the events of January 2011 – have yet to be heard; that is, a neglected social body. Kallel's sculpture expresses ambivalence with regard to the revolution, one year on, conveying the continuing suppression of diverse voices while simultaneously indicating the possibility for change.

In exploring the liminal boundaries of the body, rather than the body itself, Kallel's works are, to an extent, reminiscent of Duchamp's use of moulds and casts, as in his *Female Fig Leaf* (1950; bronze). But Kallel's works use flexible, organic materials. For *Which Dress for Tomorrow?* she selects a material which has been produced for centuries in regions from Bengal to the Middle East. Jute was not employed by Duchamp, though this organic material provides a fitting tool for the liminal processes he favoured. In its porosity, jute lends itself particularly well to materialising an ambivalent infra-thin separation, while simultaneously evoking the alternative domains of the body and the world within which it moves. Duchamp mentions the characteristic of 'porosité' ('porosity'), along with 'imbibage' ('imbibing'), in his discussion of infra-thin, frequently organic, substances (note 26v, 27). Kallel's reuse of jute to allude ambivalently to clothing and human skin resonates, moreover, with the infra-thin semantic shifts between signifier and signified, materiality and metaphor. Kallel's use of jute is, though, more reminiscent of Joseph Beuys's predilection for organic materials. The Fluxus artist exploited the contrasting sensations and emotional connotations of materials such as felt (which mixes both organic and industrial fibres). Felt – which, like jute, 'imbibes' anything with which it comes into contact – can be stifling and claustrophobic but also warm and protective. Kallel's signature material is similarly mobilised to allude to contrasting associations: jute is rigid yet porous, oppressive yet breathable, imprisoning yet (potentially) liberating. *Which Dress for Tomorrow?* plays also on the contrast between organic jute and industrial metallic wiring. The combination of industrial and organic, rigid and pliable, materials is particularly reminiscent of Eva Hesse's sculpture in which soft, 'feminine' materials evocative of human forms could be seen to subvert the geometries of male-dominated American minimalism.[30] Kallel's 'ball' of material suspended by taut threads is strikingly reminiscent of Hesse's *Vertiginous Detour*, in which a ball, hanging from the ceiling by rope, is enclosed in netting, an experiment with tension and gravity which can similarly be seen to communicate provisionally inhibited freedom (1966; acrylic and polyurethane on rope, net, and papier-mâché). This work is engaged with more explicitly in Kallel's *Sens unique* (One Way), a large sculptural ball of hair and fabrics, which is suspended using a fishing net (2012; 450 × 150 × 150 cm).[31] But this alternative anthropomorphic sphere adapts Hesse's ambivalent practice to evoke the restrictions and tensions of post-revolutionary Tunisia, as well as the uncertainties with regard to the country's future: the title of this work perhaps suggests a more pessimistic outcome than the more ambivalent contemporaneous *Which Dress for Tomorrow?*.

Kallel's works tie these dynamics to the ambivalence of the Tunisian revolution between oppression and liberation. In the context of art exploring this revolution, the affective ambiguity between malleable, organic material and taut metallic thread in *Which Dress for Tomorrow?* is reminiscent of Meriem Bouderbala's mixed media

---

[30] See, for example, Anne Swartz on Hesse's *Accession II* (1967) (Swartz, 1997).
[31] This work was exhibited at the 'Dream City' street art festival in Tunis and Sfax in 2012.

series, *The Awakened I–IV* (2010). Bouderbala evokes the bodies of martyrs of the revolution in fluid, contingent ink and wash, while they are bound and suspended by taut blood-red thread attached to sharp needles. The use of the same needles to emblazon the figures with symbols of Christianity, Islam and Judaism ties the visual-haptic 'clash' to religious conflict, while perhaps posing the same question as Kallel's sculpture with regard to the possible coexistence of diverse ways of being Tunisian. Kallel's evocation of potential liberation despite constraint through the 'skin' of an absent body finds a parallel in Mouna Karray's photographic portraits displaying her ambivalently confined and shrouded yet dynamic *present* body. Karray's series also resonates with Erruas's exploration of revolutionary dynamics through white on white (*Noir* (2013); see Chapter 4).[32]

While Erruas's *Les Drapeaux* incorporates flags and reworks these icons directly, *Which Dress for Tomorrow?* explores an allusive alternative to the potentially iconic body and dress. Kallel's evocation of constraint and violence contrasts with Erruas's investigation of fragility and a process of mourning. Erruas's work is primarily one of commemoration in relation to diverse forms of revolution in North Africa and the Middle East; that of Kallel addresses the uncertain future of Tunisia. Yet, these works converge in resonating with infra-thin dynamics while developing alternative 'languages' in which it is possible to evoke the idea of revolution between the binaries of success and failure, black and white, and beyond the bright colours and bold outlines of photographic icons.

Comparable 'revolutionary' poetics of absence can be found in art that uses glass or clear plastic screens by Aïcha Filali and Shada Safadi, though these artists develop distinctive aesthetics involving the photographic image or the use of light and shadow and depending on the spectators' movement. Aïcha Filali's work, like that of Kallel, engages specifically with Tunisia, which saw the fall of Ben Ali's dictatorial

---

[32] A precedent, which similarly 'anchors' the singular to the specific, can be discerned in the *vêtements-sculptures* of Majida Khattari. This Paris-based artist stages *défilés-performances* for which she designs ambiguous restrictive and liberatory 'veils' in the aim to forge a 'third way' between the for/against debate on the hijab in France. Kallel's exploitation of the ambivalent properties of jute is reminiscent of Khattari's explicit engagement with, yet contestation of, Beuys in her use of felt to create an oppressive yet protective 'veil': 'Kacha' ('Covering', 1996).

regime on 14 January 2011, but which continues to experience the turbulence that is inherent in the process of democracy. Shada Safadi's work, by contrast with the works I have analysed in this chapter until now, mourns and commemorates those lost in the violent ongoing revolutionary conflict in Syria. On one level, this poignant work can be taken to speak universally of the tragic loss of civilians in war, but it is most evocative of the civil war in Syria.

By contrast with the uprising in Tunisia, which led to the removal of an autocrat and to democratic elections within a year, the uprising in Syria was rapidly repressed by the state. What began as a peaceful revolt on 15 March 2011 developed, in 2012, into an intractable civil war between Assad's government and the oppositional Free Syrian Army, which is still ongoing at the time of writing. While the revolutionary uprisings in Tunisia and Egypt triggered the initial Syrian uprising, this has unfolded in distinct and more complicated circumstances. As Nader Hashemi and Danny Postel have stated, '[w]hile the conflict in Syria has its origins in domestic politics – rooted in the corruption, nepotism, cronyism and repression of 42 years of Assad family rule – its regional and international dimensions are manifold' (Hashemi and Postel, 2013a: 6). Indeed, the conflict has led to new geopolitical rivalries and global divisions between the multiple countries which have a stake in its outcome, paralysing the UN Security Council (Hashemi and Postel, 2013a: 6–7; see also Safadi and Neaime, 2016). The war has become even more complex and intractable given the rise of radical Salafi jihadi movements (Hashemi and Postel, 2013a: 8). The year 2012 in which Safadi created her work – saw the escalation of violence in Syria, the failure of the UN ceasefire attempt, and the declaration of the conflict as a civil war, on 15 July, by the International Committee of the Red Cross. A report of 14 April 2018 by Al Jazeera stated that more than 465,000 Syrians had been killed in the fighting, over a million had been injured and over 12 million – half of the country's pre-war population – had been displaced.[33] Safadi's poignant installation responds to the already extensive human cost of the war one year into the conflict.

The distinct contexts and states of 'revolution' evoked by these works set them far apart in terms of both their content and their tone.

---

[33] Dates and statistics were taken from the timelines provided on the websites of Al Jazeera and Al Arabiya: www.aljazeera.com/news/2016/05/syria-civil-war-explained-160505084119966.html; english.alarabiya.net/en/2016/03/14/Timeline-Syrian-crisis-five-years-on.html (last accessed January 2020).

Yet, they mobilise a comparable aesthetic similarly to create a space in which civilians can be represented in non-iconic ways, and to encourage alternative modes of interaction. The work of these artists resonates (unintentionally) with Duchamp's perception of glass and mirrors as infra-thin planes between two- and three-dimensionality and his preoccupation with their capacity to reflect, to reverse and to allow for the contingent. This is most famously exemplified by his work in glass: *La Mariée mise à nu par ses célibataires, même* (The Bride Stripped Bare by her Bachelors, even) (1915–23), also known as *Le Grand verre* (The Large Glass), in which he employs a complex iconography to explore male–female relations (see Marcel Duchamp, 1969).[34] At the same time, these works of 2012 call to mind enduring local practices of painting under glass or engraving glass. Both, though, develop alternatives to existing local and transnational practices to exceed iconic representations of radically different experiences and stages of ongoing 'revolution'.

Photography and video are perhaps the most challenging media in which to present an alternative language of revolution, given that it is in these media that icons of the 'Arab Spring' have tended to be constructed and disseminated. These icons have frequently focused on heroic bodies, such as 'The Girl in a Blue Bra' who was killed during demonstrations in Tahrir Square, or 'spectacular body acts' from self-immolation to nude activism, as Marwan Kraidy has shown (Kraidy, 2016). Aïcha Filali, however, uses photography to depict ordinary people and to create a space for alternative non-heroic and non-spectacular visions. This Tunis-based artist's series, *L'Angle mort* (Blind Spot, 2010–12), captures oblique back views of ordinary Tunisian people in the street and presents life-size cut-outs of them on windows or clear plastic screens (Figure 1.3). At 'Rosy Futures' at the IFA Gallery Stuttgart, for example, the figures were presented on the gallery windows, facing outwards towards the street.[35] The photographs reveal details which are usually hidden from view or simply go unnoticed: a crumpled or untucked shirt, for example, or the creases of trousers gathering around the buttocks. This project was begun in advance of the revolution and developed in relation to this new

---

[34] For an introduction to *The Large Glass*, see the catalogue entry for this work by Ronald Alley (1981).

[35] This was also the case at the IFA Gallery Berlin, where this exhibition first took place (the photograph in Figure 1.3 was taken at the exhibition in Berlin).

context. *L'Angle mort* was first presented on clear plastic screens at the Galerie Ammar Farhat, Sidi Bou Said, Tunisia, in 2010. Elitism – including that in the art world, in and beyond Tunisia – is a recurrent theme in Filali's work. As Mohamed Ben Soltane states of the 2010 series (examples of which he presents in his post-revolutionary virtual exhibition, 'Souffle de Liberté / Tunisie' (2011)): 'Ces gens qui ne font pas partie du public habituellement "très select" des galeries d'art, s'approprient un espace duquel ils sont socialement exclus. Quelques mois plus tard, en Janvier 2011 et cette fois dans la réalité, ils s'approprieront l'espace politique en étant dans la première ligne de ceux qui chassèrent le président déchu du pays' ('These people who are not usually part of the normally "very select" public of art galleries, appropriate a space from which they are socially excluded. A few months later, in January 2011, and this time in reality, they will appropriate the political space by being on the front line of those who drove the deposed president out of the country') (Ben Soltane, 2011). This exhibition was greatly appreciated in Tunisia (see, for example, Abassi, 2010).[36] Filali – like Kallel – can be seen as one of the 'non-collective actors', and her pre-2011 oeuvre as one of the many 'dispersed endeavors', which Gana perceives to have contributed to the Tunisian revolution itself (Gana, 2013: 2).[37]

At the 'Rosy Futures' exhibition, which occurred after the Tunisian revolution, *L'Angle mort* includes a photograph of a man flying the Tunisian flag above two further cut-outs of people in the street. In this image, as in the other photographs, we cannot see the man's face or the focus of his gaze; the scene itself is missing. The cut-outs below the man, in which there is no link to the protests, similarly show the backs of a couple looking downwards together at an item we cannot see and

---

[36] Asma Abassi refers to Filali as one of the most remarkable Tunisian artists. She comments on the surprise and indignation of certain spectators on realising that the faces of the people photographed could not be seen on the other side of the plastic screens. This 'blind spot', and the apparent 'banalité' of the work, Abassi suggests, 'ne nous pousse pas à une contemplation naïve, mais bien à une réflexion profonde et intelligente, toujours dans la même veine et avec la même verve auxquelles elle nous a habitués. Avec "L'angle mort", elle vous invite à voir la vie de dos"' ('engages us not in naïve contemplation but in deep and intelligent reflection, always in the same spirit and with the same verve which she has encouraged us to expect. With 'Blind Spot', she invites you to "see life from behind"') (2010).

[37] Gana takes the first expression from Bayat (2010: 14).

'Poetics of Absence' 65

a man making a positive thumb-up gesture to someone who is obscured from our view.[38] Here, we are invited to look 'behind' the iconic media images of the revolution. Revolutionary demonstrations, moreover, are allied with the ordinary through their juxtaposition with unknown people engaged in everyday activities. Filali's spontaneous photographs of unknown people can also be seen as counterpoints to the pre-revolutionary pervasiveness of iconic images of Ben Ali. Her work is reminiscent, in this way, of the Paris-based 'JR''s collaborative street art project, *InsideOut* (Tunis 2011), which involved pasting portraits of ordinary people at sites previously occupied by the former leader's photograph (see Chapter 4). But Filali more subtly explores the boundary between inside and outside by combining photography with glass.

Interpreted through the lens of the 'infra-thin', Filali's use of glass to support her cut-outs renders visible an infra-thin screen. Viewed from inside, the silhouettes of the people she photographs can be compared, to some extent, to the figures in Duchamp's *Le Grand verre*, which he imagined as shadows of a quasi-fourth-dimensional space. They also resonate with his note: 'Peinture sur verre vue du côté non peint donne un infra mince' ('Painting on glass seen from the non-painted side gives an infra-thin') (note 15, 24). But the practice of presenting images behind glass is also reminiscent of the ancient Tunisian tradition of painting under glass.[39] This enduring tradition was influenced in the eighteenth and nineteenth centuries, as Hocine Tlili details, by Italian and Turkish figurative representation (2012: 163). Filali's practice diverges from both aesthetics in presenting back-views of ordinary passers-by. Her work produces an alternative form of reversal and a different means of incorporating contingency; that is, through the spontaneous use of the instantaneous medium of photography. By contrast with the two-dimensional figures of Tunisian painting and, even more so, with the upturned mechanomorphic figures of Duchamp's *Large Glass*, Filali's photographs appear as indices of

---

[38] This hand gesture is itself reminiscent of that painted in the colours of the Tunisian flag and used as a symbol of excellence and achievement in touristic advertising. Its use in this everyday context empties it of such national symbolism (stock photo uploaded by Vepar5; online since 10 October 2013; see https://stockfresh.com; last accessed May 2017).

[39] The artist has stated that she might have been influenced by this tradition (email, 23 May 2015).

three-dimensional corporeal reality. *L'Angle mort* invents new means of visualising invisibility, which resonates with the political aim to include those who are not usually deemed worthy of representation.

As the artist states, 'je voulais donner à voir les différents caractères de la typologie des Tunisiens mais vus de dos. L'intérêt de ce support transparent et grandeur nature c'est de créer une confusion entre les spectateurs et les personnes qui sont représentées sur le verre' (I wanted to bring into view the various characteristics of Tunisian types but seen from behind. The point of using this transparent and life-size format is to create an intermingling of the spectators and the people who are represented on the glass').[40] The people represented occupy the threshold between inside and outside, art and life. Mingling with shifting reflections of the city, they seem to walk within it. The images evolve with the changing light and with the equally contingent perspectives – and reflections – of the mobile spectator, producing, we might say, an alternative experience of 'fourth-dimensional' outward, multidirectional expansion to that visualised by Kossentini's kaleidoscopic arabesque. Duchamp conceived of the infra-thin as a liminal separation either in space or in time: '*séparation* inframince – mieux que cloison, parce que indique intervalle (pris dans un sens) et cloison (pris dans un autre sens)' (infra-thin *separation* – better than partition, because indicates interval (understood in one sense) and partition (understood in another sense)') (note 9r, 22, emphasis Duchamp's). But this work materialises a separation characteristic of the infra-thin to create a space for those who have tended to be excluded from iconic visions of Tunisia and to encourage contemplation of the historical interval between the revolution and the present moment of the exhibition. The spectator and the wider *hors champ* are, moreover, incorporated in a way that indicates the porosity of, and exchange across, *cultural borders*.[41] In Filali's work, photography comes to be aligned with uncertainty and contingency, a point that is developed further in Chapter 2's consideration of 'contingent encounters'.

---

[40] The artist stated this in my email exchange with her in May 2015.

[41] The infra-thin relationship between cultures that can emerge in the experience of such art is reminiscent of Duchamp's exploration of the infra-thin separation between 'masculinity' and 'femininity' in many of his works. Indeed, his note on the infra-thin as both screen and interval continues: '– séparation a les 2 sens mâle et femelle' ['– separation has both male and female meanings') (note 9r, 22).

Evoking the distinct context of the war in Syria, a contrasting work, *Promises* (2012) by Shada Safadi (based in the Syrian Golan Heights), communicates the tragic loss of hundreds of thousands of civilians (Figure 1.4). In this haunting installation, multiple vertical transparent plastic screens poignantly display life-size images of human bodies – both adults and children.[42] The distorted white figures are etched by hand (their whiteness comes from the use of heat during the etching process), while they give the impression of imprints, as if the bodies had been laid on the clear surfaces.[43] Light is projected onto the screens, illuminating the translucent shapes and casting ghostly shadows on the surrounding walls. As the spectator disrupts the light ray and walks between the screens, their own shadows fuse with those of the dead. The artist's statement accompanying the work expresses the guilt of those who have survived, the need to remember the dead, and the necessity to continue the battle for which these people lost their lives, until freedom from oppression is achieved:

That spirit could have flown without being seen by anyone. But the horror of what happened, and its struggling out of fear, made it leave an impact that demands of us, we the ones who are alive, to give promises. We 'forget the promises we give to our dead,' we keep them for some few days and then forget. We did not see things ourselves when they happened ... We saw it after it happened, and the scene etched itself in our memory. How can we apologize for that spirit that took us out of darkness? You still exist and we were meant to stay alive, but our freedom is still incomplete; you are dead and we are the dead too.[44]

---

[42] This work was exhibited at the 'Young Artist of the Year Award' (Al Mahatta Gallery, Ramallah, 2012, and Mosaic Rooms, London, 2013).

[43] Shada Safadi confirmed the details of her process for this work in our email exchange of December 2019.

[44] Artist's statement at 'Young Artist of the Year Award', Mosaic Rooms, London, 2013. The statement makes no explicit reference to Syria, while the allusions to ongoing horror and 'our' incomplete freedom, from the point of view of the artist based in the Syrian Golan Heights, tempt us to view the work in relation to the civil war in Syria. As Shada Safadi confirmed in our email exchange of December 2019, 'all of my artwork explores the reality of the war, the border, the Occupied Syrian Golan, the distances, the family meeting between Syria and Golan in the Shouting Hill, etc. as I am from this area, my village is so close to the ceasefire line between Golan and Syria'. Reviewer of the exhibition in Ramallah, Daryl Meador, also connects the work to Syria: 'Safadi, born in the occupied Syrian Golan Heights, uses the forms to represent those lost in the Syrian uprising' (2012). This connection also emerges from the Young Artist of

Safadi's work resonates formally with diverse infra-thin practices, while it develops an alternative means of rendering visible the invisible to share an experience of loss and mourning. The use of transparent screens to visualise the liminal traces of other-worldly figures is reminiscent of Duchamp's practice in *Le Grand verre*. But in Safadi's work the dimensional passage occupied by the figures – some upright, some upturned – is assimilated to the passage from life to death. The multiplication of figures, moreover, each occupying their own screen, evokes the mindless execution of anonymous masses. The shapes' resemblance to contingent corporeal imprints resonates formally, to some extent, with Yves Klein's multiple *Anthropometries* (1960), the results of performances in which he asked women to cover themselves in 'International Klein Blue' paint before pressing their bodies against white paper. For the New Realist artist, these imprints rendered visible the border between materiality and the void, corporeality and spirituality (see Morineau, 2006). Such liminal zones and passages are, in Klein's work, suggestive of the transcendence of the earthly, corresponding with this artist's interest in Rosicrucianism. Safadi's work resonates with avant-garde practices of rendering visible the invisible, in the work of both Duchamp and Klein. But her translucent figures evoke lifeless bodies with skeletal limbs. Although these distorted forms are suggestive of contingent corporeal imprints, furthermore, closer scrutiny reveals their gradual formation through intricate loops etched by hand. Rapid modes of image production, such as body printing, or the instantaneous medium of digital photography employed by Filali, are eschewed in favour of a painstaking process that is reminiscent of the long Syrian tradition of enamelling glass. Safadi's practice echoes her words: 'the scene etched itself in our memory'. This process can be seen to contribute to the cathartic enterprise of remembrance and of making and keeping, in the artist's words, 'the promises we give to our dead'.

Safadi's *Promises* transforms mourning and remembrance into an active process which is extended to the spectator. As in Kossentini's installation, light and shadow are employed to embody the participant. In this case, their shadows merge with those of the ghostly figures; their acquired status as mobile 'porteurs d'ombres' ('carriers of shadows'),

the Year Award 2012 Brochure (in English and Arabic); available at: https://issuu.com/qattan.foundation/docs/yaya_2012_brochure.

between embodiment and disembodiment, heightens their awareness that they 'were meant to stay alive' but others were not. Their kinaesthetic experience leads to their emotional understanding of the artist's words: 'you are dead and we are the dead too'. The spectator's emotional comprehension of the work is equally encouraged through its treatment of the universal themes of death and remembrance and through the use of traces and shadows of absent bodies, rather than photographs of people in locatable environments such as we see in Filali's photographs. In both its themes and its aesthetics, Safadi's work is strikingly reminiscent of Christian Boltanski's *Théâtre d'ombres* (1984), while Boltanski's installation ambivalently provokes both sadness and laughter (see Grenier and Boltanski, 2007). In *Théâtre d'ombres*, small handmade metal figurines of skulls, ghosts and masks dangle near the gallery floor, with light spots close by to project multiple exaggerated shadows onto the gallery walls. In formal terms, the use of shadows in the work of both Safadi and Boltanski is reminiscent of ancient traditions of shadow theatre in multiple countries across the world. It also resonates with Duchamp's use of these infra-thin phenomena to evoke a quasi-fourth-dimensional space: one of his notes on the infra-thin includes a photograph displaying shadows of his ready-made objects (note 13, 25). Such a space, moreover, is evoked in the works of both Safadi and Boltanski through the effect of multidirectional outward expansion generated by the use of low-angle lighting from a single source (or group of spotlights, in *Théâtre d'ombres*). In the work of both artists this alternative location is assimilated to the domain of the dead. Yet, Safadi's work produces a markedly different tone from Boltanski's 'danse macabre'. The shadows of *Promises* are identified with the bodies of those lost during a historically specific war. Safadi's work is closer, at least in content and tone, to other works by Boltanski which evoke the death of Holocaust victims while also exploring human suffering universally.[45]

Reminiscent of Erruas's work, Safadi's poetics of absence constitutes a form of mourning. Safadi employs a distinctive use of white but does so similarly to evoke the liminal zone between life and death. She also develops a comparable painstaking, yet perhaps cathartic, process. Safadi's work, by contrast, appears to focus exclusively on loss, functioning primarily as a testimony to the tragic results of revolutionary

---

[45] See, for example, *Réserve* (1990).

conflict. Yet, it can also be seen to gesture towards the future in its transgression of the boundaries between the disembodied and the embodied, and via its message that 'our freedom is still incomplete'. *Promises* forges a means of evoking the dead, and the revolutionary cause for which they fought, which avoids the potentially iconic images produced by the media. Closer to media images, certain recent artwork exploring the Syrian war exposes the extreme violence inflicted on civilians, such as Tarek Tuma's portrait painting of Hamza Bakkour, the thirteen-year-old boy shot in the face during a siege in Homs in February 2012.[46] Such artwork is reminiscent of photojournalism and filmed reportage in its function to shock the international public. Installations such as that of Safadi provide a necessary counterpoint to such iconic language, engaging the spectator intellectually, physically and emotionally in cross-cultural experiences of opacity, and calling for democracy – not only in Syria and the wider Middle East and North African region, but in diverse situations across the globe.

Comparable to Erruas's *Les Drapeaux* and Kallel's *Which Dress for Tomorrow?*, these works by Filali and Safadi resonate with infra-thin dynamics, and with a range of transnational and local practices, while 'anchoring' such dynamics. At the same time, through *L'Angle mort* and *Promises*, these artists develop alternative poetics of absence by combining photographed or painted anonymous figures with transparent screens. These spatially more extensive installations involve the spectators kinaesthetically and generate reflections or shadows, which heightens the experience of instability and contingency.

The 'infra-thin critique' in these works, and in the installations by Kossentini and Fatmi, can be situated in relation to wider aesthetics of resistance.[47] In rendering visible the invisible to avoid, and often explicitly contest, icons, clichés or other visual languages associated with order and authoritarianism, these works are reminiscent of certain art exploring (neo-)colonialism or globalisation. I have already discussed Fatmi's earlier uses of the spinning arabesque as precedents for the dimensional shifts in his later work and in that of Kossentini.

---

[46] Exhibited at '#withoutwords: Emerging Syrian Artists', P21 Gallery, London, 2013.

[47] My focus, here, is on the cross-cultural, though precedents can also be found in work that negotiates divisions between perceived 'feminine' and 'masculine' practices through poetics of absence, as I have suggested through references to earlier work by Safaa Erruas and Sonia Kallel.

Critical 'poetics of absence' can be discerned in works that forge an alternative, non-reductive visual language with which to convey experiences of exile through immigration. Zineb Sedira captures shadows in light boxes to evoke such an experience for Algerian women (*Exilées d'Algérie: Amel, Fatiha, Salia, Zoulikha and Aïcha*, 2000), while Hamid Debarrah employs photographic positive and negative in his 'double' portraits of male immigrant workers (*Faciès inventaire: chronique du foyer de la rue Très-Cloîtres à Grenoble* ('Face Inventory: Chronicle of the Hostel on the Rue Très-Cloîtres in Grenoble') (2001). In a divergent way to Kallel, Saadeh George creates resin 'casts' resembling skin to explore the fragility of identity and the effects of displacement in *Today I Shed My Skin: Dismembered and Remembered* (1998; photography, photo etching and resin) (see Lloyd, ed., 1999: 52). Exploring alienation in a globalised frame, Kader Attia's numerous fragile aluminium moulds of veiled figures bowed in prayer seem to signal an equivalence in religion and consumerism as alternative forms of (empty) refuge (*Ghost*, 2007). Filali's work is reminiscent of Samta Benyahia's use of gallery windows as the support for her deep blue *moucharabieh*.[48] This Arabo-Andalusian architectural screen, which in North Africa was traditionally designed to separate gendered spaces while allowing the women to see through its openings, is transposed to emphasise the porosity of the boundaries between cultures on either side of the Mediterranean. Alternative aesthetics of revolution do not simply and suddenly emerge with the revolutions that began in 2011. Yet, these works develop new practices in response to this shift in context and to the iconic language of 'revolution'. They explore conceptual and sensorial shifts, passages between dimensions or between presence and absence, or exchanges between spectator and object, specifically to evoke both past and future, to commemorate while looking forwards and to communicate uncertainty yet also possibility.

Infra-thin Critique and Transnational Criticism

Diverse works exploring the Arab Uprisings, or their distinct manifestations in Tunisia and Syria, resonate with infra-thin dynamics. They allude doubly – or multidirectionally – to apparently stable, separate

---

[48] Samta Benyahia has been using this pattern since 1992.

identities or discourses, while rendering visible the space or interval between them. But, in these works, such dynamics are 'anchored' in relation to specific cultures and historical moments. Singularising infra-thin practices come to be associated with resistance to iconic visions in contexts of ongoing revolution or emerging democracy. They create a space for alternative voices, visions and understandings of distinct revolutionary situations. These works hover not only between the specific and the singular, and between metaphor and materiality, but also between the translatable and the untranslatable, politics and poetics, in their evocation of an infra-thin *critique*.

The infra-thin critique can be employed as a tool for analysis of aesthetics of revolution and resistance in alternative contexts and in a wide range of art forms, from installations or videos inclusive of multiple elements and dimensions to the most minimal of sculptural or ready-made objects. Encompassing the ideas of the screen and the interval, this notion can be used to examine diverse uses of space and time – within the work of art itself or between different versions of the work as it travels from one geographical and historical context to another. As I suggested at the outset, though, despite its proximity to Duchamp's notion – and, in certain cases, its explicit reuse of his practices – this artwork cannot be seen simply to call for a 'turn back' to certain European modernist tropes as critical tools. For, in addition to 'anchoring' infra-thin practices reminiscent of those of Duchamp or his successors, it frequently employs or recalls divergent enduring local, regional or diverse transnational practices to generate the instability that is characteristic of the infra-thin. It suggests passage, exchange or contingency through practices from weaving or the use of jute to the ancient, cross-cultural tradition of shadow play or the motifs of Arabo-Andalusian furniture. It resonates with diverse variants of modernism, continuing the transcultural process that modernisms tend to involve. This artwork seems rather to call, as I suggested in my introduction to this book, for a critical approach that is itself transnational, transhistorical and multidirectional.

In a range of work exploring the revolutions in Tunisia, Syria and beyond, moreover, infra-thin dynamics are generated through alternative combinations or new practices to convey revolutionary dynamics of constraint and liberation, but also fragility and uncertainty. This work forges aesthetics in which it is possible to question the tendency to think of the revolutions – and of 'revolution' more widely – in binary terms of success or failure. This art allows for an understanding of 'revolution' that – moving beyond this term's implication of a completed cycle – accommodates transition, negotiation and diversity. These works indicate different relationships to activism, but they do not themselves promote a straightforward political message. Instead, this art creates a space – and an interval – between politics and poetics. Through diverse means of connecting presence and absence, it engages with the revolutions while encouraging spectators to reshape their memories of them and to imagine alternative futures for countries from Tunisia to Syria.

The dynamic between the specific and the singular, the translatable and the untranslatable, stability and instability can be discerned in the works I explore throughout the remaining three chapters. Many of those works resonate with art that evokes an infra-thin critique through presence and absence, and visual and other sensorial elements. The feature that unites the works in this chapter with all those in this book, though, is the creation of a shifting space between the work and the spectators. In Chapter 3, I explore this space further through works that not only involve the spectators physically but also encourage a range of participants actively to contribute to making the work. I also examine this interface in Chapter 4 in relation to works that evoke the relationship between presence and absence in alternative ways. In the next two chapters, I focus on the dynamic between stability and instability in relation to what I call 'contingent encounters of resistance'. I argue that a diverse corpus of artwork, converging with that explored above, adapts and anchors a range of existing local and transnational practices – or develops new practices – to evoke an ongoing revolution between freedom and fragility, certainty and uncertainty. Yet, as I show, this art exploring the revolutions undermines or avoids icons or iconic spaces specifically through contingent encounters between stable and unstable forms or substances, parameters and processes or artist and participants.

2 | Contingency and Resistance: Exceeding Icons through Matter and Motion

Icons and iconic images, as I indicated in my introduction to this book, convey the revolutions simplistically as completed, and present a people as ideologically unified in their vision of their country's future. Art can, however, move beyond such images to reveal the unsaid, the unheard or the unseen of 'revolution'. Such art interacts ironically or ambiguously with iconic objects, structures, faces or spaces. Otherwise, it creates an alternative to iconic imagery, alluding indirectly to the rigid interpretations that icons foster, by presenting or performing habitually marginalised spaces or bodies in ways that resist their easy reuse for ideological purposes. Iconic visions are exceeded, in many works of art exploring the revolutions, through encounters between stable and unstable forms or substances, parameters and processes or artists and participants. The dynamic between stability and instability is, in such cases, produced by allowing contingent elements to enter the work and partly to determine its shape. Hela Lamine, for example, produces distorted portraits of Ben Ali by using a decaying mixture of bread and water in *Nous ne mangerons plus de ce pain-là* (2011; Figure 0.2). Nadia Kaabi-Linke reworks the black Salafist flag, which has been reappropriated by terrorists, by embroidering its usually white calligraphic inscription with real jasmine, which wilts and loses its scent during the course of the exhibition (*Smell*, 2012; see: https://commons.wikimedia.org/wiki/File:Smell_(2015)_%E2%80%93_Nadia_Kaabi-Linke.jpg). Mouna Karray projects static images of Ben Ali together with the unedited soundtrack of a conversation between a taxi driver and his passenger as they observe changes on the streets of Tunis (*Live*, 2012). Majd Abdel Hamid commissions women from the Palestinian village of Farkha to weave portraits of the Tunisian martyr, Mohammad Bouazizi (*Mohammad Bouazizi*, 2011; Figure 0.3).

2 Contingency and Resistance

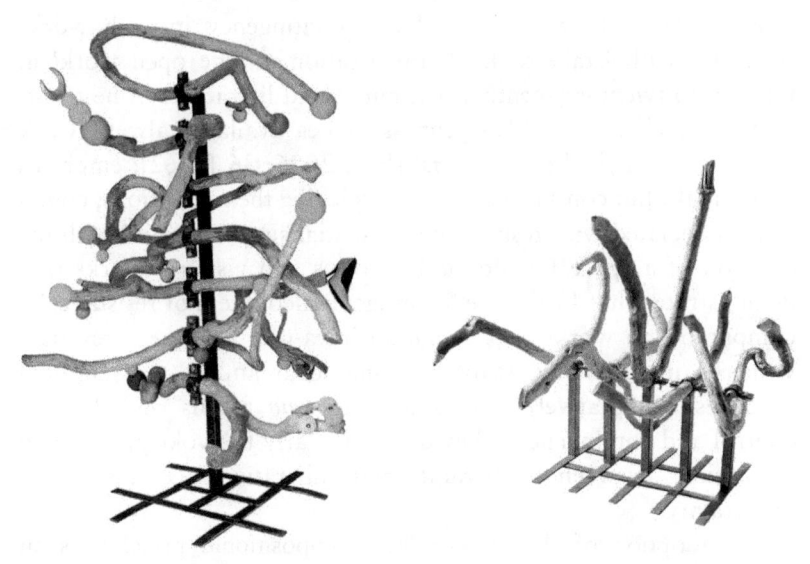

Figure 2.1 Aïcha Filali, *Bourgeons en palabres* and *Bourgeons d'i(n)vers* (2011), courtesy of the artist

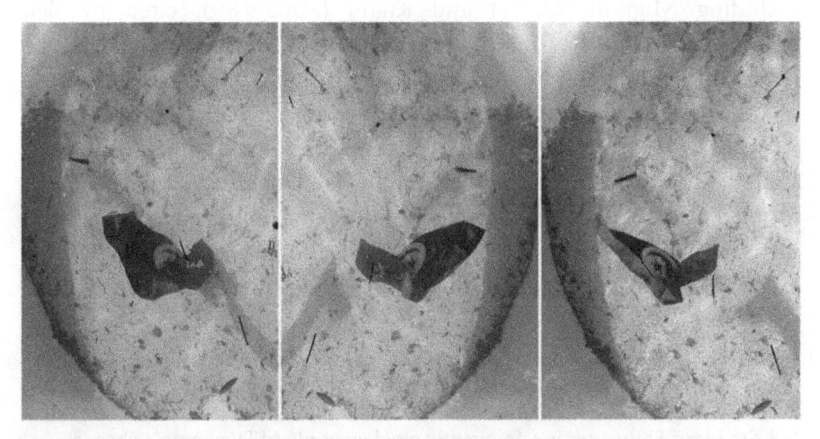

Figure 2.2 Meriem Bouderbala, *Flag Nymphéas* (2012), photographs 1–3 of 6, from left to right, courtesy of the artist

The balance between control and contingency in such works resonates with Umberto Eco's theorisation of 'the open work' in relation to twentieth–century art, music and literature: '[t]he *possibilities* which the work's openness makes available always work within a given *field of relations*' (Eco, 2006: 36 [1962]; emphasis in original). But contingency, in art exploring the revolutions, comes to be associated with resistance to essentialising views and with the creation of a space for alternative voices and visions. Works that demonstrate what I call here 'contingent encounters of resistance' – comparable to works that evoke an infra-thin critique – resonate with, or intentionally adapt, existing local and/or transnational practices. Alternatively, artists develop *new* means of balancing control and contingency. They do so similarly to evoke an ongoing revolution between constraint and liberation, certainty and uncertainty.

The adoption of chance as a key compositional principle is an enduring and diversely transnational phenomenon. It is, though, frequently seen by Western scholars to have emerged in the early decades of the twentieth century and to be associated with European and North American artists (such scholarship calls to mind the tendency to present knowledge from the West as universal, discussed by authors including Mignolo (2011) and Kilani (2002: 89), cited by Ben Soltane, 2012: 219). *Chance Aesthetics*, edited by Meredith Malone (2009), for example, investigates the use of chance, and its relationship to determinism, in work by artists including Marcel Duchamp, Jean Arp, André Breton, and later works by Jackson Pollock and John Cage.[1] A frequently cited example is Duchamp's *3 Standard Stoppages* (1913–14): he ironically fabricated unique instruments of measurement by releasing three one-metre-long pieces of string at a height of one metre.[2] Jackson Pollock is well known for having dripped

---

[1] The expression 'aesthetics of contingency' has also been used in relation to art and literature on the *subject* of contingency: see Lyons's study of Baudelaire, Pascal and Mallarmé (2014).

[2] *3 Standard Stoppages* is a frequently cited example of Duchamp's chance aesthetics. This work, intended as a ludic challenge to the authority of the metre, consists of the irregular wooden templates the artist produced using the random lines made by the free-falling string. Duchamp's questioning of the authority of the metre, and his production of an alternative, personal system of measurement, was influenced by German philosopher Max Stirner's anarchistic *L'Unique et sa propriété* (1845; French edition published 1899).

and flung paint across his canvases, albeit in a different spirit and involving a lesser degree of chance. John Cage explored the unexpected possibilities of the accidental by flipping coins to produce musical scores. Yet, as other critics have suggested, contingency in art has existed for centuries and beyond Europe and North America. Jackson Pollock's paintings, for example, have been compared to eighth-century Chinese gestural ink painting and to the kinaesthetic practice of Chinese calligraphy (see Lachman, 1992; Westgeest, 1996). It is well known that Cage also produced compositions by consulting the I Ching, the ancient Chinese divination text. Some works of art exploring the Tunisian revolution resonate (or engage directly and ironically) with certain European or North American modernist chance aesthetics. But they frequently draw, in addition or alternatively, on enduring regional practices including Arabic calligraphy, ceramic production or weaving. Although these practices were not originally motivated by a desire to harness the effects of 'chance' as such, contingency is inevitable in their processes: they continue, frequently, to rely on the artist's hand or gestures and non-industrial tools and/or on fluid or formless organic materials. The contingency involved in the practice of Arabic calligraphy is suggested by artist and calligrapher Hassan Messoudy, who indicates its convergences with graffiti. He emphasises the importance, in both practices, of corporeal gestures performed in sync with breathing (Messoudy, 2011: 31). The process of hand-making textiles also depends to some degree on chance, as is indicated in a further illuminating transhistorical and transmedial comparison by film theorist Laura U. Marks. Marks suggests that the glitches in certain low-resolution video from North Africa and the Middle East resonate with imitation textile fabrication, which uses fewer knots per inch (Marks, 2014: see especially 263–70).[3] But art exploring the revolutions through such practices draws on them *directly*. It deliberately uses the effects of these – or European or North American – contingent processes, moreover, to exceed iconic visions. The same can be said of its uses of public space and/or participation.

Tunis-based curators Christine Bruckbauer and Patricia Triki comment, as I mentioned in my introduction, on the significance of the

---

[3] Marks's focus, here, is on the aesthetic qualities of 'glitch' and what low-resolution video reveals about conditions on the ground.

proliferation of participatory art in public space in Tunisia, given that this was monopolised by former heads of state through statues or posters of them, or streets named after them (Bruckbauer and Triki, 2016). They situate post-revolutionary participatory art in relation to local and wider Maghrebi art practices, including enduring uses of public space as a site for storytelling, dancing, music and the fourth-century Tunisian tradition of satirical shadow puppet theatre.[4] Participation, though, they say, is new in Tunisian art. This may be true of participatory work that involves a direct critique of power; for example, Moufida Fedhila's performance on the Avenue Habib Bourguiba, encouraging people to vote for 'Super-Tunisian' (*Super-Tunisian St'art*, 2011) and JR's photographic project to replace Ben Ali's portrait with those of ordinary Tunisians (*InsideOut* 'Part 1 – Tunis', 2011; see Chapter 4). A precursor, though, as Aurélie Machghoul notes, can be found at the biennial art festival, Dream City, directed by Selma and Sofiane Ouissi, which began in Tunis in 2007 (Machghoul, 2013; Bruckbauer and Triki also refer to this festival). Dream City emerged from the necessity the Ouissis saw for a specifically Tunisian contemporary art created for public space and for a new way of seeing this space (Machghoul, 2013: 30). Yet, much older precedents for participatory art can be found in the artisanal practices of weaving or ceramics, which have long entailed participation.[5] Other works, by contrast, adapt aspects of twenty-first-century transnational participatory *social* and digital practices, such as producing, uploading, 'liking' and commenting on touristic snapshots or selfies.

I explore contingent encounters of resistance across two chapters. The use of such participatory practices is the subject of Chapter 3. There, I also examine in further detail the use of local or regional artisanal practices. I focus, in the current chapter, on work that employs formless, frequently organic, materials and substances, or

---

[4] The context for this discussion is the exhibition they co-curated, entitled 'The Turn: Art Practices in Post-Spring Societies' (Vienna, 2016). This focused on socially engaged art in the public space, including work such as Moufida Fedhila's performance, in which the artist called for people to vote for 'Super-Tunisian'.

[5] Critics of participation in art tend to focus on 'Western' production and to view the origins of this phenomenon in early twentieth-century modernism, while commenting on its development and expansion since the 1960s (see, for example, Eco, 2006 [1962]; Dezeuze, 2010; Bishop, 2012).

the peripatetic mode. This work's involvement of spectators or passers-by anticipates my discussion, in the next chapter, of diverse forms of participation and means of renegotiating space. Certain work, moreover, combines the contingent practice of weaving with participation or reveals the convergence of organic materials and the peripatetic mode. Scholarship on participatory art has often tended to separate this from other uses of chance and, moreover, to distinguish between participation, collaboration and interactivity, as I will discuss. Yet, it might be more productive to see diverse relationships between control and contingency, which allow for different degrees of chance to shape the work, on a continuum.

Works exploring the revolutions through contingent encounters, like those evoking an infra-thin critique, frequently diverge from existing practices partly because they combine them with icons or iconic spaces. Certain aspects of these works might call to mind European modernist practices, of which the artists will be well aware; yet, they are also distinct from these practices, reflecting readings of the world through shifting local, regional and global lenses (Katchka, 2013: 500).[6] The use of formless materials in many works responding to the Tunisian revolution might call to mind Georges Bataille's work. Yet, he saw in the 'informe' a means of emphasising pure materiality, evacuated of metaphor (Bataille, 1970: 217). The dynamic between materiality and metaphor is fundamental to the works exploring the Tunisian revolution that I analyse below. These works hold in tension poetics and politics. Art historian Caroline A. Jones suggests that Bataillean anti-form has become open (albeit ambivalently) to metaphorical reading, since its merging with existentialism in post–World War II Paris in the work of artists such as Wols, Dubuffet and Fautrier. As she states, 'Within the Sartrean context, anti-compositional *informe* was doomed to be interpreted as a "gesture," an existential Act.'[7] Formlessness in

---

[6] Kinsey Katchka makes this point regarding a multiperspectival reading of the world (rather than only via European or American lenses) in relation to 'African artists', including those of Africa's diasporas.

[7] Jones's understanding of the formless counters the tendency to exclude art that can be seen to represent from this category; such attempts to preserve what Jones believes is an artificial distinction between form and formless were evident, as she remarks, at the *Informe* exhibition produced by Yves-Alain Bois and Rosalind Krauss at the Pompidou Centre in 1996, and in their accompanying book: *L'Informe: mode d'emploi* (Bois and Krauss, 1996). (See Caroline A. Jones, 2006: 132.)

art from this context did not always lend itself to interpretations of it as existential, though it actively sought to encourage a metaphorical reading (rather than passively being 'doomed' to such a reading). Fautrier's series of sculptures, *Les Otages* (The Hostages; 1943–44; bronze and lead), for example, uses formlessness to commemorate the anonymous masses of hostages, while drawing delicate profiles simultaneously to mourn individuals (see Dempsey, 2000). The association of formlessness with the anonymous masses, in Fautrier's work, is encouraged by the work's title and the use of figuration. In the work on the Tunisian revolution that I consider here, formlessness and form also coexist. But in this work exploring contemporary Tunisia, formlessness comes to be associated with resistance, and this is precisely because it appears together with icons or objects indicative of dictatorship or alternative kinds of extremism.

Works exploring the revolution by filming or photographing in the peripatetic mode similarly harness contingent effects for the purposes of resistance to icons or iconic spaces. The use of the peripatetic mode resonates, to some extent, with the Situationist practice of the *dérive*: '[literally, "drifting"], a technique of rapid passage through varied ambiances ... In a dérive one or more persons during a certain period drop their relations, their work and leisure activities, and all their other usual motives for movement and action, and let themselves be drawn by the attractions of the terrain and the encounters they find there' (Guy Debord, 1956, trans. Ken Knabb). Forms of *dérive* can be found in the work of a wide range of artists, including John Miller, Matthew Buckingham, Raymond Depardon and Sophie Calle.[8] Works exploring the revolutions, though, exceed Debord's definition of the *dérive*. They tend to depend on journeys at varying speeds, sometimes involving deceleration rather than 'rapid passage'. They visualise a specific space and historical moment of revolution, moreover, as opposed to 'varied ambiances'. Of the *dérive*, Debord stated: '[c]hance is a less important factor in this activity than one might think: from a dérive

---

[8] See, for example, Sophie Calle's *Filature parisienne* (1978–9) and *Suite vénitienne* (1980) (both published as *A Suivre*, Doubles-jeux, livre 4 (Arles: Actes Sud, 1998)), and Raymond Depardon's *Errance* (2004). A wide range of examples of the *dérive* could be seen at the Palais de Tokyo's exhibition, 'Les Dérives de l'imaginaire' (2012–13).

2 Contingency and Resistance

point of view cities have psychogeographical contours, with constant currents, fixed points and vortexes that strongly discourage entry into or exit from certain zones' (Debord, 1956). Chance is also diminished in these works, but in ways that reflect the particular revolutionary conditions in which they were produced. Routes can be determined by traffic jams due to demonstrations or by checkpoints indicative of restrictions on freedom. At the same time, chance is heightened, as we will see, through alternative practices.

I focus, in this chapter, on art exploring pre- and post-revolutionary Tunisia – from the injustices of Ben Ali's regime to the protests against Mohamed Ghannouchi's interim government in February 2011, the divided response to the moderate Islamist Ennahda party elected in October of the same year, and conditions under the centrist secular party Nidaa Tounes elected in 2014. I begin by analysing diverse examples of 'revolutionary formlessness'. Aïcha Filali's pair of sculptures, *Bourgeons en palabres* and *Bourgeons d'i(n)vers* (2011; Figure 2.1), is formed of twisted branches which bud incongruously with sculpted or ready-made objects indicative of diverse political voices. I compare Filali's installation to works in which a contingent organic process is rendered visible: Lamine's perishable portraits of Ben Ali in *Nous ne mangerons plus de ce pain-là* (2011) and Nadia-Kaabi Linke's flag embroidered with jasmine (*Smell*, 2011) are examined alongside works by Meriem Bouderbala and Lara Favaretto. Bouderbala's *Flag Nymphéas* (2012; Figure 2.2) depicts the Tunisian flag sinking gradually into a reflective pool of water. Lamine and Bouderbala rework national icons of revolution by combining digital, and apparently stable, modes of representation – scanning and photography – with substances that obey their own natural laws. Lara Favaretto, like Kaabi-Linke, uses materials that evolve during the course of the object's exhibition. Favaretto's large cube of brown confetti, *As If a Ruin* (2012), shifts and scatters as the spectator breathes on the object and walks around it. In the second part of this chapter I examine primarily two works of video art which employ the peripatetic mode in divergent ways to generate unpredictable microvisions of Tunis. Karray's video installation, *Live*, in which portraits of the former leader are shown while we hear the conversation between a taxi driver and his passenger, is compared to Ismaïl Bahri's pre-revolutionary *Orientations* (2010). This work anticipates Karray's peripatetic aesthetics in exploring the streets of Tunis by filming the images reflected in a cup of ink, which the artist holds as he walks. I argue that these works involving shifting materials or the artist's displacement in public space find their closest precedents in early twenty-first-century art that resists neo-colonialism or other sources of power in a globalised frame or in local Maghrebi contexts. I also show that, at the same time, these works produce new combinations of existing contingent practices or invent alternative contingent encounters of resistance. Contingent encounters, we will see, convey Tunisia as shifting and plural, and involve diversely located spectators in the process of rethinking an ongoing revolution.

Forms of Revolution and Revolutionary Formlessness

Work by Filali, Lamine, Bouderbala, Favaretto and Kaabi-Linke reveals diverse means of incorporating and harnessing the contingent effects of organic materials and processes to resist clichés and to create a space for alternative voices and visions. Aïcha Filali's pair of sculptures, *Bourgeons en palabres* and *Bourgeons d'i(n)vers* (collectively entitled *Bourgeons*), was produced in 2011, in the months following the deposition of President Ben Ali on 14 January (Figure 2.1). Reminiscent of the installations by Kossentini and Erruas examined in Chapter 1, this work communicates the ambivalence and turbulence of nascent democracy, conveying new-found freedom but also precariousness. Yet, it presents alternative, sculptural means of balancing the visual and the haptic, the translatable and the untranslatable. Filali's work reveals a process of incongruous sculptural 'grafting', incorporating an organic material – tree branches – which is conjoined with carved or industrially fabricated objects.

The twisted branches of *Bourgeons*, though literally constrained by heavy black metal clasps and bolts, bud with diverse, disjunctive sculpted or ready-made objects. The branches of the first sculpture, *Bourgeons en palabres*, grow into the tips of multiple coloured pencils, a metaphor for the contrasting emerging voices which jostle to be heard in the wake of Ben Ali's departure. This sculpture also evokes freedom of expression in Tunisia since the revolution, as the artist has commented (cited by L'Orient-Le Jour / Agences, 2012). The second sculpture, *Bourgeons d'i(n)vers*, evokes the emergence of contrasting Islamic and Islamist voices ('la composante islamique/iste(?)' ('the Islamic/ist(?) component', the artist states) that had equally lain dormant throughout successive periods of singular rule.[9] The title puns on the word 'din', which means 'religion' in Arabic.[10] The branches of this 'tree' – also held together with black metal – bud surrealistically with green and gold Islamic symbols, a matching green high-heeled shoe and an old limescaled tap. The branches allude to organic, contingent growth, communicating metaphorically the impossibility of suppressing 'untranslatable' voices. The organic matter is no longer 'in process', but the twisted forms of the actual branches employed by Filali recall their history of literal restraint, and growth in spite of this, which inspired the artist to use them as the material for her work. The viewer becomes aware of this on reading the artist's accompanying statement:

Un arbre de notre jardin, contraint pendant de longues années par une structure de fer pour l'embellissement d'un kiosque, a vu ses branches se raidir, se tordre, se contorsionner jusqu'à durcir et se vider de leur sève. A la faveur d'un élagage radical et tardif, voilà qu'apparaissent, dénudées des quelques feuilles qui en couvraient la couche extérieure, des branches, noueuses, torturées, qui se sont directement imposées à moi comme matière – à; donc préservées pendant quelques années, en instance, pour leur intérêt plastique et affectif.

Une révolution plus tard, les choses se sont naturellement mises en place ... sous forme de sculptures de l'après. Et voilà que les branches se remettent à vivre. Certaines de leurs extrémités bourgeonnent à nouveau, et évoluent vers des objets inattendus. Apparaissent alors en miroir, les germes dormants, enfouis dans le terreau qui les porte.

Toute ressemblance avec la situation d'un pays qui a initié les révolutions arabes, un certain 14 janvier 2011, est tout à fait intentionnelle. (emphasis in original)[11]

---

[9] Filali states this in the accompanying note at the exhibition 'Dégagements, La Tunisie un an après' (Institut du Monde Arabe, Paris, 2012).
[10] The artist confirmed this for the report on the exhibition by L'Orient-Le Jour / Agences (2012; no author provided).
[11] This statement appeared in the accompanying note at 'Dégagements, La Tunisie un an après' (IMA, Paris, 2012; emphasis in original).

(The branches of a tree from our garden, constrained for many long years by an iron structure to decorate a pavilion, began to stiffen, twist and contort themselves until they hardened and lost their sap. And, as a result of a radical and belated pruning, there appeared, stripped of the few leaves that covered their exterior layer, branches, knotted, tortured, which imposed themselves on me directly as a material to [use]; preserved, therefore, for a few years, in waiting, for their plastic and affective qualities.

One revolution later, things naturally arranged themselves ... in the form of sculptures of the aftermath.

And that's when the branches began to come back to life. Some of their extremities started to bud again, and they grew into unexpected objects. Opposite, dormant sprouts then appeared, buried in the ground surrounding them.

Any resemblance with the situation of a country that initiated the Arab revolutions, one 14 January 2011, is completely intentional.)

Filali's sculptures evoke the emergence of new life and a new 'Tunisia', while giving back a voice and a space to those who were long silenced and obscured by the official histories and visions of the country. *Bourgeons* gives particular attention to the theme of political diversity. The sculptures emphasise democratic plurality and inevitable resistance to political hegemony and singularity, while they also signal conflict and instability. Filali's creations point specifically to the presence of contrasting positions. The carved red, blue, green, yellow and black pencil buds of *Bourgeons en palabres* could be perceived positively to prefigure a multicoloured script of distinct, yet intertwined and coexistent, voices, which join together in relative harmony to 'write' a new and plural Tunisia. The second, interconnected, 'tree', which grows disjunctive ready-made objects, is perhaps more evocative of tensions and disharmony – specifically among proponents of political Islam – while still avoiding a one-sided presentation of the revolution and its aftermath. The budding, yet redundant, well-worn tap could be seen to allude to the resurgence of an outmoded, perhaps fundamentalist, brand of theocratic politics, intimating that it has no more to offer, while the Islamic crescent object and the high-heeled shoe (both green, the traditional colour of Islam) might be taken to evoke conservative and liberal (*ijtihad*) positions, respectively, within political Islam. This visual juxtaposition of interconnected, yet distinctive, positions resonates with Olivier Roy's identification of the same three broad camps to demarcate the views of Muslim religious scholars and intellectuals in the centuries-old debate regarding Islam and democracy (Roy, 2012; see also Marzouki, 2013). Filali's heterogeneous objects – which, moreover, exhibit different textures and shades of green – appear to point to a nuanced alternative to the dichotomy constructed between 'Western' democracy and radical forms of Islamism. Presented as a pair, *Bourgeons* could be seen to convey the compatibility – and indeed the interdependence – of particular, and evolving, versions of political Islam and democracy. (While some in Tunisia accused the moderate Islamist party Ennahda of doublespeak, Nadia Marzouki argues that its discourse on the concept of civic state ('dawla madaniyya') emerges from the enduring debate surrounding their compatibility (Marzouki, 2013).[12]) Alternatively, the separate trees could appear to evoke the need for a distinction between the religious and political spheres, reminiscent of the views of proponents of *laïcité* for Tunisia. *Bourgeons* allows for both readings, moving beyond the tendency to polarise secularism and religion in debates regarding the country's governance.[13]

Filali's *Bourgeons en palabres* evokes uncertainty regarding the country's political future. Like Kossentini's *Le Printemps arabe* and *Heaven or Hell*, this work evokes the instability and fragility that are necessarily inherent in an emerging democracy and the time inevitably required for democracy to unfold fully (see Dakhlia, 2011: 114; Khouri, 2014: 13–14). At the same time, it reveals an alternative means of conveying the complexity and ambivalence of 'revolution' and 'democracy' between the binaries of success and failure. These binaries are at times associated reductively with secularism and religion or even 'Western' democracy and radical Islamism, as critics such as Dakhlia (2011) and Andrea Khalil (2011) have shown. Filali allows her work to be determined, to some extent, by the contingent effects of organic matter, as well as found industrial objects fabricated by

---

[12] Roy (2012) stresses the compatibility and increasing interdependence of political Islam and democracy since the Arab Uprisings began in late 2010.
[13] An example of scholarship that questions the Islamist/secular divide can be found, as I indicated in the introduction to this book, in Andrea Khalil's indication of the common goals for women in Tunisia, at least in urban contexts (Khalil, 2011).

unknown makers for a utilitarian purpose. At the same time, the artist balances contingency with control, and materiality with metaphor, by combining the tree branches with objects she chooses, by imposing a metal structure on them, and by reshaping them by hand. Contingent encounters, in this work, question inflexible perceptions of the nation and allow for the view that identity is ungraspable and subject, inevitably, to evolution. It uses organic, haptic, affective forms and materials to point to a fragile and uncertain reality but also to forge an ambivalent 'language' with which to evoke the potential for a democracy that is independent of a Western model and free from internal extremisms. Fragility, yet inevitable resistance, is similarly evoked in works that render visible multiple stages of the contingent process of creation or that allow such a process to evolve throughout the course of the exhibition by using perishable or ephemeral materials.

In *Nous ne mangerons plus de ce pain-là* (2011), Tunis-based Hela Lamine presents a row of seven photographic portraits of Ben Ali, which appear increasingly distorted from left to right to the point of becoming almost unrecognisable (Figure 0.2). The original portrait was made with a mixture of bread and water and allowed to decompose over time. The series of seven images that we see mounted, ironically, in gilt frames are photographs of scans of the same portrait at different stages of its gradual decomposition. Each is underlined by a golden plaque, engraved with the dates of the election and each re-election of Ben Ali, from 7 November 1987, through to the date of his enforced departure: 14 January 2011.[14] Lamine's work 'revises' the history of Ben Ali's leadership, so that moments of apparent political power and popularity are exposed as markers in the history of his decline. The former president's fall from grace is subversively indicated by his depiction using the humble diet of bread and water – which the people refused to consume (their opinion is voiced through the title,

---

[14] Hela Lamine has stated that she chose to present seven images, given the symbolism of this number, 'the lucky number of the ex-president, which would lead him straight to ruin in this work' (cited and translated in Bruckbauer and Triki, 2012: 114–15). At the exhibition 'Rosy Futures' in Stuttgart (2013), the artist exhibited a further scanogram of a piece of grilled and water-soaked bread arranged to resemble the Tunisian flag, which appears to convey the fragility of Tunisia in the immediate aftermath of the revolution (see Bruckbauer and Triki, 2012: 114–15).

which functions metaphorically and literally). The title uses a French expression, while it recalls the slogan chanted in Arabic by protesters in Tunisia on 14 January 2011: 'Khobz ou mé, ou Ben Ali, lé' ('Bread and water, and Ben Ali, no'); it conjures the artist's personal memory of demonstrating at that time.[15] This chant, like the bread used to make this work, resonates with the Bread Riots in Tunisia in the 1980s, to which I return below. The decaying portrait – reminiscent of Dorian Gray – points to the reality of corruption and deception, which is obscured by official images of the former regime. Lamine's image of Ben Ali becomes darker and greener in colour, and its boundaries are literally exceeded as hard plaques of mould begin to grow.

Franco-Tunisian artist and curator Meriem Bouderbala (also based in Tunis) similarly uses the instantaneous medium of digital photography and a different icon (the Tunisian flag) together with an alternative contingent process and organic substance in *Flag Nymphéas* (2012; Figure 2.2). In an interview some seven years after she created this work, the artist reveals how her choice to move away from figurative art (she is particularly well known for her ambivalent photographic images of her body) came from the need she felt to avoid images of 'women of the revolution': 'Au moment de la Révolution, quand on m'a demandé de descendre dans la rue et de faire des photos des «femmes de la révolution» je n'ai pas pu. J'ai refusé parce que je savais très bien que l'image serait récupérée ... Pour la nommer je n'ai fait qu'une photo «Flag Nymphéas».' ('At the time of the Revolution, when I was asked to go to the street and take photos of "women of the revolution" I couldn't. I refused because I knew very well that the image would be recuperated ... To name [the Revolution] I took only one photo: "Flag Nymphéas".') (in interview with Inès Ben Azouz, 2018). Bouderbala's concern resonates with the need, expressed by Jellel Gasteli, to avoid producing 'icons of revolutionary exoticism' (2012; see also Michket Krifa, in interview with Wafa Gabsi, 2012).

Bouderbala's row of six large photographs (90 × 60 cm) depicts the flag floating in an evolving blend of water, sky and light, which – like the title – refers ironically to Monet's *Nymphéas*. In their touches of red, pink and yellow produced by fragments of vegetation floating on

---

[15] See the artist's text accompanying this work on her website: https://helalamine.com/2011/03/01/khobz-ou-me-pain-eau/

the shallow pool, and their reflection of sunlight, greenery and the sky beyond, these images recall Monet's palette and balanced compositions. The composition of three of the photographs can be compared directly to works including *The Water Lily Pond* (*c*.1917–19, Albertina, Vienna)), in which the sky emerges on the left-hand side behind the dark green silhouette of the tree reflected in the water. Bouderbala's painterly images echo Monet's aim to merge water and sky in the absence of spatial cues such as a horizon or a bank.[16] Yet, the tranquillity evoked, in Monet's paintings, by 'the illusion of an endless whole',[17] is disrupted, in Bouderbala's photographs, by the bright red national icon. In contrast to Monet's monumental paintings, which are hinged together to encompass the viewer and to create 'the refuge of a peaceful meditation',[18] the images of *Flag Nymphéas* are distinct, separated by an interval of blank wall, and the series reveals a shifting composition. The flag is depicted from different angles, the sky emerging alternately on the left or right of the image; the photographs can be apprehended as three pairs, each showing the flag within half of the same circular pool. The semicircular compositions, though, are asymmetrical, because the work presents a temporal sequence. It consists of a series of snapshots taken while the flag drifts in the water, gently rolling up or unfurling as it sinks to the bottom. *Flag Nymphéas* alludes ironically to Monet's paintings to convey the fragility and uncertainty of contemporary Tunisia. Rather than provide a refuge conducive to meditation, it implicates the viewers. It calls for them to relate Bouderbala's poetic work to the political context, even while it refuses to make a clear political statement.

From one perspective, *Flag Nymphéas* appears to evoke pessimistically the current situation in Tunisia and to intimate that the revolution has failed (Bouderbala created the work at the time when Ennahda won the elections, in October 2011, which some perceived in terms of a failure of the revolution; see Ben Azouz, 2018). The flag's movements

---

[16] Monet's words regarding his aim to provide 'the illusion of an endless whole, of water without horizon or bank' are cited by The Museum of Modern Art (2004 [1999]: 98).

[17] Monet, cited by The Museum of Modern Art (2004 [1999]: 98).

[18] Monet, cited by The Museum of Modern Art (2004 [1999]: 98). See especially his monumental triptych works on curved walls at the Musée de l'Orangerie, Paris.

in contact with the water appear to suggest a country – or at least a government – in decline. Its shifts can be seen as a critique of the current confusion, of a government that is adrift. The first part of the artist's statement, which appeared alongside the work, can be understood to encourage this reading: 'Mon pays s'enfonce et se noie, la surface étale de l'eau révèle sa lente immersion. Il n'y a plus de révolution populaire, il ne reste que la récupération par un «mode révolutionnaire» que des élites en mal d'émotions se partagent avec avidité. La guerre est toujours menée par les mêmes' ('My country is getting into deeper and deeper water and drowning; the water-covered surface evokes its gradual immersion. Popular revolution no longer exists – only hijacking via a revolutionary mode that the elites greedily share in their quest for sensations. War is always waged by the same people.').[19] Echoing the first part of Bouderbala's statement, the sinking flag can be seen to signal the country's depleting revolutionary energy, its decline towards inertia and stagnation. This impression is enhanced by the fragments of dead vegetation floating on the surface of the water (in contrast to the full bloom of Monet's lilies). Yet, visually, the flag sinks only if read from right to left; if viewed in this direction – the direction encouraged by the circular layout of the exhibition – the flag appears to drift on the surface of the water before gliding downwards. Its colour darkens as it descends and in the last image it touches the ground, the crumpled fabric obscuring the star and crescent that define the object as the Tunisian flag. Yet, standing before the work, we might read in either direction (echoing the directions of Arabic or French). From left to right, Tunisia appears to rise again; the flag unfurls to 'bloom' fully when it reaches the surface of the water. We know, logically, that the process employed to create the work involved a downward movement dependent on gravity; but images of the stages of this natural process have, if the work is read from left to right, been rearranged; time has been manipulated in the exhibition of the work. The final sentence of Bouderbala's statement can, moreover, be seen more optimistically to indicate the possibility for an alternative Tunisia to emerge: 'Le visage de la Tunisie d'aujourd'hui est celui de l'art

[19] Artist's statement at '25 ans de créativité arabe' (Institut du Monde Arabe, Paris, 2012–13). The English version of the artist's statement ('25 Years of Arab Creativity'), which I have used here, was supplied, alongside an Arabic version, in the English/Arabic version of the catalogue for the exhibition at the Abu Dhabi Festival in 2013 (2013: 64).

quand il affirme sa quête sublime et son errance' ('The current face of Tunisia is like that of an erring art on a quest for the sublime').[20] The artist's comment, in her interview years after she created *Flag Nymphéas*, signals the perception she had had of both pessimism and optimism in her ambivalent flag: 'c'était ma perception de la révolution tunisienne. C'est un drapeau qui sombre, c'est une nation qui se noie *et se régénère*' ('it was my perception of the Tunisian Revolution. It's a sinking flag, it's a nation that's drowning *and regenerating*') (in interview with Ben Azouz, 2018; my emphasis).

This work – like many others emerging from this context – forges a language of 'errance' ('wandering') (to reprise the artist's term), which might be taken to mean a language of experimentation and freedom, through its use of a contingent process in conjunction with natural elements that are subject to change. It creates a new space between water and sky, surface and depth, in which Tunisian identity can be renegotiated. The apparently stable language of the flag converges with fluidity and movement, as well as unevenness. This impression of unevenness is enhanced by shifting light and shadow on the object, its evolving colour as it drifts downwards or upwards, and the intermittent obscurity of its defining symbol when the material curls inwards. Even if the work is read from right to left, the flag that touches the ground (still wavering, rather than having sunk entirely) suggests that the people – those who propelled the revolution – are only lying dormant. The evocation of movement through a combination of contingent natural elements (water, the sky and light), the shifts in composition and the possibility of viewing in both directions suggest the provisional nature of the country's confusion and its evolution away from current turbulence. This work, too, resonates with Dakhlia's observation regarding the inherence of instability in democracy, whether emerging or established (2011).

Flag Nymphéas reveals an alternative means of exceeding the iconic language of the flag to that of Erruas's installation *Les Drapeaux*, alongside which it was exhibited at the Institut du Monde Arabe (2012–13).[21] While Erruas's work involves the contingent kinaesthetic process of weaving by hand, Bouderbala's flag is disconnected from the

---

[20] I use the remaining line of the artist's English version of her statement for this work, as printed in the English/Arabic version of the catalogue for '25 Years of Arab Creativity' (2013: 64).

[21] '25 ans de créativité arabe', IMA, Paris, 2012–13.

artist's hand, and shifts due to the combined effects of gravity and water. Nadia Kaabi-Linke's installation *Smell* (2012) reworks a flag indicative of an alternative source of power – that which has been appropriated by the extremist Islamist movement in North Africa – by using a perishable material and the contingent enduring process of weaving.[22] The artist embroiders the usually white calligraphic Shahada (the Muslim confession of faith) with real jasmine, which wilts and loses its scent during the course of its display (see: https://commons.wikimedia.org/wiki/File:Smell_(2015)_%E2%80%93_Nadia_Kaabi-Linke.jpg). The gradual attenuation of the scent of jasmine evokes continuing repression in Tunisia in alternative forms. This sensorial shift appears to question whether Ben Ali's authoritarianism will simply be replaced by that of religious extremists.[23] The flag, which has become a visual icon of Islamist extremism (both local and global), appears to lose its power. The same can be said for the flower which had been appropriated by Ben Ali's regime and yet has often been invoked by the international media in reportage on the so-called 'Jasmine Revolution'. The piece evokes fragility and uncertainty, but also a multidirectional critique.

A further dimension, unforeseen by the artist, emerged in the reception of this work, which has only been exhibited once, at the Musée de Carthage, Tunisia, in 2012. As Nadia Kaabi-Linke has related, she remembers that people liked the work. There were also 'somewhat reserved' reactions, given the use of the sacred Shahada – '[m]ais rien de bien grave car j'ai représenté ces mots avec un symbole que les gens apprécient à l'unanimité en Tunisie' ('but nothing really serious since I represented these words with a symbol that's appreciated unanimously by people in Tunisia').[24] Yet, there was also a response the

---

[22] Exhibited at 'Chkoun Ahna' (meaning 'Who Are We?' or 'About Us' in Tunisian Arabic) (Musée de Carthage, Tunisia, 2012). See documentation supplied on the artist's website by Timo Kaabi-Linke: www.nadiakaabilinke.com (last accessed July 2013).

[23] Regarding the intention behind this work, Tn News cites curator Timo Kaabi-Linke, the artist's husband: 'the idea was to write the "credo of the new Salafi movement with the symbolic flower of last year's change." Through this, the artist sought to convey the idea that change can never come to an end, that change is an ongoing process. "One must be vigilant, so that it does not fade away,"' (Timo Kaabi-Linke cited by Tn News (no author named), 2012).

[24] My citations of the artist in this paragraph are from our email exchange of December 2019.

artist did not expect. The guardian of the museum, who considers himself to be a Salafist, liked the work so much that he asked the artist if he could keep it after the end of the exhibition: 'Il m'avait promis avec émotion qu'il allait prendre soin de l'oeuvre et remplacer les fleurs fanées par des fleurs fraîches tous les jours' ('He promised me emotionally that he was going to take care of the work and replace the wilted flowers by fresh flowers every day'). The artist was moved by this response, which caused her to reflect further on the work's possible meanings and on her own perspective:

J'ai aimé l'ambivalence que recèle ce travail que Hafedh m'a permis de voir. J'ai compris à quel point ma vision était restreinte et «jugemental» et à quel point une personne qui se considère salafiste peut être beaucoup plus humble et ouverte qu'une personne qui se croyait éclairée, ouverte et moderne. / Je remercie Hafedh qui m'a donnée une belle leçon de vie et d'art pour toute ma vie.

(I liked the ambivalence contained by this work, which Hafedh enabled me to see. I understood how restrained and 'judgemental' my view had been and how someone who considers himself Salafi can be far humbler and more open than someone who thought themselves enlightened, open and modern. / I'm grateful to Hafedh, who has given me a good lesson in life and art for the rest of my life.)

Hafedh's interpretation calls to mind, in an alternative way to Filali's sculpture, the range of Islamist (including Salafist) positions and the complexity of the frequently polarised (Islamist/secular) debates surrounding Tunisia's future. (Jihadi Salafists in Tunisia are 'a minority within a minority', as Gana, following Fabio Merone and Francesco Cavatorta, has affirmed (2013: 25).[25]) It also reveals the extent to which such open, ambivalent work can allow, democratically, for alternative, sometimes conflicting, voices and visions which might exceed the expectations of the artist. Hafedh's response, which effectively restores the sacred value of the Shahada, moves beyond its appropriation by extremists and can be seen to extend the work's critique to the assumptions that are often made within and beyond Tunisia regarding this flag, Salafism, Islamism and indeed Islam. It calls to mind Mignolo's emphasis on the subjectivity and contingency of knowledge, and the locatedness of the 'knower', as well as Kilani's similarly crucial reminder that '"L'histoire

---

[25] On the heterogeneity of Tunisian Salafism, see the chapter by Merone and Cavatorta (2013) in Nouri Gana's edited collection.

universaliste du monde prouve qu'elle n'est qu'une version particulière de l'histoire"' ('The universalist history of the world proves that it is merely one particular version of history') (Mignolo, 2011; Kilani 2002: 89, cited by Ben Soltane, 2012: 219).

In this work, Kaabi-Linke manipulates the real flower, 'writing' with it and then allowing the organic matter to evolve. This piece evokes translatable visual and verbal languages while exceeding them and allowing for the *un*translatable through a perceptible contingent process of transformation – material and olfactory.[26] The contingent, subtle and gradual process of transformation can be seen in terms of an alternative language in which it is possible to call for 'democracy', while allowing for different definitions of this word. An ephemeral material and its contingent transformations over time are also central to Turin-based artist Lara Favaretto's sculptural work, *As If a Ruin* (2012).

As If a Ruin engages not with a flag or other national icon but with the more abstract visual language of the cube.[27] Favaretto's cube is made of brown confetti, which shifts, falls and scatters around the base of the sculpture as the spectator breathes on it and walks around it, collecting confetti on the soles of their shoes (see Clément Dirié, 2013: 106).[28] In this work the contingent encounter between the cube and the ephemeral confetti is doubled by that between this material and the spectator's movements. This precarious work ambivalently conveys both the collapse of Ben Ali's regime and the country's uncertain

---

[26] The use of real jasmine to allude to the Tunisian revolution and the Arab Uprisings is reminiscent of Latifa Echakhch's sculpture, *Fantôme*, in which she juxtaposes a shirt with garlands of withering jasmine in a poignant commemoration of Mohammed Bouazizi (part of the artist's exhibition, 'Tkaf', Kamel Mennour, Paris, 2012).

[27] *As If a Ruin* is thus more reliant than other works, including those by Lamine, Bouderbala and Kaabi-Linke, on the context – curatorial, but also historical and perhaps cultural – in which it is exhibited. Alternatively, or in addition, it depends on an accompanying text that refers to its first appearance with works produced in response to the Tunisian revolution: 'Chkoun Ahna' (Musée de Carthage, Tunisia, 2012). Such a text was presented with the work at 'Ici, ailleurs', a thematically broader exhibition of works exploring the Mediterranean (La Friche la Belle de Mai, Marseille, 2013).

[28] Favaretto has commented on her wider interest in the effects of organic elements in her work: 'I select objects that add parallel lives to my installations, objects that already have a history, especially those that have been submitted to various kinds of energy, power, and weather conditions – all agents that intervene on the materials that compose each artifact' (cited by Dirié, 2013: 106).

future.[29] The sombre colour of the confetti might be taken to signal that the celebrations are over, while its ephemerality communicates the current fragility of Tunisia. Similar to Kossentini's reappropriation of the arabesque-Rotorelief, Favaretto's cube, which might call to mind 1960s American minimalist art or the ancient Ka'aba in Mecca, appears to symbolise alternative forms of hegemony – political and cultural, but also social cohesiveness in Tunisia. (This work, as curator Timo Kaabi-Linke states, was originally a site-specific piece inspired by the destruction of Carthage, but many Tunisian visitors were convinced that it represented the Ka'aba (Timo Kaabi-Linke, 2013).[30]) The process of outward scattering echoes the shattering in Kossentini's work. The shift from form to formlessness can similarly be seen, here, to pose the question as to whether the revolution was a success or a failure, while also making space for the less black-and-white idea that it is still in process.

While Filali incorporates organic matter that has already undergone a contingent process, these four artists set in motion an encounter between an apparently stable icon and an organic material. But the result of this process is, at least to some extent, unpredictable. In Kaabi-Linke's and Favaretto's work the encounter is unmediated and continues in the spectators' presence. In all four works the parameters imposed serve, paradoxically, to highlight contingency. Both Lamine and Bouderbala intervene after the process to produce photographs of multiple stages of the encounter and show these simultaneously. They balance contingency with control by selecting, framing and rearranging images of the process, as well as by adding text beneath or alongside the photographs. Their presentations of series of images draw our attention to the process, to subtle movements – of both object and composition – and to nuances in meaning, just as they create a space for alternative voices and directions for Tunisia. In their works, the instantaneous medium of photography, which is often associated with transparency and authenticity, is contested through its use to depict a gradual and organic process. Photography, which has often been used to produce clichés and 'icons of revolutionary

---

[29] Clément Dirié relates the work's fragility and inevitable disappearance to the uncertainties of the 'Arab Spring' (Dirié, 2013: 106).

[30] The source of inspiration in Carthage was lost in the work's re-exhibition at 'Ici, ailleurs' in Marseilles and no reference was made to it in the curatorial note or the exhibition catalogue.

exoticism', comes, in these works, to be aligned with uncertainty and instability.

The contingent processes employed in all these works are reminiscent, to some extent, of European and North American modernist aesthetics. The use of decaying, perishable materials or of processes that escape the artist's control resonates with process art of the 1960s and 70s and its precursors. Lamine's procedure is reminiscent of Man Ray's photograph of dust 'breeding' on Duchamp's *Large Glass* (*Dust Breeding*, 1920).[31] Some of Duchamp's notes on the infra-thin, moreover, refer to contingent organic processes: 'glissage - / Sechage – collage / viscosité - / cassage. / Brûlage / fondage (dans les liquides avec le sucre pax.) / Porosité – imbibage) ...' ('sliding - / Drying – sticking / viscosity - / breaking. / Burning / melting (e.g. in liquids with sugar) / Porosity – imbibing) ...'] (note 26v, 27).[32] Lamine's mixture of bread and water produces a viscous substance and undergoes further mutations upon prolonged contact with air, or the process of 'sechage'. Kaabi-Linke's focus on scent resonates with Duchamp's interest in contingent sensorial shifts and elements that exceed the visual: 'Odeurs plus inframinces que les couleurs' ('Odours more infra-thin than colours') (note 37, 34). Kaabi-Linke combines alternative means of incorporating contingency by using this perishable material together with the local and regional practices of embroidery and calligraphy. Her incorporation of this material heightens the contingency already involved in these enduring practices. Yet, in these works exploring the

---

[31] The full title of Man Ray's photograph is: *Dust Breeding (Duchamp's Large Glass with Dust Notes)*.

[32] Contingency frequently emerges as a key element of Duchamp's infra-thin: it is also central to processes discussed in Chapter 1, including reflections, shadow and light and fading colours. Critics have tended to discuss Duchamp's chance aesthetics as an alternative means of generating the singular, distinct from the infra-thin. See Thierry Davila (2010: 48–51). Davila introduces Duchamp's use of chance as an 'autre forme': 'Outre celle de l'art et de l'inframince, cette quête de la singularité prend plusieurs autres formes ...' ('Another form: in addition to that for art and for the infra-thin, this quest for singularity takes several other forms ...') (48). Despite Davila's separation of chance from the infra-thin, the relevance of this concept to *3 Standard Stoppages* is suggested by the critic's consideration of Duchamp's individual variations on the metre in terms of 'de petites differences, d'écarts producteurs de formes' ('small differences, intervals productive of forms') (51).

revolution, this organic matter does not simply refer to itself. Used, in Lamine's series, to produce a famous image of the former leader, it becomes a metaphor for corruption. It also evokes the Tunisian bread riots of 1984 against Bourguiba's economic policies, which, as Gana states, prepared the ground for Ben Ali's constitutional coup three years later (2013: 22). The bread mixture also resonates with the revolutionary chants of Tunisians in January 2011; thus, it connects 'dispersed endeavors' – the *r*evolutionary – to the revolution (to reprise Gana's expression, 2013: 2). The contingent process becomes a means of resisting Ben Ali's dictatorship. In Kaabi-Linke's work the jasmine serves, similarly, not only for its material properties but also for its symbolism. The jasmine anchors the work in relation to the revolution. The gradual attenuation of scent in this work appears to question whether Ben Ali's authoritarianism will simply be replaced, while it exceeds the apparently stable black-and-white language of revolution and that of religious extremism, if the flag is seen as symbolic of this (it literally moves beyond black and white). Hafedh's response to this work, which involves restoring the scent and the sacredness to the Muslim inscription, also moves beyond black and white both literally and metaphorically, though by allowing for a reconsideration of rigid views of the re-emergence of Islamist voices in Tunisia. In Bouderbala's *Flag Nymphéas*, contingency is introduced via the gesture of dropping the icon into the water, a procedure which calls to mind Duchamp's releasing of one-metre-long pieces of string. It is also reminiscent of certain Dadaist gestures, including Tristan Tzara's 'creation' of poetry by emptying a bag of jumbled words cut out of a newspaper article. The dropping of an object into water also resonates (in practice, if not in spirit or intention) with Yves Klein's more recent work in which he exchanged his 'immaterial pictorial sensitivity' (a quality which remained undefined) for gold leaf, which he then threw into the Seine (1962).[33] Crucially, however, in contrast to the photographs of Klein's performance, the artist and the action of dropping the flag are absent

---

[33] Klein exchanged his 'immaterial pictorial sensitivity' – a quality which remained undefined – for gold leaf, which he then threw into the Seine (10 February 1962; this was one of several 'sales ceremonies'). In each case, the purchaser was asked to burn their receipt in keeping with the spiritual quality of the work. (See Goldberg, 1979: 94.)

from the perceptible part of Bouderbala's work. The visible, contingent process is that of the flag gliding through water. Diverging from all three of these examples of chance aesthetics, Bouderbala's work privileges the object over the gesture and uses an icon that binds the contingent process to contemporary Tunisia.

These works, distinct from connections of formlessness with pure materiality in the work of Bataille, hold in tension materiality and metaphor. They are distinct, furthermore, from Fautrier's series of sculptures *Les Otages*, in which the association of formlessness with the anonymous masses is encouraged by the work's title and the use of figuration. In this work exploring contemporary Tunisia, formlessness comes to be associated with resistance, and this is precisely because it appears together with icons or objects indicative of dictatorship or alternative kinds of extremism. By contrast with Fautrier's delicate profiles, which are drawn into – and appear to emerge from – his formless masses in *Les Otages*, this work holds form and formlessness in tension. That is, it incorporates, or alludes to, a distinct, external language of order and exceeds that language, evolving beyond it, as well as beyond the artist's control. In these ways, these works hold in tension the poetic and the political. Their closest precedents can perhaps be found in works that employ organic substances to contest languages of power in a globalised frame. In Mounir Fatmi's video work *Manipulations* (2004), for example, a Rubik's cube is handled until it becomes a black cube and then melts into a formless black liquid, exceeding what appear in his work as 'Western' and 'Eastern' symbols of order. Lara Favaretto's shifting disintegrating cube resonates particularly with this work.[34] In her work, and others exploring contemporary Tunisia, though, the dynamic between form and

---

[34] See also Kader Attia's series of black paintings of the *Ka'aba*, which evoke the structure of the cube at the top but descend into wavering verticals and drips (for example, *Black Cube II*, 2005).The order embodied by the cube is also questioned in Kader Attia's video *Oil and Sugar* (2007; 4'30), in which oil is poured onto two towers of white sugar cubes. The crumbling of the two towers, which become an amorphous shifting substance, can be seen to echo the collapse, on September 11, 2001, of the symbols of capitalist hegemony that formerly dominated the Manhattan skyline. The interaction of oil and sugar also evokes the search for alternative sources of energy in the face of dwindling resources (Kader Attia, cited in Durand, 2010: 76.) The cube – particularly the white cube of the art gallery and the Minimalist cube – has long been contested in art.

formlessness echoes the revolutionary tension between constraint and liberation, yet also uncertainty. It evokes an alternative space and a (shifting and provisional) 'language' in which the revolution can be debated and rethought.

The peripatetic video works of artists such as Mouna Karray and Ismaïl Bahri similarly incorporate iconic images, and allude to iconic public space, such that contingency comes to be associated with resistance. These works might seem distant from those involving organic materials and processes. Yet, aesthetics of revolution in both types of work depend on contingent movement – from the gradual shifts undergone by fabric in water, wilting flowers or decomposing bread to journeys through space on foot or at higher speeds. Certain videos, moreover, reveal a convergence of shifting haptic organic materials or phenomena and unedited footage captured in motion. At the same time, they demonstrate alternative means of exceeding icons and encouraging a rethinking of iconic space by restricting the spectators' viewpoint and privileging contingent auditory or haptic encounters.

Revolutions in the Peripatetic Mode: Micro-visions and -voices of Tunis

Video and photographic work reveals diverse uses of the peripatetic mode to generate contingency in ways that encourage a reimagining of sites and sights of the Tunisian revolution. The peripatetic mode is frequently combined with parameters involving the frame or the type of shot. In the online work *Deux minutes de Tunis* (2011), for example, Oussema Troudi conveys the demonstrations against Ghannouchi's interim government via fifty-one videos filmed on foot, on the metro or on the train, each for two minutes, with a static frame and from a restrictive angle (Mohammed Ghannouchi had been a member of Ben Ali's party, the Rassemblement Constitutionnel Démocratique (RCD); protesters sought a clean break with the deposed president's regime). As I have shown elsewhere, these constraints imposed by the artist paradoxically allow his images of Tunis to be shaped by contingent everyday life and passers-by (Shilton, 2016). Contrasting with iconic images seen on television and social media, the historic sit-in at the Kasbah is conveyed in this work via sounds and peripheral sights such as people's feet, rubbish or remnants of a fire on the ground, a popcorn cooker, or a helicopter surveying from above. In such works the journey itself is at times implicit. Troudi's videos produced at the demonstration are filmed while standing still, by contrast with the high-speed footage in others he films from a train in the suburbs of Tunis. Yet, these spontaneous images evoke the artist's circulation in public space. The same can be said of Aïcha Filali's collection of photographs of people in the streets of Tunis in *L'Angle mort*. In my discussion of this work, in Chapter 1, I focused on the effects of contingent shifting reflections of spectators and the environment on the glass overlaying the images. Yet, contingency is also incorporated in *L'Angle mort* through the art process, which combines the peripatetic mode with the view from behind unknowing passers-by. Wassim Ghozlani's *Postcards of Tunisia* (2010–11) unites photographs taken in rural Tunisia, while his collection similarly conveys the artist's displacements on foot. His off-centre photographs of everyday life and industry or close-ups of natural elements convey spontaneity and a lack of cultural specificity, by contrast with carefully constructed exoticist postcards. These collections by Ghozlani and Filali, which were both initiated in 2010, reveal the presence of contingent encounters of resistance involving the peripatetic mode in Tunisian art prior to the revolution. The peripatetic mode, whether implicit or explicit, leads to contingent images that contrast with icons of Tunisia and the revolution.

Distinct from Debord's theory of the *dérive*, such work often moves beyond urban environments and frequently emerges from journeys at varying speeds or at a decelerated pace. These videos or photographic collections are closer to early twenty-first-century works that seek to explore Algerian or Moroccan spaces in ways that avoid images of exoticism or violence, while countering internal censorship. Katia Kameli, for example, films while travelling at various speeds and on different modes of transport to evoke the diversity of Algiers and its surrounding areas in *Bledi, a Possible Scenario* (2004).[35] The sequences she films from a car or on foot in the city, for example, incorporate visual and verbal traces of Algeria's multi-layered history and of personal stories, together with scenes of everyday life. Yto Barrada uses restrictive high-angle views and close-ups in *Le Projet du Détroit* (1998–2004) to investigate treacherous journeys from Tangiers to

---

[35] This film is available on the artist's website at: http://katiakameli.com/production/bledi-a-possible-scenario/.

Gibraltar through 'tentations' ('temptations'), as opposed to the commonly depicted and named 'tentatives' ('attempts').[36] Her large-scale monochrome photographs for the series 'Dormeurs' [Sleepers], for instance, each depict a man sleeping on the grass while waiting for an opportunity to cross the Straits. Focusing on the ground again, Barrada captures wild flowers or grass, everyday objects, or people's feet throughout her video for the multimedia work *Iris Tingitana* (2007), the name of a flower specific to the region. This flower becomes, through Barrada's technique, a symbol of resistance to the eradication of local particularities through rapid economic development. Yet, more recent work exploring Tunisia combines such parameters in alternative ways or it invents new means of generating contingent encounters of resistance. Videos by Karray and Bahri (who are both based between Tunis and Paris) demonstrate striking alternative methods of restricting the spectators' vision and using other senses to convey a specific space and historical moment.

Mouna Karray's six-minute video, *Live* (2012), is shaped by the uninterrupted real-time audio footage of a conversation between a taxi driver and his passenger as they travel through Tunis, commenting freely on the former regime and the current transitional government led by Mohammed Ghannouchi. This soundtrack jars with the simultaneous slide show, projected throughout the work, of static, propagandist images of the deposed president (see https://mounakarray.com/live/live.html).[37] Karray (2012) tells us in a note alongside the work, 'Depuis le 14 jan 2011, les Tunisiens s'expriment dans la rue librement et le taxi est devenu une forme d'"espace public" où chauffeur et client peuvent discuter sans crainte' ('Since the 14th Jan. 2011, Tunisians express themselves freely in the street and the taxi has become a kind of "public space" where driver and passenger can discuss without fear'). Their voices are alternately privileged – through modifications in volume and subtitles in French – with those on the radio and the chants

---

[36] Restrictive framing or camera angles are often used, and combined with alternative modes of transport, in Bruno Boudjelal's photographic collection, *Jours intranquilles: chroniques algériennes d'un retour (1993–2003)*, which was published as a book in 2009. See also Nadia Ferroukhi's series, *Chroniques algériennes*, 2000–present: www.nadia-ferroukhi.com/v3/crbst_18.html). Boudjelal's and Barrada's works also include found images, which are an alternative means by which the artist relinquishes a certain measure of control over the work, as will be discussed further in Chapter 3. I have analysed these works by Kameli, Barrada, Boudjelal and Ferroukhi elsewhere (Shilton, 2013a).

[37] Last accessed June 2020.

of demonstrators in the street. The conversation itself unfolds spontaneously in response to visual signifiers of upheaval and transition observed en route. The driver points out 'les Fords de Leïla', referring to the former ownership of such international firms by the family of Ben Ali's wife, Leïla Trabelsi.[38] He commends the recent transformation of the Fords into police cars. Meanwhile, a further indicator of radical change emerges as the presenters of a new radio programme invite people to express their opinions on controversial topics, such as the reintegration into social and professional life of prisoners who have been granted an amnesty. The translation in the subtitles turns to give precedence to the cries of demonstrators outside as they call for the dissolution of what remains of the RCD, the only ruling party since 1988. These voices from the street trigger heated commentary from the taxi driver with regard to Ben Ali's former prime minister, who remains at the head of the interim government: 'il faut virer Ghannouchi ... C'est dans l'intérêt de la Tunisie qu'il parte. Sinon ça va se gater pour de bon' ('we have to get rid of Ghannouchi ... For the sake of Tunisia, he has to go. If not, it's going to be spoiled for good'). A counterpoint to these political discussions is provided by the track of a woman singing a love song, which is interspersed by the fragmented, everyday exchange between the male driver and the female passenger as she directs him to her destination. As Mouna Karray has commented, '[j]'avais envie de mettre en valeur la parole, qui est en marche, en vitesse, et une image de propagande très statique, qui ressemble à une fiction, coupée du réel' ('I wanted to emphasise speech, which is in motion, at speed, and a propagandist image, which is very static, which seems fictional, cut off from the real') (cited by L'Orient-Le Jour / Agences, 2012).

The static, iconic images of Ben Ali, which have long constituted the view of 'Tunisia' that has been presented both internally and externally, are disrupted by this democratic plurality of intertwined, contrapuntal voices. The visions conjured verbally throughout this taxi ride, moreover, indicate political perspectives that go beyond those embodied by these icons; imaging is exceeded by imagining. The soundtrack highlights the new status of the same images as signifiers of a past regime; they expose the former government's corruption and

---

[38] On the corruption fostered by the extended families of Ben Ali and his wife in the context of glaring socio-economic disparities and the unemployment of more than a third of the country's youth, see Gana (2013) and Murphy (2013).

its manipulation of the people. Viewed together with these revolutionary voices, these former visual signs of apparent stability become signifiers of instability. Carefully selected images of Ben Ali pledging allegiance to the nation with hand on chest or listening to the people with a hand behind his ear are imbued with irony in this new audio-visual context. Comparable to Lamine's series, other icons of political stability, intended to elicit support, come to function as markers in the history of Ben Ali's decline, like the widely disseminated photograph of the former leader at the foot of Bouazizi's hospital bed. The status of these images as veneer, and their role in perpetuating a myth, is emphasised visually in the close-up, towards the end of the video, on the distinct, uniform dots of colour that construct Ben Ali's face. The gradual zoom-in invites us to scrutinise these seemingly authentic photographs and to look beyond the façade that they create. The work presents a discrepancy between the official, fixed images and the diverse, shifting 'reality' that they have long attempted to obscure, the alternative 'Tunisia' that emerges through sound.

The auditory insistence on plurality in this work is coupled with the use of the peripatetic mode. That is, the inextricably linked practices of travelling and recording in 'real time' give rise to an uninterrupted polyphony of 'live' – or, more precisely, spontaneous – dissonant, untranslated and even 'untranslatable' voices, which hail from alternative, unofficial spaces. The political discussion is combined with an everyday practice, while the work demonstrates that an ostensibly ordinary taxi ride takes on – unavoidably in the Tunis of 2011–12 – a political character. The journey itself can be construed in terms of a political intervention. The combination of 'dissenting' voices and movement within the capital city is reminiscent of de Certeau's concept of an 'urban text' produced by 'pedestrian speech acts' (de Certeau, 1990 [1980]), while dissidence (and dissonance) is here magnified by the speed of car travel. Travelling at higher speed, which has been connected to social superiority by Susan George (1998), can be associated in Karray's work with a revolutionary reversal of political power dynamics. Travelling and literal speech coalesce in what can be seen as a democratic reappropriation of a panoptic urban system which conspires to obscure opposition to political singularity. This work invents an audiovisual language of travel to articulate instability and ungraspable diversity.

Karray's choice of video is appropriate, given the history of this medium's status since the mid-1960s as 'television turned against itself'

(Hall and Fifer, 1990: 19). Her disjunctive use of static images and 'travelling' voices disrupts the passive, unquestioning mode of image consumption that is associated with television, providing a wider critique of the use of this medium to perpetuate myths. Her principal target, though, is static photographic imaging. Like Lamine's *Nous ne mangerons plus de ce pain-là*, *Live* exposes and resists not simply the iconic images of Ben Ali but the very language of photography – its fixity, its control of the viewer's gaze, its implicit authoritative proclamation that 'ça a été' – by incorporating contingency into the art process.[39] This work conveys an irreducible Tunisia and an unfinished revolution through a contingent encounter between vision and voice, stasis and travel.

Ismaïl Bahri similarly counters the stability and power that are usually associated with image-making through video and photography by evoking an alternative Tunisia between visibility and invisibility, and between fixity and movement. Bahri is cited by Mohamed Ben Soltane as one of the talented Tunisian artists who live abroad and are becoming increasingly involved in the art scene in Tunisia (Ben Soltane, 2012). (Ben Soltane makes this point in his list of the positive developments made possible by the revolution 'au-delà des hésitations et des polémiques actuelles inévitables dans une période de transition démocratique' ('beyond the current deliberations and polemics inevitable in a period of democratic transition') (2012).) By contrast with Karray, Bahri films while walking or at a standstill. He constrains the spectators' vision by filming, in *Orientations* (2010), through a cup of ink or, in later videos such as *Film à blanc* (2013–14) or *Foyer* (2016), by attaching a sheet of paper in front of the camera lens. Through such rudimentary elements he evokes and deconstructs the process of image-making through print or film. In the post-2010 works, these elements might seem to obscure and abstract Tunisia at a crucial moment in the country's history. Adnen Jdey has aptly described Bahri's exhibition 'Instruments' (2017) as a gesture that 'ouv[re] grand les yeux sans promesse de dévoilement' ('opens the eyes without promising to unveil anything') (Jdey, 2017). *Film à blanc* was produced amid the funeral procession of an assassinated politician of the opposition, Mohamed Brahmi, in July 2013. When filming among demonstrators, in *Film à*

---

[39] Photography's proclamation that 'ça a été' was first discussed by Roland Barthes (1980).

blanc, Bahri was interrogated by some who warned him that he should record this important moment in Tunisia's history.[40] Yet, as the artist states, these 'instruments' become 'activateurs d'attention' (Jdey, 2017). *Film à blanc* and *Foyer* (2016; shot in 2014–15) register the *hors champ* (that which lies physically beyond the frame of the image), moreover, in a way that more powerfully conveys instances of the country's history than would an iconic photograph or audiovisual representation, which run the risk simply of reproducing 'revolutionary exoticism'. Bahri has expressed 'une certaine méfiance' ('a certain wariness') with regard to political subjects, while he admits to being drawn by the challenge of dealing with them in a nuanced manner (Ismaïl Bahri in interview with Olivier Marboeuf (2013a)). Bahri created *Orientations* before the revolution, but this video anticipates his later experiments in revolutionary contexts.[41] As we will see, his interest in images as they transform – in their suspension between matter and image – which could be seen already in this video of 2010, converges in striking ways with that of artists who develop non-iconic means of evoking the revolution. *Orientations*, in which the peripatetic mode is most evident, can be seen to anticipate Karray's aesthetics in *Live*. Both artists combine the practices of filming and travelling/wandering in a way that exceeds authoritative visions of Tunis and questions the very language in which images are constructed through audiovisual media.[42]

Orientations (approx. 20′) incorporates contingency by filming through ink while walking. The movements of the fluid substance and the fragmentary, unstable images it conjures are directly linked to the movements of the artist's body. The circle of black liquid in the cup functions as the 'eye' or 'lens'. The artist describes his journey as 'une marche de myope' (a myopic walk). He allows his trajectory to be determined by the images he perceives in the ink. As he walks, the

---

[40] See Ismaïl Bahri in interview with Rodolphe Olcèse (2013).

[41] Formerly displayed at: www.ismailbahri.lautre.net/ (last accessed 2014; an extract of a different version of the video is viewable at this site). Stills of *Orientations* can be found at: www.ismailbahri.lautre.net/files/ismail-bahri-orientations-2010.pdf.

[42] This work has been displayed at exhibitions such as 'Lumière noire' (Staatliche Kunsthalle, Karlsruhe, Germany, 2012), 'Précipités' (Galerie Les Filles du Calvaire, Paris, 2012) and 'Le geste premier' (BBB Centre d'Art, Toulouse, 2013). It can also be viewed on the artist's website www.ismailbahri.lautre.net/ (last accessed May 2014).

rippling, uncontrollable substance, which spills over the edges of the cup, registers blurred flickering images. The artist stops intermittently to pose the cup on the ground, allowing the liquid provisionally to stabilise and register upturned fragments of architecture and satellite dishes, foliage and the sky beyond, or advertising posters with smiling faces and brightly coloured slogans. Thus, fragments of the *hors champ* are allowed to enter the frame. Further clues to the surrounding environment emerge in the sounds of chirping birds, barking dogs, whistling passers-by and the hum of traffic. Within the frame of the video we also see a kerb lined with decaying leaves and diverse consumer waste, and occasionally the boot of a parked car or the feet of a passer-by. An unintended turning point occurs when the process is interrupted by two onlookers who each begin a dialogue with the artist. This draws our attention to further, previously concealed, aspects of the *hors champ*.[43]

Anticipating Karray's *Live*, urban space is reworked through wandering – which, here, we experience through sound and image – and via contingent 'pedestrian speech acts'; Bahri's work converges more closely with de Certeau's concept by foregrounding the actual practice of walking. 'Tunis' emerges between the visual and the kinetic, stability and 'errance'. *Orientations* might be seen to anticipate Bouderbala's words, while it forges an alternative aesthetic of 'errance'. This work converges with her *Flag Nymphéas* in using a fluid substance. In one shot, Bahri similarly shows the Tunisian flag. His images are reflections, but the flickering, uneven flag he captures anticipates Bouderbala's depiction of this icon through a rippling, shimmering pool. In both works the *hors champ* is incorporated through a shifting reflective surface. In Bahri's work the ambivalence between inside and outside, near and far, emerges more emphatically. The artist's hand and the impact of his movements are visible. The unstable movements of the body contribute to the images registered by the contingent substance. The reflections in the ink indicate what lies beyond the frame of the video, while that which we perceive within the frame is what usually constitutes the *hors champ*: the unofficial vision of the city and the processes by which images are constructed.

---

[43] This video has been shown either as a single-channel work, or as part of a two-screen installation, alongside or opposite a sixteen-minute video depicting a different version of a similar process (which unites a number of journeys) without the interruption of the passer-by.

The contingent journey makes visible the consumer waste (empty bottles, packets and cigarette butts) that is usually obscured – and that is the end product of the process set in motion – by the advertising billboards glimpsed through the ink. The sequences of uninterrupted walking and unedited real-time footage also register the surrounding sounds of nature and human life. Further aspects of the *hors champ* are communicated when the artist encounters two passers-by. They question him regarding his practice, as well as his origins and ethnicity. The conversation is in *Darija* (Tunisian Arabic) with subtitles in English. He is prompted to provide a commentary: 'I am watching the reflections in the glass'; 'I am filming the glass'; 'it gets bigger and shows the city upside down'; 'it shows all you can see in a different way'. We also learn that the artist appears to these passers-by as a 'Westerner':

– You're not Tunisian?
– Yes, yes, I am Tunisian.
– But you live abroad?
– In Tunisia and in France.
– But mostly there ... your accent and your skin

These conversations produce a shift in register and unpredictably locate the work within wider concentric circles.

Orientations points to the inevitable unreliability of perceiving and representing by exposing a selective process of inclusion and exclusion. It draws attention to the process of image-making itself by employing ambivalently the advanced technology of digital filming to expose a simple process, using rudimentary materials: ink and a plastic cup. It deconstructs the audiovisual language used by cinema, video and television, emphasising the component parts of lens, light, motion and time.[44] The use of black liquid in *Orientations* can be seen to allude to the vitreous humour within the eye itself and to the mechanics of seeing. Alternatively, it can be perceived as the matter used to produce images, verbally or visually, through print media. By contrast with the immediately legible images in the news or on billboards, the images registered by Bahri emerge and evolve without stabilising. Comparable to the uses of water, bread or jasmine discussed above – and to the infra-thin aesthetics analysed in Chapter 1 – these images explore the passage between formlessness and form.

[44] Anaël Pigeat makes a similar point regarding Bahri's use of video across his oeuvre: (2013, 406; translated by C. Penwarden: 48).

Revolutions in the Peripatetic Mode 107

Emerging contingent images, between signifier and referent, are also central to Bahri's post-2010 videos *Film à blanc* and *Foyer*. These works, in which the artist inhibits vision by fixing a blank sheet of paper in front of the lens, register aspects of the revolution's aftermath. The more recent video, *Foyer*, places more extreme limits on the spectators' vision than *Orientations* and is filmed at a standstill – at least, at the outset. Yet, it is reminiscent of the earlier video in that the practice of filming outside leads to a contingent encounter, which we hear but do not see. *Foyer*, filmed at a coast in Tunis, was originally intended as an exploration of light (Bahri, 2017).[45] Fleeting glimpses of the environment at the lower edge of the frame appear, depending on the unpredictable movements of the sheet of paper in the wind. But the central chance element shaping this work comes to be the contingent encounters between the artist and those who approach him, extending the brief exchanges of *Orientations*. Bahri's words emphasise the active role of passers-by in forming the work and almost in film-making, themselves: 'Au fur et à mesure, ils ont commencé à ... projeter sur cette feuille de papier énormément de choses et d'une certaine manière à se faire du cinéma' ('Gradually, they started to ... project so many things onto this sheet of paper and, in a way, to make a film for themselves') (Bahri, 2017). The artist relinquishes control, allowing the film to record its surroundings: 'Le film, *il s'est de lui-même sans trop, ni que je le veuille ni que je m'en rende compte, peuplé* de ce qui l'entoure et *s'est impressionné* comme une pellicule vierge s'impressionne de la lumière qui l'entoure en fait' ('The film, *of its own accord without any real conviction, and without my wanting or realising it, populated itself* with what surrounded it and *exposed itself* like a blank photographic film exposes itself to the light surrounding it, actually') (2017; my emphasis). The film is not just a passive receptacle but a vehicle: '*elle s'affecte* de ce qui l'entoure et *elle révèle* quelque chose' ('it's affected by [literally, '*it affects itself* by'] what surrounds it and *it*

---

[45] In an interview shown on video at Bahri's exhibition 'Instruments' (Jeu de Paume, Paris, 2017), the artist highlights how this work emerged partly by accident: 'C'est un film qui est arrivé un peu par accident, ... j'essayais de faire un projet autour de la question de la lumière' ('The film kind of happened by accident ... I was trying to do a project on the subject of light'). The credits tell us the film was made in Tunis, and this is presumably apparent to Tunisian viewers from the accents of passers-by; the exact location of *Foyer* is not known, though a reference is made to Ibn Khaldoun Street, which will be familiar to some viewers.

reveals something') (2017; my emphasis). Reminiscent of *Orientations*, Bahri's use of a camera in public space leads to a spontaneous conversation about the process of filming.[46] Again, the conversation also raises the question of the artist's relationship to Tunisia.[47] This work, though, comes to reveal particularities of this moment in post-revolutionary Tunisia, after the election of Nidaa Tounes in 2014: those who approach the artist comment that the people made a mistake, that they had thought it would be better after Ben Ali. This film about filming comes, moreover, to reveal specifically the conditions of filming in Tunisia at this time. Police arrive to question the artist and take him to the police station. The artist is questioned as to what he is filming and his camera is inspected. The police relax when they realise that he has not filmed the police station and that he is Tunisian; they turn to lament the emergence of terrorism and fear since the revolution, as well as the tarnished image of Tunisia in France. This film which seems, at first, to show 'nothing' – at least visually – reveals ironically the anxiety surrounding image-making in the aftermath of the revolution. In this work, the artist's practice of filming with the chance element of a sheet of paper, the wind and the shifting light triggers contingent encounters with passers-by. Between these encounters at a standstill we witness his exchange with the police and his unintended displacement as he is taken to the police station. The camera continues to record, uninterrupted, revealing fragmented images of the ground and the sounds of the wind. The peripatetic mode emerges here as unplanned and coercive: a kind of 'anti-*dérive*'. The practice of filming while moving comes to be associated with constraint. The artist's freedom to continue to film is, in addition, closely linked to the absence of images; he is allowed to film because the blank sheet of paper is perceived to censor the image. At the same time, sensorial elements beyond the visual are ignored. This video reveals the freedom, albeit within certain parameters, to 'se faire du cinéma', democratically opening expression (verbal and creative) to ordinary people.

---

[46] Passers-by ask what the paper is for, what the point is and whether there is a message, for example. In response, the artist explains that the wind decides what will and will not be seen.

[47] When the artist speaks Tunisian Arabic a passer-by says he had thought he was French. When he is interrogated by the police he reveals that he lives and works in France as an artist and teacher; he is, again, also prompted to describe his art process in detail.

In *Film à blanc*, the video Bahri produced at the funeral procession of Mohamed Brahmi, constraints on vision are combined with silence, by contrast with *Orientations*, the later *Foyer*, or Karray's *Live*. The artist films, as for most of *Foyer*, at a standstill in a public space, but in the middle of a moving crowd indicative explicitly of political unrest in the months following the revolution. The sheet of paper covers all but the edges of the image. We glimpse, via this outline, the moving procession of agitated bodies, the colours and patterns of their clothing, and the red-and-white Tunisian flag. Our vision of this historical moment is limited, but it is conveyed by the haptic. The excitement and tension of the evolving crowd is registered by the sheet of paper, which reveals protestors' shadows and quivers when bodies press against it.[48] The white sheet functions as a canvas for the contingent shifts of the world beyond, reminiscent of the receptive surfaces of Robert Rauschenberg's *White Paintings* (1951).[49] It emphasises the screen between the spectator and what is viewed. This work is reminiscent of the uneven, haptic surfaces on which the fleeting images are registered in *Orientations*. Both videos can be seen to transform the camera from an instrument of vision into an instrument of touch. Yet, they explore an alternative dimension to that explored by film theory on 'haptic visuality', the idea of an almost touchable filmic 'skin' (see Laura U. Marks, 1999). These videos foreground the tactility of the 'lens' – in this case, of the screen itself – intimately binding it to corporeality in ways that weaken the artist's control over the work of art. They highlight the uneven and contingent interface between subject and object by connecting the 'lens' or screen to the unstable movements of the body: 'visuality' is haptic, kinetic and kinaesthetic. In *Orientations* the palpable lens is visibly linked to the artist's 'blind' walking body, the ink recurrently overflowing and staining his wavering hand. In *Film à blanc* the contingent encounter occurs between the screen and the unpredictable corporeal movements of others. By impeding vision and suppressing sound, this work embodies spectators and thereby intervenes in the passive, unquestioning process of image consumption that is encouraged by television. The work

[48] On the artist's process for this work, see Ismaïl Bahri in interview with Olivier Marboeuf (2013b). Available at: www.khiasma.net/magazine/filmer_a_blanc/ (accessed February 2014).
[49] It was John Cage who perceived Rauchenberg's *White Paintings* as receptive screens: 'airports of the lights, shadows and particles'. (See Cage, 1961: 102.)

alludes to the event while also encouraging spectators to consider the processes of looking and representing. If the event is 'missed' in the conventional, televisual sense, it is reframed, reworked and re-experienced through a haptic contingent encounter, which questions the hierarchy between viewer and viewed.[50]

While wary with regard to political subjects, Bahri has signalled his interest in the ways in which they might be evoked:

> [J]'essaye de capter et de cadrer certains signaux et flux de «ce qui arrive» pour les passer à travers le filtre de mes petites expériences. Parler de filtre m'intéresse parce qu'il s'agit peut-être un peu de cela: fabriquer des appareils de captures vidéographiques très élémentaires que traversent flux et images prélevées (que ça soit de journaux ou de signaux télévisés) pour les cadrer d'abord, les altérer ensuite, et pour en prélever, peut-être, une forme d'essence ... Cadrer c'est aussi réduire le flux à une certaine échelle, plus petite, à l'échelle de ma table de travail mais aussi à une échelle plus humaine, celle d'une possible pensée et celle d'un autre rythme. Dans ce sens, cadrer c'est rendre plus intelligible quelque chose qui nous dépasse. (Bahri in interview with Marboeuf, 2013a)

(I try to capture and frame certain signals and flux of 'what's happening' to pass them through the filter of my own experiences. Speaking of a filter interests me because that's perhaps kind of what it's about: fabricating very basic videographic capturing devices which are traversed by flux and appropriated images (whether from newspapers or televised signs) to frame them, first, and then modify them, and to extract, perhaps a kind of essence ... To frame is also to reduce the flux to a certain scale, smaller, to the scale of my work table but also to a scale that's more human, that of a possible thought and that of another rhythm. In a way, to frame is to render more intelligible something which is bigger than we are.)

---

[50] An alternative approach to representations of the revolution can be found in Bahri's *Film* (2011–12), in which ink is deployed, reminiscent of *Orientations*, to generate images through a simple process. This work consists of a series of silent videos, each depicting a triangular strip of newspaper which unfurls on contact with an ink-covered surface – a process inspired by Marcel Proust's image of Japanese origami that opens out to disclose a previously hidden universe when placed in cups of water (see Stuart Reigeluth, ed. 2013: 42–43). Thus, upturned fragments of images of demonstrations, and text in Arabic or English, gradually emerge from the darkness, as if by magic. Language – here, both visual and verbal, of print media and digital video – is once more destabilised by being combined with a contingent process. Ink, in this work, alludes to the materiality of writing and image production, abstracting language from the meanings it generates.

Bahri's words resonate with the aims of other artists who strive to find new ways to deal with the 'unrepresentable' subject of the Tunisian revolution. Reminiscent of many of their works, Bahri's practice often involves alluding to iconic visual languages or symbols and undermining them; in his case, reappropriating and 'filtering' them – by reframing or altering by other means. The artist's intervention in the stream of images 'reduces the flux' in the sense of presenting a micro-vision, a fragment of an image between appearance and disappearance; that is, 'une possible pensée' between signifier and signified. This practice of filtering images and highlighting their passage, their suspension in process, can already be seen in *Orientations*. The 'autre rythme' that this involves can be seen in terms of a deceleration – by walking and pausing in *Orientations* or, in *Film à blanc* and *Foyer*, by coming to a standstill. The artist's deceleration is reminiscent of the concept of 'vertical travel', the term Michael Cronin employs to characterise 'temporary dwelling in a location for a period of time where the traveller begins to travel down into the particulars of place either in space ... or in time' (Cronin, 2000: 19). In *Orientations*, *Foyer* and *Film à blanc* the artist-traveller's vertical journey allows for the exposure of 'the particulars of place' (in space), which are habitually obscured by clichéd panoramic views of the city or its architecture. His accidental encounter with passers-by, which unpredictably discloses further elements (spatial and temporal) beyond the lens, is a consequence of this decelerated journey on foot.

Bahri reflects, in the same interview, on his mode of intervention as a possible mode of political 'engagement'. Commenting on the 'flux' of information and ink, the artist stresses the importance of the ambiguous degree he strives to obtain between images and matter, holding these in tension. The ambiguity in his work comes from bringing the elements

au degrés [*sic*] précis où images et matières s'incarnent sans coaguler. D'où m'on [*sic*] intérêt pour les images équivoques, qui apparaissent, qui passent tout en demeurant. Il y a une attention à rendre sensible et intelligible le moment où quelque chose du flux bascule vers d'autres formes. Une tentative de penser ces images dans leurs transformations, peut-être, pour ne pas leur laisser le temps d'être annexées ... dans ce sens[-]là, le révolutionnaire dans son devenir m'intéresse. (Bahri in interview with Marboeuf, 2013a)

(to the precise point where images and matter incarnate each other without coagulating. That's where my interest in equivocal images, which appear and which pass by while remaining, comes from. My process involves taking care to render sensible and intelligible the moment where something of the flux shifts towards other forms. An attempt to think these images in their transformations, perhaps, to avoid allowing them the time to be annexed ... in that sense, the revolutionary in its state of becoming interests me.)

Bahri's interest in ambiguous, equivocal, transitional images between presence and absence, stability and instability, or in matter that emerges without solidifying, is reminiscent of the sensorial and formal shifts that are central to contingent encounters in works by artists such as Kaabi-Linke and Favaretto, as well as Fatmi's earlier *Manipulations*. Bahri's interest in images as they transform, before they can be 'annexed', is already perceptible in *Orientations*. As Marboeuf observes, this work avoids the 'innate violence in the act of naming, of catching hold of what is nameless, bringing it out of the shadows and fixing it in place ... with Orientations ... there is a question of touching from a distance, showing without naming, without repossessing in a definitive way' (Bahri in interview with Marboeuf, 2013c). Bahri's practices provide alternative means to communicate not the revolution but the emergence of 'the revolutionary': 'le révolutionnaire dans son devenir'.[51]

The works of Karray and Bahri, while using the contingent peripatetic mode, are distinct from the *dérive* as defined by Debord. Indeed, considering them in the light of Debord's definition of this concept highlights the particularities of the space and historical moment in which they film. Bahri's journeys involve deceleration and vertical travel rather than 'rapid passage'. Through his eventual displacement in *Foyer* the peripatetic mode is linked with coercion, contrary to the suggestion of inherent freedom in Debord's *dérive*. Bahri's works explore a limited terrain, as opposed to 'varied ambiances'. In Karray's work the destination is known in advance. Chance is diminished in these works, but not because 'cities have psychogeographical contours, with constant currents, fixed points and vortexes that strongly discourage entry into or exit from certain zones' (Debord, 1956). The movements – and moments of stasis – recorded tend to indicate a particular space and historical moment of revolution (with the exception of Bahri's pre-revolutionary *Orientations*). The rhythm

---

[51] The idea of 'le révolutionnaire dans son devenir' resonates with Stuart Hall's emphasis on the concept of identity as a process of 'becoming' (see Hall, 1990: 225).

of the journey central to Karray's work is controlled by the demonstrations against the interim government, which impede the flow of traffic. The dialogue is triggered partly by the sights and activities encountered. The conversations captured by Bahri's *Foyer* allude to ongoing disillusionment, unemployment, censorship and the rise of insecurity in Tunisia three years after the revolution. The practice of filming and travelling is used in contrasting revolutionary contexts: Azza Hamwi's *A Day and a Button* (2015) reveals the particularity of restrictions on circulating in Damascus through a woman's use of a hidden camera, which captures a moment of forbidden entry and the ever-present threat of bullets and shelling. (In the brief shot which shows the traveller's passage being denied, we see two men saying 'Forbidden, young lady'. Further indications of obstacles to circulation are revealed verbally. The narrative, in which the traveller reflects on identity, refers to the constant demand to present ID cards after a fragment of music alludes to the presence of checkpoints.) At the same time, chance is heightened in these works through alternative means, which distinguish them also from early twenty-first-century works visualising Algeria or Morocco (or Syria, in the case of Hamwi's video).[52]

In the contexts of Algeria and Morocco, which did not experience revolutions in 2011, art investigating peripheral spaces and stories subtly gestures towards alternative ways of thinking.[53] The works I have mentioned, by Kameli and Barrada, explore Algerian or Moroccan spaces while avoiding 'naming', 'fixing' or 'repossessing' such spaces through all-encompassing 'scenes' or 'types' (as can be seen in the extensive colonial postcard series, entitled 'Scènes et Types', c.1900, by photographers including Lehnert and Landrock). The same could be said of pre-2011 works exploring Tunisia, including Ghozlani's *Postcards of Tunisia* and 2010 exhibitions of Filali's

---

[52] In the Syrian context, Azza Hamwi's poetic journey around Damascus resonates with Joude Gorani's film of a journey on the city's outskirts to expose the gap between ideology and reality in *Before Vanishing* (2005).

[53] As John P. Entelis argues, Algeria was the first country in the MENA region to experience an 'Arab spring', at least two decades earlier, but that democratic moment was rapidly brought to an end by a military *coup d'état* (Entelis, 2011). On the extent of constitutional reforms in Morocco following the February 20th Movement of 2011, see Maghraoui (2011).

L'Angle mort. Karray's *Live* is comparable to Kameli's *Bledi, a Possible Scenario* (2004) in which she allows a part of her shifting vision of Algiers to depend on the speed of a car and the flow of traffic.[54] Karray's taxi journey also resonates with Khaled Benaïssa's *Babel* (2006), which films a conversation in a taxi in Algiers, though his video – like that of Kameli – conveys diversity through both sound and image.[55] Kameli's longer film conveys a diverse and shifting picture of Algiers by oscillating between documentary and fictional modes through the use of colour and black-and-white, high- and low-speed footage, digital video and Super 8, and interviews and soundtracks (from local rap and *rai* to transglobal electronica). Karray, by contrast, uses unedited, real-time footage. The spontaneous conversation she records diverges from the staged performance of *Babel*. In conveying a city exclusively through sound, *Live* resonates with Hassen Ferhani's *Les Baies d'Alger* (2006), in which the multiple voices of telephone conversations are accompanied by a view over the rooftops and outward towards the bay.[56] But this video by Ferhani, which explores the subject of surveillance, does not involve a journey. Karray invents an alternative contingent encounter by combining the auditory with the peripatetic mode. Her heightening of spontaneity and contingency, through these means, is crucial in the context of Tunisia's ongoing resistance to authoritarianism.

Bahri's *Orientations*, *Film à blanc* and *Foyer* resonate with other sequences in Kameli's *Bledi*, which are filmed on foot or involve periods of vertical travel. Kameli's pedestrian journeys tend to take place in crowded areas and her trajectory is determined, in parts, by the women she follows. In *Orientations*, by contrast, Bahri films on a side street and his movements depend on the images reflected in a cup of ink. The crowd depicted in the later *Film à blanc* determines this work, though people engage physically – yet unknowingly – with a static camera. While Kameli's pedestrian journeys involve fleeting

---

[54] This film is available on the artist's website at: http://katiakameli.com/production/bledi-a-possible-scenario/.

[55] Benaïssa's video highlights social and ethnic diversity by bringing together a French-speakingg woman (a 'tchi-tchi'), a Kabyle man with a stutter, and a taxi driver who refuses to speak despite the man's repeated questions.

[56] This reverses the recurrent all-encompassing view of the bay in colonial postcards and film. Ferhani's *Les Baies d'Alger* and Khaled Benaïssa's *Babel* were both produced as part of a video workshop led by Katia Kameli in 2006.

contingent exchanges through looks, Bahri's decelerated or vertical journeys, in all three works, lead to longer encounters – auditory or haptic.[57] This artist's use of restrictive angles is reminiscent of the high-angle views and close-ups employed recurrently by Barrada in *Iris Tingitana* (2007) or her earlier series, *Le Projet du Détroit* (1998–2004).[58] But Bahri 'touches from a distance' distinctively by combining restrictive angles or a blank sheet of paper together with walking and/or a shifting substance or natural phenomena. Bahri's journeys depend on a 'blind gaze', reminiscent of Pak Sheung Chuen's installation, *A Travel without Visual Experience* (2008), which presents this artist's journey through Malaysia blindfolded. Chuen's installation is determined by a more extreme weakening of visual perception: it consists of the photographs the artist took without seeing.[59] Bahri's work, by contrast, focuses on the mechanics of seeing and representing and on the passage between matter and image. Thus, in all three of his works considered here, Tunis emerges between visibility and invisibility, resonating with the subtle infra-thin passage between presence and absence while emphasising this 'gap' through framing and contingency (of a substance, a body in movement, and a public space). Although *Orientations* was produced before the revolution, it explores a dynamic that would become central in Bahri's later experiments in 'blank filming' and, as we will see in Chapter 4, in diverse evocations of Tunisia through the body and space.

Conclusion

This art exploring contingent encounters frequently adapts, innovatively combines or develops existing means of generating chance, from local, regional or wider transnational spaces. By contrast with these existing strategies, however, it often incorporates or alludes to icons,

---

[57] Longer exchanges can be seen at the beginning of Kameli's *Bledi*, when she interviews travellers on the ferry from Marseilles, but these are planned encounters in the documentary mode.

[58] Barrada frequently devotes a large part of her images to the ground, capturing wild flowers or grass, everyday objects, or people's feet, in *Iris Tingitana* (2007). The Iris Tingitana, a flower specific to the region, becomes, in Barrada's images, a symbol of resistance to the eradication of local particularities through rapid economic development, as I mentioned above.

[59] In a dark room, which can only briefly be illuminated by the flashes of the viewer's own camera, they too experience a 'journey' without sight.

symbols or spaces that encapsulate external and/or internal essentialising perspectives on the revolution or Tunisia's future. Contingent encounters, in these works, do not only involve the interaction between the control exercised by the artist and the contingent effects of organic materials or processes. These works refer – sometimes unintentionally – to visual or verbal icons or languages of order and authoritarianism and explore the space between or beyond them. It is through these references that contingent forms or formless shifting substances, uneven and fragmented images or auditory or haptic spontaneity and participation are anchored in relation to post-2010 Tunisia and come to evoke resistance to reductive notions of identity and 'revolution'. It is in seeking to avoid 'icons of revolutionary exoticism' and/or (in pre-2011 works that anticipate revolutionary aesthetics) the neo-colonial or internal dictatorial impulse to name, fix and repossess that art invents alternative means of balancing control and contingency. These diverse works 'harness' contingent movements, from the gradual, almost imperceptible shifts undergone by organic substances to the actions and displacements of the body – of the artist or participants – in interaction with a material, a space or an exhibited object. Contingent encounters are tied to revolutionary dynamics of constraint and liberation, but also cohesiveness and fragility. They also question binary thinking regarding the revolution in terms of success or failure and allow for an understanding of 'revolution' that accommodates transition, negotiation and diversity. Such contingent encounters highlight a state of metamorphosis which, comparable to the passages explored in Chapter 1, encourages spectators to reshape their memories of the revolution and to imagine alternative futures for Tunisia.

This space for alternative memories and projections is created, in other works, through a contingent encounter between artists and artisans, performers, video makers or members of the public – at the stages of the work's production, exhibition and/or its reception in different formats and contexts. Chapter 3 focuses specifically on this type of encounter and the use of diverse forms of exchange to exceed iconic visions of the revolutions and of the revolutionary, more widely.

3 | Contingent Encounters: Artists, Artisans and Amateurs

Alternative aesthetics of revolution emerge, as we have seen, through contingent encounters between stable and unstable forms and formless matter, or between parameters established by the artist and processes that exceed their control. I focus in this chapter on the contingent encounters that can also occur between the artist, or artists, and a range of people, from artisans and amateur video-makers or performers to members of the public. Majd Abdel Hamid directly involved female weavers from the Palestinian village of Farkha and displayed their portraits of the Tunisian martyr Mohammad Bouazizi alongside his own (*Mohammad Bouazizi*, 2011; Figure 0.3). Artisans and their practices are included *in*directly, by contrast, in Selma and Sofiane Ouissi's video performance (*Laaroussa*; 'doll' or 'bride', 2011), which is shaped in some measure by the gestures and unedited audio footage of female ceramicists at work in Sejnane, Tunisia (Figure 3.1). Spectators are involved in a process of 'reordering space' in Collectif Wanda's architectural installation *Le Ciel est par-dessus le toit* (2012–13; Figures 3.2 and 3.3), or in making alternative images of Tunisia today in a photo/voting booth created by Mouna Jemal Siala and Wadi Mhiri (*Parti Facelook / Parti Facelike*, 2012–13; Figure 3.4). How does such work develop our understanding of contingent encounters as means to produce non-iconic visions of revolution? How, in responding to specific contexts of revolution, might this work spur a rethinking of conventional definitions of participation in art? In what ways does it develop existing practices, or invent new practices, to communicate alternative experiences and perceptions of revolution?

Critics have distinguished between participation and collaboration in art. As Christian Kravagna states,

Collective [collaborative] practice describes the conception, production and implementation of works or actions by several people with no principal differentiation among them, in terms of status. Participation, on the other

118   3 Contingent Encounters: Artists, Artisans and Amateurs

Figure 3.1 *Une poétique du geste* (A Poetics of the Gesture): *Laaroussa* (2011). Concept, composition and choreography Selma and Sofiane Ouissi / direction CéCiL Thuillier / editing Nicolas Sburlati / sound design David Bouvard.
© Dalila Yaakoubi-Les adc

Figure 3.2 Collectif Wanda, *Le Ciel est par-dessus le toit*, Dream City 2012–13 (exterior view) by L'Art Rue.
© Manuela Maffioli

Figure 3.3 Collectif Wanda, *Le Ciel est par-dessus le toit*, Dream City 2012–13 (interior view) by L'Art Rue.
© Sarra Zarrouk

Figure 3.4 Left-hand image: Mouna Jemal Siala and Wadi Mhiri, mock campaign poster for *Parti Facelook / Parti Facelike* (2012–13). Courtesy of Mouna Jemal Siala. Right-hand image: installation view (author's photograph)

hand, is initially based on a differentiation between producers and recipients, and focuses on the participation of the latter by turning over a substantial portion of the work to them, either at the point of conception or at a later stage in the work. (Kravagna, 2010: 241)

In a new-media context, Beryl Graham similarly asserts that full collaboration – 'working jointly with' – implies the production of

Figure 3.5 Sonia Kallel, *Tisser la médina*, Dream City 2012–13 (Tunis). Courtesy of the artist

something with a degree of equality between the participants, rather than participation within a system designed by somebody else (Graham, 2010: 293). Both critics also differentiate between participation and interactivity. Graham describes as 'interactive' situations in which the spectator navigates bodies of data, arranging the content generated by an artist, but does not have a creative impact (286).[1] The works I discuss below (when they do not involve a lasting creative impact) tend to resonate more closely with Kravagna's nuanced definition of interactivity, which, in his view, 'allows for one or more reactions to affect the work – usually in a momentary, reversible and repeatable manner – in its appearance, but without fundamentally changing or co-determining its structure' (Kravagna, 2010: 241). But, as Anna Dezeuze suggests, works of art that require the spectator to 'do it yourself', can cross the perceived boundaries between participatory and interactive art: 'The separation between content on the one hand, and form or structure on the other, on which these distinctions rely is not … always clear cut in do-it-yourself artworks, which

---

[1] Graham draws, here, on the work of Ann Sargent Wooster (1990) and a statement by artists Thomson and Craighead (Forde, 2001).

specifically set out to challenge the differences between object and process, between the work in itself and the experience of the work.' (Dezeuze 2010: 6). Dezeuze, like Bishop, questions the distinction some critics have made between 'self-reflexive autonomous practices' and community-based projects, which are intended to lead to solutions regarding specific political or social issues (Dezeuze, 2010: 7; Bishop, 2006, 2012).[2] Art exploring the revolutions through contingent encounters often similarly blurs the boundaries between participation and interactivity, between object and process (or what Grant Kester has called 'dialogical practices'; Kester, 2004) and, moreover, between poetics and politics. But it crosses these categories in ways that respond to a specific local and/or regional context. While some critics have acknowledged that participatory art is a global phenomenon, scholarship on participatory art has tended to focus on Western Europe and to identify precedents in earlier twentieth-century art that respond to periods of upheaval or movements for social change in the West. In exploring specific moments of oppression and revolution in North Africa and the Middle East, works such as those I address in this chapter can be seen to encourage new perspectives on both the aesthetics and the ethics of participatory art.

This art often involves producing tangible objects, from wall hangings to video art or online photographic collections. But involvement of others in such work can be direct or indirect. It can be provisional or leave a lasting trace, affecting the work's internal composition or the framing and arrangement of its individual parts. The dynamic between control and contingency can evolve through, and hold in tension, different stages of the work, from an exchange that produces its raw material to a process that extends beyond its initial exhibition. It can shift between different formats or between galleries, public sites and online fora. This work, moreover, uses different degrees and stages of participation specifically to provide a contingent alternative to icons or iconic spaces. Reminiscent of work incorporating organic materials or unpredictable processes, this work anchors contingent practices through reference to particular images, sites or local traditions. It also develops aspects of enduring or more recent local or transnational practices – from weaving or ceramics to interactions characteristic of

---

[2] Examples of such criticism can be found in Kester (2004) and curator Nicolas Bourriaud (1998).

social media – to generate contingency. In this case, though, contingency is heightened through the involvement of others from within and beyond the space or community being explored.

Participatory art – by contrast with chance aesthetics – is frequently assumed to be political. Art that incorporates or alludes to icons or iconic sites in revolutionary contexts does encourage spectators to connect the work to politics, but it questions the assumption that participatory art has an 'intrinsic or fixed political affiliation' and that collective authorship is inherently 'good', cohering with the views of Foster and Bishop (Bishop, ed., 2006; Foster, 2006 [2004]: 195; Bishop, 2012: 8). It might be expected, in art that explores the emergence or potential for democracy, that participants are allowed a substantial role in the creation or, at least, the production of a work. While many projects are inclusive, certain works raise the question as to whether such art can run the risk of marginalising its participants in privileging the artist's control over contingency. In other works, though, the parameters are deliberately loosened to allow effectively and democratically for plural, and potentially conflicting, contributions.

Participatory art produced since the Tunisian revolution can be situated in relation to local and Maghrebi art practices, including the traditions of public storytelling, dancing, music, and satirical shadow puppet theatre, as I indicated in Chapter 2 with reference to Bruckbauer and Triki. I mentioned that a precursor could be found in the biennial art festival, Dream City, directed by Tunis-based choreographers and dancers Selma and Sofiane Ouissi, as Machghoul has stated (Machghoul, 2013). The Ouissis launched this festival in Tunis (in 2007) as 'une démarche artistique citoyenne et collective pour se réapproprier un espace public confisqué par le politique' ('a civic and collective artistic method of reappropriating a public space confiscated by the political') (Ouissi and Ouissi, 2007). Exchange between, and movement of, artists and spectators was already central to these works, as the Ouissis detail in their editorial for this first festival: 'En investissant des lieux insolites de la médina, les artistes ne se contentent pas d'agrémenter un parcours mais *interpellent le passant et l'accompagnent sur son trajet*' ('In occupying the unusual parts of the Medina, the artists are not simply enlivening a route; they interpolate the passer-by and accompany them on their journey') (2007; my emphasis). (As indicated in the introduction to this book, the Arabic-speaking artists of the work I am analysing tend to create with both local and international audiences in mind and, therefore, often to comment on or present their work in French or English. The Dream City programmes produced by the Ouissis also include many titles in Arabic and occasional descriptions for performances only in Arabic or Tunisian *Darija*.) The Ouissis' project, *Laaroussa*, moreover, which resulted not only in the video I mentioned at the outset but also in many works that involved female ceramicists directly in their production, began before the revolution, in October 2010 (I will provide details of some of these works below). Yet, more distant precedents can be found in the artisanal practices of weaving or ceramics, which have long entailed participation. In work exploring Tunisia by involving artisans and their practices, the production of an object – material or digital – is particularly important as a means to preserve, and/or draw attention to, a struggling tradition. Other works adapt aspects of online practices of exchange via photographs. Whether engaging with centuries-old practices or twenty-first-century transnational social and digital rituals, in outdoor, indoor or virtual spaces, such art develops alternative aesthetics to communicate experiences and perceptions of revolutions in specific local contexts. Criticism on art and the Tunisian revolution has frequently focused on interventions in public space. Such art, crucially, reclaims this space that was previously subject to censorship (see Ben Soltane, 2012; Karoui, 2012; Ounaina, 2012; Triki, 2013). In this chapter, however, I bring together works shown in physical and virtual public spaces, as well as in galleries. These works are, in my view, inseparable, and all the more so given that they move, frequently, between private and public, inside and outside, blurring the boundaries between those sites which are conventionally viewed as separate and commonly associated with either art or activism.

I begin this chapter by examining works that involve others at the stage of production, or during an exchange that precedes that stage, focusing primarily on contrasting means of evoking encounters between artists and artisans. I address means of developing participatory weaving practices to heighten contingency and to forge a transversal Palestinian–Tunisian connection in Hamid's *Mohammed Bouazizi*. I compare Hamid's wall-hanging to two works that involve artisans and their practices indirectly to explore neglected practices and spaces in Tunisia: Selma and Sofiane Ouissi's video performance *Laaroussa*, and Sonia Kallel's *Tisser la médina* (2012–13), an audio tour and video installation exploring the endangered profession of silk weaving in the Tunis Medina (Figure 3.5). The second part of this chapter addresses art that involves spectators (who can, in turn, become producers) at the stage of the work's exhibition and, at times, in subsequent presentations of the work online. I examine how they are implicated in 'reordering' the space of the Tunis Medina in Collectif Wanda's *Le Ciel est par-dessus le toit* (2012–13). This installation exemplifies the continuing existence of the more subtle type of work which appeared in the public space of the Medina in earlier Dream City festivals, engaging spectators – often physically or/and interactively – to think about space or society in alternative ways. I also analyse how spectators are encouraged to participate more actively by making alternative, contingent 'icons' in two indoor installations. I compare the co-production of images of Tunisia in Jemal Siala and Mhiri's *Parti Facelook / Parti Facelike* to the spectators' ambivalent role as photographers of the revolutions in Tunis, Cairo and Damascus in Febrik's *The Watchtower of Happiness* (2012). These two installations employ participatory methods which are, in different ways, reminiscent of the social and digital practices of producing, uploading, 'liking' and/or commenting on touristic snapshots or selfies. Finally, I compare how art involves others – through textile-inspired practices, unedited or found footage, or physical or virtual means of display – to explore distinct contexts and themes of revolution, including the loss of demonstrators in Egypt and civilians in Syria and the experience of refugees. Across cultures, media and formats, I argue, art develops wide-ranging distinctive participatory contingent encounters to encourage an understanding of particular revolutionary conditions and to spur further resistance.

Artists and Artisans: Textiles and Transnational Resistance from Ramallah to Sidi Bouzid

The wall-hanging, *Mohammed Bouazizi* (2011; Figure 0.3), by Ramallah-based artist Majd Abdel Hamid and eight female weavers from Farkha, a village near the West Bank town of Salfit, draws on a local tradition and involves artisans directly. At the same time, it invents a particular form of participation, which involves minimal contact between the artist and the participants. Hamid uses participation to heighten contingency as a means to rework an icon of the Tunisian martyr whose self-immolation was one of the catalysts for the revolution. He also engages female weavers from this locality as a means of exploring an alternative to European or North American aesthetics. This grid of nine portraits dialogues ironically with Andy Warhol's grid of silk-screened images of Marilyn Monroe in *Marilyns* (1962), while forging – via the use of a Palestinian tradition – what we might see as a transversal participatory aesthetic of revolution. This is a gallery-based work: it has been exhibited at the French Cultural Centre in Ramallah and the Mosaic Rooms in London (2012–13).[3] Hamid's transversal aesthetic appears ironically within institutions that originate from vertical transnational connections. In Ramallah, though, it gave rise to a particular use of space, which the artist recorded and uploaded to YouTube.

Diverging from participatory art – and from traditional methods of co-producing textiles in workshops or, more recently, in refugee camp projects – Hamid maintains a distance from the artisans. The artist did not communicate with the eight weavers and was not present as they worked. He spoke to just one woman (Um Mahmoud) and she distributed the work to the other weavers (see Cosmic Vinegar, n.d.). The artist states that he did not feel his presence was important and suggests that this meant he 'did not enforce a power structure on the production process (…) I tried to be a participant rather than an instructor.' (Hamid, in interview with Cosmic Vinegar, n. d.). Hamid explains elsewhere that, for cultural reasons, he did not feel comfortable going to women's houses and speaking to them one on one; he details his process as follows:

[S]o what happened was i went there and told her this is my project, this is the one that i've embroidered, i had one ready, and i told her i want 8 of these, this is the color pallette [sic] but please feel free to combine any three colors you want. and basically she curated the whole thing. she got together a group of women, she was telling them what to do – do this, do that – and i did the exhibition. (Hamid, 2015b; lower-case letters in original)

The gap between artist and artisans was widened by the freedom Um Mahmoud was given to interpret the work and decide what to communicate to the weavers, without the artist knowing what she said (see Cosmic Vinegar, n.d.). In addition, she communicated with each artisan individually, presumably leading to variation in her explanations and each weaver's interpretations of them. Each contributor to the work, including the artist, wove their portrait individually. The artist had a greater role than the other weavers in the creation of the work:

---

[3] The piece was exhibited as part of the Qattan Foundation's Young Artist of the Year Award of 2012.

he conceptualised the piece and arranged its nine parts. The piece is 'participatory', rather than 'collaborative', as it maintains the essential distinction between artist and participants, if we follow the definitions provided by Kravagna and Graham. A hierarchy of roles is inevitable in participatory art. The lack of contact and exchange between artist and participants, in the creation of this work, might be seen to strengthen this hierarchy – as might the work's display solely under the artist's name, though the curatorial note does tell us that the portraits were woven primarily by Palestinian women in Farkha. When viewing the work, we do not know the details of the process, including the role of the artisan who orchestrated the work, and the artist's portrait remains indistinguishable from those of the other participants. From one perspective, this obscures the women's individual contributions. From another perspective, the fact that the artist's portrait remains unidentified democratically levels the multiple contributions of artist and participants (the weavers, at least). These ambiguities indicate the risks involved in producing participatory art, cohering with the view that such art is not *inherently* oppositional or democratic (Bishop, ed., 2006: 8; Foster, 2006 [2004]: 195; Bishop, 2012). At the same time, though, they highlight the specific context in which this work was produced. The distance between artist and participants, which might explain the anonymisation of their contributions, paradoxically heightened the women's freedom and individuality. It increased the potential for contingency in their portraits, which questions the essentialising views of revolution perpetuated by icons. The artist was keen to avoid a mechanical medium that rapidly and efficiently produces identical copies; he chose embroidery partly because this would lead to variations in the nine portraits (Hamid, 2015b). The production of contingency specifically via the indirect engagement of women weavers from Farkha, moreover, can be explained further by the need to forge an alternative to what Hamid perceives as 'Euro-centric aesthetics' and to engage local audiences (see Cosmic Vinegar, n.d.).

This work exceeds an icon of the Tunisian revolution, while the indication of the artisans' status as Palestinian women, in the accompanying note, brings further connotations of resistance to the work. It is important to the artist that spectators know the work was co-produced and that they are aware of the weavers' location and gender.[4] This roots

---

[4] Knowing this draws our attention, first of all, to the subtle differences between the portraits, as well as bringing into the foreground the perspectives of those

the portraits in the history of embroidering traditional dresses with the Palestinian flag and other icons during Israel's ban on the flag and on artwork employing its four colours in the 1980s and early 90s (Asad, 2016).[5] Hamid uses the enduring 'domestic tool' of embroidery as he perceives it as a non-patriarchal medium. As he states in relation to his more recent series of images of the conflict in Syria, embroidered solely by the artist, 'It's not about me being a man and doing embroidery ... It's about the medium itself being, I wouldn't say *maternal* – I really don't like this word – but it's really not patriarchal' (Hamid, cited by Asad, 2016; emphasis in original).

Hamid engages directly with a 'Western' work of art in alluding to Andy Warhol's numerous renowned silkscreens of Marilyn Monroe, which he produced in the months following this icon's death in 1962.[6] Warhol employed the method of silkscreening both for its 'assembly-line effect' and for the contingent variations that it produced (Warhol and Hackett, 1980: 22). His various repetitions of an image of Marilyn Monroe of 1953, using this method, comment on the construction and commodification of personas in American culture (moma.org, n.d.; see also Whiting, 1987).[7] Hamid refers ironically to Warhol's *Marilyns*, multiplying an icon in bright colours, each time with full red lips. Yet, he develops a contrasting technique and process to explore an icon of revolution in a contemporary Tunisian context. He opted not for silkscreen printing but for embroidery as, he says, 'an autonomous performance in private space, an attempt to investigate the creation of the paradoxical "pop" star' (Hamid, 2016). The ambivalence in his work between the icon to which he alludes and the multiple contingent 'home-made' portraits might be seen to evoke the complexity of the Tunisian revolution – between liberation and uncertainty, and between monolithic and diverse, subjective visions of the country's identity. Warhol, by contrast, chose the method of silkscreening partly as a means of avoiding a 'home-made' appearance (Warhol and Hackett, 1980: 22). He celebrated this method for being 'quick and chancy'

who are not normally included in political discussions or in art exhibitions, local or international.

[5] On resistance through Palestinian 'flag dresses', see Allenby (2002: 105–6; cited in Asad, 2016).

[6] At the Mosaic Rooms the portraits were presented separately, rather than as part of a grid, losing the direct reference to Warhol's work, though the use of blocks of colour is still reminiscent of the 1960s North American pop aesthetic.

[7] The image was a publicity photograph for the film *Niagara*, taken by Gene Kornman in 1953 (tate.org, n.d., b).

(Warhol and Hackett, 1980: 22). Hamid also generates 'chance', but by setting in motion a long process combining an enduring local manual practice and involving others in the work's production.

Contingency is produced in this work, in part, through the process of weaving by hand. Hamid conceives of embroidery as a sculptural practice. As he says: 'there's ... this very intimate relationship when you do embroidery because you use your hands, you actually sweat on it, ... you're using it, you're touching it the whole time, it's not like painting with a brush. ... it's more like a sculpture actually' (Hamid, 2015a). These portraits of Bouazizi exceed the iconic through their sculptural, haptic qualities; the same can be said of Erruas's embroidered flags in *Les Drapeaux* (see Chapter 1). The visible weave and irregular outlines, the traces of the handmade process, similarly evoke fragility and delicacy, by contrast with the bold photographs often found in media reportage. The pixilated appearance, the wavering lines and the irregular features of the multiple portraits are intended to elicit a deeper emotional and intellectual response.[8] Hamid's more recent series of images exploring the conflict in Syria similarly remakes media photographs in embroidery (*Screenshots*, 2016). These images become 'more harrowing because of the sense of unreality the medium imparts' (Asad, 2016). In the works of Hamid and Erruas, the irregular stitches are traces of the kinaesthetic, corporeal practice of weaving. But the stitches in Hamid's work also indicate a participatory process which takes further this confrontation of the iconic. These stitches indicate the 'haptic *texture*' of the work, the term used by Kester to describe the process of social interaction and exchange in collaborative art (Kester, 2011; my emphasis). But, contrasting with the works discussed by Kester, Hamid minimises contact with the participants. He also privileges the art object produced by that (indirect mode of) exchange, rather than shifting the centre of the work to a process which can only be understood afterwards through documents.

Hamid's technique, like that of Erruas, evokes both fragility and resistance to various essentialising visions. In her press release for the exhibition, 'Unravelled' (Beirut Art Center, 2016), which included Hamid's *Screenshots*, Rachel Dedman draws attention to the inherently marginal and critical nature of embroidery: 'Embroidery has always been a practice of the periphery, so when an artist includes it

---

[8] Asad comments on the pixilated appearance specifically of Hamid's series of images reworking photographs of the conflict in Syria (2016).

in his or her practice, it brings to the surface of art a critical dimension' (Dedman, 2016). In Hamid's case, the practice of embroidery is tied specifically to the Palestinian resistance and this local practice is redirected, across time and space, to resist iconic visions of the Tunisian revolution and Tunisian identity, as well as 'Western' canons and histories of art.

It was the handmade 'domestic' appearance of the work that triggered an unexpected response from some spectators when it was exhibited at the French Cultural Centre in Ramallah.[9] Five Muslim men began to pray out loud spontaneously before the portraits of Bouazizi. Hamid states: 'I talked to them afterwards and it was simple: they just felt it was comfortable enough to pray there. The embroideries made the space look homey.' (Hamid, in interview with Cosmic Vinegar, n. d.). This contingent response highlights the work's difference from iconic language, which aims to produce a unified reaction, often by shocking the spectators. The artist recorded this response and uploaded the video to YouTube. In this format, a further layer is added to the work. Our attention is drawn to the unplanned 'performance', the surrounding space and the wider local viewing context of Ramallah – beyond the French institution within which it is displayed. The work's display on the Web can be seen as an alternative means of moving beyond the vertically transnational relationship that is indicated by the French Cultural Centre. At the same time, the video of the wall-hanging together with these spectators in Ramallah emphasises the transversal Palestinian–Tunisian connection that was already present at the stage of production.

By incorporating this particular iconic image, and involving others in its remaking, Hamid's use of embroidery not only complicates conventional oppositions between perceived masculine and feminine practices, and between art and craft.[10] It also holds in tension fragility and resistance, ocularity and the haptic material object, as well as its 'haptic texture' – while creating a particular '*anti*-dialogical' practice paradoxically to heighten autonomy and freedom. The method of participation used and the anonymised presentation of the work are not without risk. Yet, through this contingent process the work does counter the single authoritative icon of revolution. The product of the women's individual contributions is a shifting portrait of the martyr.

---

[9] It was shown at this Centre as part of the annual Palestinian Young Artist Award (2012).

[10] Dedman points to embroidery's situation between such perceived opposites (2016).

It draws attention to Bouazizi as an individual rather than a hero. It is suggestive of fragility and uncertainty in the aftermath of the revolution, and of a lack of consensus surrounding Tunisia's future, by contrast with the tendency in the media to 'ossify perspectives' by iconising Bouazizi's story (Iskandar, 2014: 136–7). It also points to the possibility of including marginalised voices and visions in the process of commemorating the revolution. The stitch, comparable to the infra-thin 'hinge' explored in Chapter 1, evokes materially a space beyond icons and iconic languages, allowing for alternative visions and ways of perceiving. It is also the point of connection between communities and cultures that are usually seen to be divided. Through Hamid's dialogue with Warhol's famous work, he intervenes in the canon, while also negotiating an aesthetic distinctive to a specific context and to an alternative transnational, transversal relationship. His use of embroidery comes partly from the desire to preserve an enduring practice (Asad, 2016). But he develops this practice to produce an aesthetic of revolution. He uses the contingency inherent in the medium and heightens this through a particular mode of participation at a distance. He combines both to produce an aesthetic with which it is possible to allow for alternative perceptions of Tunisian and Palestinian culture.

Reminiscent of Hamid's *Mohammed Bouazizi*, works produced in Tunisia by Selma and Sofiane Ouissi and Sonia Kallel explore and involve an enduring local practice. Their works, by contrast, emerge from a long period of direct contact and exchange with a community of artisans. Yet, these works move further from conventional definitions of participation, since artisans and their practices are incorporated indirectly.

Performing Encounters, Weaving Spaces: Tunis/Sfax/Sejnane

The Ouissis' video, *Laaroussa*, and Sonia Kallel's *Tisser la médina*, do not engage directly with icons. They provide an alternative to iconic sites and 'spectacular bodies' by highlighting, instead, neglected spaces and communities through subtle visual, auditory and kinaesthetic means. In exploring marginalised sites and ordinary people they converge with the pre-revolutionary work to which I referred in Chapter 2, by artists such as Wassim Ghozlani and Aïcha Filali. Indeed, plans for the wider project, *Laaroussa*, as I have noted, began in 2010, in advance of the revolution. At the same time, their works reveal new directions for aesthetics of resistance in the wake of Ben Ali's deposition, as a means of continuing the work of the 'real' revolution; that is, by furthering the aim for greater cultural and socio-economic inclusiveness. The ways in which these works include artisans diverge from conventional definitions of participation and interactivity. Yet, both depend on, and bear the traces of, a direct exchange. The artists control the work, but they shape it by using the sounds, voices or gestures of artisans and their processes. Their works are abstractions of an earlier, directly participatory, process, which can be seen as an integral stage of the works. In an alternative way to Hamid, they hold in tension object and process, though the process is dialogical in this case. In Kallel's work, moreover, artisans who 'participated' at the first stage can become involved more directly as spectators at the stage of the work's exhibition. Through their innovative uses of a participatory exchange with a local community and practice these artists develop alternative aesthetics of revolution.

Selma and Sofiane Ouissi's twelve-minute video, *Laaroussa*, was produced in the context of their project with a community of female ceramicists in Sejnane, northwest Tunisia, which aimed to encourage development in this rural area and was intended to lead to a cooperative initiated and directed by the women.[11] The video shows the two artists kneeling together on the earth as they mime the potters' actions, accompanied by sounds of them preparing, kneading and shaping the clay (Figure 3.1). The video's title, *Laaroussa*, which it shares with the wider project, is the name given to the ceramic dolls which have been made by women in this region for centuries. The text presented with an extract of this video online comments on the ceramicists' 'savoir-faire séculaire'.[12] The project involved a programme of five workshops over five months (between February and June 2011), which encouraged women who had previously worked in isolation to share their expertise

---

[11] It was not possible to establish the cooperative, as a social economist could not be found to take this forward. The project led, though, to the sale of Sejnane pottery across Tunisia, which had not previously been the case, and numerous organisations came to work with the potters. Sejnane pottery also came to be recognised by UNESCO and is now included in the heritage of humanity (Béatrice Dunoyer, email of 13 November 2018). I am very grateful to Béatrice Dunoyer, and Selma and Sofiane Ouissi, for answering my questions regarding the project *Laaroussa*. For further details of the project, see Dunoyer et al. 2011.

[12] As presented at l'artrue.com (last viewed in July 2018).

and experience. It resulted in several works produced by the women or together with the Ouissis (who work between Tunis and Paris) or other artists based in Tunisia or France. The video *Laaroussa* was first shown with a selection of these works in an outdoor exhibition in Sejnane in June 2011. It has appeared at exhibitions including the Triennial, 'Intense proximité', in 2012 at the Palais de Tokyo, Paris. The works have also been shown – in part or in whole – in a section dedicated to the project on the artists' website, l'artrue.com.

The video *Laaroussa* is not, in itself, participatory in a conventional sense. Yet, it depends on the artisans' actions. The artists' performance is shaped by the women's gestures and by unedited audio footage of them making the traditional ceramic dolls. These central features of the work are rooted in the long process of direct exchange between the artists and ceramicists. The audio footage was made during this period and, although the women do not participate directly in producing the video, we hear them participating at this earlier stage of the work. The sounds of their gestures, moreover, establish the pattern and rhythm of the artists' actions. During the workshops, the artists also learned the women's movements by imitating and repeating. Their performance is a corporeal interpretation of those gestures. It is derived from this enduring local practice. This video does not involve the women directly in making an object. Yet, comparable to Hamid's participatory wall-hanging, this work uses a local practice to produce an alternative aesthetic or, in this case, corporeal 'language'. Indeed, in the text accompanying the video on l'artrue.com, the Ouissis articulate their performance in terms of a language, calling it a 'processus d'écriture chorégraphique' ('a process of choreographic writing'), an 'alphabet gestuel entre danse et ouvrage' ('a gestural alphabet between dance and work'). Their choreographic writing brings together the usually separate fields of sculpture and dance, and of ancient ceramic practices and contemporary digital video art; that is, the local and the transnational. Through this work the artists hold in tension their role and that of their 'objects' and, moreover, direct and indirect forms of participation. The video work lasts twelve minutes, and yet it is inextricably connected to the directly participatory project of several months. The sounds and gestures allude to this process. Rather than document their direct exchange with the women, as frequently occurs in the exhibition of community-based participatory work, this video transforms it into a work of art. Viewing the video in the context of the project website, moreover, can alter our understanding of the encounter it presents between artists and artisans. There, an extract of the video is shown alongside documentary videos, photographs and short texts. It emerges as one of a range of works, which gives more emphasis to the participatory process from which the object emerged.

At international exhibitions, such as the Paris Triennial at Palais de Tokyo (2012), the video *Laaroussa* is exhibited with minimal details of the project. We learn only that the performance was inspired by women ceramicists in Sejnane as part of the artists' project to encourage development in this region following the revolution. The longer text accompanying the 1′40 extract online, though, gives more emphasis to the contingent encounter that produced it and to the women's indirect contribution. It highlights, together with the title and description – 'Une Poétique du Geste: "Laaroussa"'; 'vidéo chorégraphique de Selma et Sofiane Ouissi' – the importance of the gestures explored by the artists as the basis for an original type of choreographic writing 'entre danse et ouvrage'. The text refers to the artists' learning and repetition of these gestures at the workshops. In doing so, it situates the work in relation to a longer temporal experience of exchange, drawing attention to the connection between the poetic and the social, 'dialogical' process that led to it: the 'haptic texture'. The abstract space created in the video is more firmly 'rooted' in the area around the town of Sejnane through photographs of the artists working with the women in the same landscape and via the detail that the work was first exhibited *in situ*: an accompanying image shows an outdoor screening of the video from behind the heads of the spectators. The text on the webpage from which this text and image are accessed, and the video extract, explicitly ties the works of art produced by the project to the sociopolitical. It reveals how the project brought together previously disconnected communities of ceramicists around Sejnane and the artists' aim for it to lead to a cooperative run by the women. We also learn that, to the exhibition of June 2011 in Sejnane, the artists invited what they call 'un public urbain' (including politicians, journalists, businessmen, Tunisian cultural services and people from beyond Tunisia) – the aim being to 'promouvoir une politique de décentralisation de l'action artistique' ('promote a policy of decentralisation of the artistic intervention').[13]

---

[13] We learn that the works were then exhibited at Dar Bach Hamba in the Tunis Medina (July–August 2011), at the Automnales de Genève (Switzerland,

The women's contingent contribution, and the *hors champ*, are also given more emphasis by the positioning of the link to this video alongside those to other works, which involve greater degrees of participation. This video is, moreover, reduced to an extract and the link to it appears among rows of links to other works; it is not given more time or space than the other works, or a more privileged position in the sequence. *La Robe idole de Sejnane*, for example, is a monumental sculpture conceptualised and directed by Sonia Kallel, but involving numerous women in the production of the small ceramic squares from which it is composed.[14] The majority of works presented on the page for the project's 'Acte 1' were conceptualised and directed by the Ouissis or other established artists. The women also worked with a Nantes-based group including migrant women embroiderers, Collectif La Luna, however, to compose and produce *Cartographie*, a 'map' of the *Laaroussa* project's 'topographie sociale'. This work brought together women from five areas around Sejnane, as well as diverse techniques (sewing, embroidery and drawing) and materials (tissue, earth, paper, wool and paint).[15] The usually authoritative language of map-making was questioned through the use of contingent materials, reminiscent of Hamid's reworking of iconic photographs. Yet, the process was, in this case, collaborative, rather than participatory, given the balanced division of labour (conceptual and physical); the materials were chosen by the embroiderers and all directions were given by the potters.[16] The text for the work *Les Poupées à plusieurs mains*, similarly suggests the collaborative nature of the process by underlining the preceding exchange and sharing of methods by the women who had formerly worked in isolation. As the description tells us, this is 'une œuvre collective des femmes potières' ('a collective work by the women potters'). Like *Cartographie*, it was triggered by the Ouissis' project, but it was conceptualised and produced by the women. In the same row there is a link to the 'composition vocale de

---

November 2011) and at the B'chira Art Center in Sidi Thabet (March 2012). The Ouissis bring their work and project to a public space through the outdoor exhibition in 2011 and, later, through their website.

[14] A similar dynamic can be found behind the large sculptural necklace directed by Tobi Ayédadjou, entitled 'Perles de Sejnane'.

[15] These details can be found in the text accompanying a photograph of the work.

[16] All the potters participated at some point (Béatrice Dunoyer, email 13 November 2018).

Saloua Ben Salah', who is individualised through the use of her name and the accompanying image of this singer.

The slideshow of photographs occupying the upper third of the page, moreover, emphasises the women's contribution: most are close-ups of their clay-covered hands kneading, shaping or firing the clay dolls. One photograph shows Selma Ouissi and a woman potter kneading the clay together, highlighting directly the exchange that preceded the poetic gestural dance in the video. The documentary video in the middle third of the page shows the women participating in a workshop and producing pottery together. In a reversal of the text for *La Robe idole de Sejnane*, which is labelled as the 'œuvre plastique de Sonia Kallel', a part of this video focuses on the women forming the squares and the upper section of the headless figure, while the artist does not appear in the frame.[17] These works are less controversially 'participatory' than the video, when they are not collaborative or individual. Yet, it is difficult to separate the video performance from the participatory process that influences its content and form – particularly, though not only, when it is viewed online.

The specific ways in which the video *Laaroussa* allows a rethinking of the conventional distinction between object and process emerge in response to the transitional revolutionary context in Tunisia. While this work is not conventionally participatory, it, like Hamid's *Mohammed Bouazizi*, uses a participatory practice to open a space for alternative voices and visions of the country and to develop a localised aesthetic. In addition to avoiding iconic sites by drawing attention to a neglected rural area, the Ouissis avoid representing the women directly. Instead, the artists perform their encounter with the community. In this way, they counter the marginalisation of these women in Tunisia while avoiding the risk of producing sentimental images of women working, such as those which can be seen in classical European or North American painting or Orientalist postcards of water-bearers with titles such as 'Algérie: Femme Arabe portant sa cruche d'eau' ('Algeria: Arab Woman Carrying Her Jug of Water').[18] While, in the video, the artisans cannot be seen, the space that the artists negotiate beyond essentialising visions of Tunisia is anchored in

---

[17] The text alongside this video lists the artists and collectives involved in the project and specifies their origins (detailed above).
[18] Such postcards could be found in the colonial 'Scènes et Types' series (*c.*1900) to which I referred in Chapter 2.

the specific context of Sejnane. This work is 'territorialised' innovatively through movement, sound and material: the artists perform in literal contact with the earth, their hands covered with drying clay. When framed online by different types and extents of participation, moreover, the 'haptic texture' is given as much emphasis as the haptic, shifting the balance between artists and artisans, as well as between poetics and politics.

Kallel's audiovisual *Tisser la médina* also emerged from a directly participatory community-based process, while the work itself similarly involves artisans and their practices indirectly. This work exploring the endangered profession of silk weaving in the Medina of Tunis comparably incorporates sounds – and, in this case, images – of the process of weaving, as well as the stories of artisans. The contingent encounter in this work also evolves – not by being reframed online but by directly involving artisans and spectators at two of its stages, in addition to the initial period of contact. As the artist has explained,

Tisser des liens entre ses habitants, entre ses rues et ses places, entre ses souks et ses maisons m'a conduit vers ceux qui tissent: les soyeux qui ont fait la gloire du vieux Tunis. Un monde inconnu s'est ouvert à moi, un monde dans lequel je me suis investie toute entière ... Un monde merveilleux par la musique de ses «nouls» chatoyant par l'éclat de sa soie, et si triste cependant car en totale déperdition ... [emphasis in original][19]

(*Weaving links between* [the Medina's] *inhabitants, between its streets and its squares, between its souks and its houses led me towards those who weave: the silk manufacturers who were once the glory of the old Tunis. An unknown world opened itself to me, a world I completely immersed myself in ... A world made remarkable through the music of its 'nouls'* [weaving looms], *shimmering from the brightness of its silk, yet so sad because completely disappearing ...*)

This work, reminiscent of the Ouissis' video, not only demonstrates an alternative means of drawing on, and preserving in some way, an enduring local process. It also uses participation to provoke a rethinking of space – in this case, the iconic urban site of the Tunis Medina. It was exhibited as part of the Dream City festival (2012), the theme of which was 'liberté' and the aim of which was precisely to 'repenser

---

[19] This text appears in the third person in the Dream City brochure in the first lines introducing Sonia Kallel's work. I reproduce the citation as sent to me by Sonia Kallel in an email of December 2019.

l'urbain' ('rethink the urban'), to 'interroger la ville d'un point de vue artistique en y associant ses habitants' ('interrogate the city from an artistic point of view by linking its inhabitants to it') (Machghoul, 2012b). Sonia Kallel's *Tisser la médina* begins with a tour of the Medina during which spectators are taken, by a guide, to the sites of several surviving *foundouks* (workshops) (Figure 3.5).[20] Their tour is shaped by the stories of some ten weavers in their workshops, as well as commentary by the artist, to which they listen via headphones. The audio tour is followed by a video installation, which relies on the contingent sounds and images of an old weaving loom. After viewing the installation, the spectators are given a map of the Medina, showing the locations of the workshops and encouraging them to visit the sites of this disappearing tradition *in vivo*. *Tisser la médina* does not run the same risks as Hamid's wall-hanging and the Ouissis' video. It was neither conceptualised nor produced by the weavers, but it incorporates their unrehearsed, uninterrupted stories, in addition to bearing other audio and visual traces of the exchanges between the artist and the weavers, as well as their environments. While Hamid minimised communication with his participants, Kallel's work – closer to *Laaroussa* – emerged from a period of eight months of contact with all the silk-makers in the Tunis Medina. During this time the artist established a relationship with the artisans, conducted interviews and recorded sounds of their working environments (Machghoul, 2012b).[21] Aurélie Machghoul characterises the process of collecting this data ('toutes les données possibles se rapportant à la profession de soyeux' '(all the possible data related to the silk-making profession')) as 'quasi anthropologique' (2012b). The aim, though, converging with the projects of the Ouissis and of Hamid, is for the encounters between artist and artisans to lead to a tangible work of art, rather than a scientific study or a documentary report – or what Kester has referred

---

[20] Kallel's multi-part work was reconstructed and adapted, in two further iterations of Dream City 2012, to the sites of Sfax and L'Estaque, near Marseilles. My knowledge of the first two versions of the installation depends on a combination of my experience of the installation as shown in L'Estaque and conversations with Sonia Kallel (to whom I am very grateful), as well as reviews and documentation. I comment below on the process of 'loss' and 'gain' involved in recreating the installation in different sites. I do the same for the installation by Collectif Wanda, which I also experienced in L'Estaque.

[21] For details of the exchange between Kallel and the weavers that preceded the work, I rely on Machghoul (2012b).

to as a collaborative 'conversation piece' (Kester, 2004). Kallel draws attention to this disappearing profession through a sensorial experience. The artisans participate indirectly through various means.

First, the audio tour depends on their narratives, as well as the locations of the *foundouks*. The spectators' journey through space is accompanied by a journey in time, as the artisans reflect on the changes undergone by their profession. The tradition is dying out as a result of 'les capitalistes [qui] vendent beaucoup plus cher qu'ils achètent' ('the capitalists [who] sell for much more than they buy'), as one artisan states. As he reflects, 'la plupart des soyeux sont morts'; 'On n'arrive plus à satisfaire la demande. Maintenant, il ne reste plus rien ici' ('most of the silk manufacturers are dead'; 'We can't satisfy the demand anymore. There's nothing left here, now'). This weaver indicates his need to continue working at the age of eighty to survive, despite the physical strain of the work. But he also highlights his passion for weaving: when he's working, he says, 'j'oublie tout. Je ne pense à rien d'autre que le fil' ('I forget everything. I think of nothing but the thread'). He compares his work to art, music or a religious pilgrimage. The stories unfold amid the sounds of old weaving looms and of birds, which indicate the distance of this working method from mass industrial production. The artisans contribute the material for the tour, rather than conceptualising or producing that stage of the work. Yet, the voices we hear in the present are traces of the direct past exchange. These two stages of the work, and, therefore, direct and indirect modes of participation, are held in tension. The space of the Medina is reshaped, for the spectators, by these spontaneous stories and sounds of hidden sites.

The poetic video installation contrasts with the outdoor kinaesthetic audio stage, and its documentary mode, and is further removed from the dialogical process in which both parts emerged. Yet, it similarly still bears the traces of that process and of the ancient practice of silk weaving. Indeed, it relies on the contingent sounds and images of a working weaving loom, which the artist recorded. The video, through which Kallel honours the profession of silk weaving, displays the beautiful rhythm created by the threads, which is orchestrated by the movement of the artisan's body.[22] It is rooted in, and encourages contemplation of, the socio-economic reality of silk weavers and others

---

[22] Sonia Kallel provided these details in our email exchange of December 2019.

whose profession is endangered. In this case, the stages of direct and indirect participation emerge through oscillation, and ambivalence, between representation and abstraction. The screen displays the white threads of a filmed loom shifting, on a black background, as they morph intermittently into an abstract cube or grid, or vertical and diagonal lines reminiscent of Frank Stella's minimalist paintings (*The Black Paintings*, 1958–60). The digital patterns shift to the regular rhythm of an old loom similar to those heard in the artisans' *témoignages* (testimonies). The medium of digital video evokes the use of technology and large-scale production in the textile industry, which is lamented in the artisans' stories. Yet, the contingent elements are not erased by digital imaging. They also influence the digital patterns and contemporary work of art. The enduring local tradition resists absorption into the global capitalist system. The exchange between art and craft is echoed by the shifts between different modes of representation, holding in tension documentary and abstraction, three-dimensional depth – indicated when the crossing lines suggest the inner workings of a weaving loom – and two-dimensional surface. The relationship between these contrasts is complicated by the coexistence of static and shifting lines and the camera's movement across the pattern in alternative directions and at different levels of focus. This piece holds in tension the practices of artist and artisan, balancing their processes in a way that resists internal neglect of aspects of the country's cultural heritage as well as hegemonic forces in the wider worlds of economics and art.

Contingency is incorporated in this work primarily through the indirect participation of the artisans and the sounds of their working environment. The unedited footage is arranged by the artist in ways that allow it to shape the work. But the contingent encounter extends to the spectators. During the audio tour their journey depends on the artisans' spontaneous stories and the sites of the *foundouks*, as well as the artist's own trajectory: '[l]a scénarisation de la bande sonore a été basée sur le trajet que j'ai réalisé à la découverte des artisans, et sur les histoires de vie, d'un métier et d'une passion' ('the scriptwriting of the soundtrack was based on the journey I undertook to discover artisans, and on the life stories, those of a profession and of a passion').[23] The spectators' experience of this stage of the work calls to mind the

---

[23] Sonia Kallel related this detail in our email exchange of December 2019.

definitions of 'interactivity', above, in that their contribution is provisional and reversible. Through their movements the spectators embody the alternative perception of the Medina that emerged through the encounter between artist and artisans, and their environment. They highlight and connect the neglected sites of an ancient tradition and crucial part of Tunisia's cultural heritage. This act of walking in a way that encourages a reimaging of the space is reminiscent of Certeau's 'urban speech acts' (1990 [1980]). But the spectators experience space (and time) as they listen to the artisans' spontaneous narratives; theirs are what we might call receptive 'urban listening acts'. The spectators' involvement in the work is, at this stage, guided (rather than controlled), even while their physical movements indicate a contingent space and perspective. At the end of the work, though, the map they are given, marked with sites and images of the *foundouks*, allows them to select which sites to visit and to explore them in the order and at the pace they choose. This does not leave a lasting trace on the environment (at least, as far as we know) and is, therefore, reminiscent of Kravagna's definition of interactivity. Yet, the direction of the work depends, at this point, on the spectators. These journeys are – or would be (if recorded) – more reminiscent of the spatially and temporally anchored '*dérives*' we have seen in Tunisian video work using the peripatetic mode, including Karray's *Live* (see Chapter 2). Kallel relinquishes more control, however, in triggering this live 'performance' by the spectators. The map itself supplies a visual and tangible summary of the alternative space produced between control and contingency. It also acts as a trigger for contingent and diverse experiences dependent on the spectators' interactions with the environment and the artisans they meet. As the artist has revealed, each spectator experienced the tour in a certain way: the inhabitants of the Medina for example (according to testimonies) were very affected by the dilapidated state of the workplaces, of which they were unaware despite being from this Medina.[24] While some spectators contacted the artist to say they had visited some of the workshops, their experiences remain unrecorded and largely unknown.[25] Yet, this opening of the work to alternative possibilities itself suggests an endless process of 'weaving' the Medina

---

[24] The artist communicated this to me in our email exchange of December 2019.
[25] Sonia Kallel referred to these messages from spectators in our email exchange of January 2017.

and a complex web of connections. This web is made even more complex by the fact that some of the artisans themselves participated, visiting fellow silk weavers; this work allows the initial participants to intervene in different ways and at different stages of the work. Kallel's work fosters exchange between the artisans, as well as between these neglected producers of the country's heritage and the spectators (from within and beyond Tunisia). *Tisser la médina* focuses on weaving but, by contrast with Hamid's wall-hanging, it is not the (collective) act of weaving that produces contingency. Rather, the work is formed – and space is metaphorically *trans*formed – through footage of weaving and the spontaneous narratives of artisans, as well as the spectators' movements (first, guided and, then, free). Kallel innovatively combines weaving and mapping to highlight neglected sites and 'weave' them together, 'reordering' space.

Tisser la médina was reconstructed and adapted, in two further iterations of Dream City 2012, to the sites of Sfax and L'Estaque, near Marseilles. A photograph recording the first stage of the installation in Sfax (linked to an article by Tunisian artist, writer and cyberactivist Ismaël on this version of Dream City, 2012) shows spectators seated in an enclosure wearing headphones.[26] The stories of weavers in Tunis were not combined, in this case, with a tour of the Medina, though they might have encouraged reflection on the similarly difficult conditions for wool and cotton weavers in Sfax and on their passion for their profession. As the artist has commented, the idea was for the spectators to travel via the (inevitably modified) audio track; the history of this profession is not the same, but the passion for the profession is present, just as it is in the memories of artisan fishermen in L'Estaque.[27] In the installation's more radical transplantation to Dream City in L'Estaque (2013) the audio stage was, as in Sfax, static (it involved listening to the stories of weavers on headphones in the garden or, when raining, in an enclosure outside the room in which the video was screened) and the final kinaesthetic exploration of the site of production was, inevitably, also lost. Yet, the work continued to resonate with the context for which it was originally created, the metaphorical weaving process extending to incorporate a new and diverse audience. In France

---

[26] The photograph can be found at: https://universes.art/en/nafas/articles/2012/dream-city-sfax/img/04 (last accessed January 2020).

[27] As the artist detailed in our email exchange of December 2019.

'Dream City' was subtitled 'Voyage à l'Estaque de Tunis à Marseille', promoting a transnational consciousness of the two cities in the spectators throughout their tour. Kallel's work could still raise awareness of this community and the need to preserve this artisanal tradition – and perhaps others beyond Tunisia. It could promote, moreover, a reimagining of Tunisia that exceeded simplistic external images of a completed and unified revolution.

These works by Hamid, the Ouissis and Kallel are diversely viewed, listened to and/or experienced kinaesthetically, but all are shaped by artists and participants, and evolve as they shift from one stage of the work to the next and/or between formats and contexts. In these ways they question neat divisions between object and process, between participation and interactivity, and between direct and indirect modes of involvement. They also develop particular localised uses and aesthetics of participation. These artists draw attention to a neglected enduring practice. At the same time, they use aspects of that practice in a new way to produce a means of conveying the revolution or of continuing its work. These pieces focus specifically on the Tunisian context, while indicating solidarity between urban and rural localities within and across borders – vertically or transversally – by involving others. Contingent contributions to the work of art occur, in these cases, at the stage of production. Kallel's *Tisser la médina*, as we have seen, additionally includes spectators at the stage of the work's exhibition. In other works, contingent encounters of resistance occur principally with spectators at the stage of the work's exhibition and, in some cases, evolve beyond this stage – invisibly or visibly. Contingency, moreover, is generated through the use of more recent, often transnational, practices.

Faces and Spaces of Resistance: Contingent Icons of Tunisia, Egypt and Syria

While Sonia Kallel invites spectators to weave an alternative route through the Medina of Tunis, Collectif Wanda encourages them to reimagine the Medina's spaces from its rooftops (Figures 3.2 and 3.3). Also shown at the first Dream City after the revolutionary events of 2011, *Le Ciel est par-dessus le toit* evokes 'Liberté' specifically by encouraging contingent encounters between spectators and an architectural installation. Involving spectators provisionally in reimagining the space of the Medina, this work is reminiscent of conventional definitions of interactivity. Unlike Kallel's work, it does not shift between usually separate categories of involvement. It does, however, demonstrate how interactivity – like direct and indirect modes of participation – can come to be associated with resistance and, specifically, to continue the work of the Tunisian revolution. The installations by Tunis-based Mouna Jemal Siala and Wadi Mhiri (*Parti Facelook / Parti Facelike*) and by the London-based collective Febrik (*The Watchtower of Happiness*) are participatory gallery-based works. Yet, they too invent particular modes of involving the spectators as a means to encourage a rethinking of Tunisia and other sites during, or in the wake of, revolutionary demonstrations. In different ways, these works encourage spectators to make their own contingent 'icons'. They also demonstrate the ways in which encounters can shift when parts of the work move beyond the gallery to the public spaces of the street or the Web.

Contingent encounters in Collectif Wanda's *Le Ciel est par-dessus le toit* question the order and certainty that are usually seen to be embodied by architecture. This work, by a group composed primarily of architects, including the permanent members Feriel Lejri, Ahmed Blaïch and Malek Jrad, creates an alternative physical space, evoking the freedom to think in alternative ways.[28] It resonates with street art that produces means by which ordinary people can 'reclaim' space. Yet, it provides a contrast to provocative participatory projects in the media of performance, photography and graffiti (including Fedhila's *Super-Tunisian St'art* and JR's *InsideOut*, to which I referred in Chapter 2) in its minimalist architectural aesthetic (JR's project, as well as examples of graffiti and street dance, will be discussed in Chapter 4). The installation consists of three simple white house-like structures positioned in a row on a rooftop of the Medina (when presented at Dream City in Tunis, 2012). The identical ephemeral structures consist of thin white walls and a roof, a doorway with a light white curtain in place of a door and a square glassless skylight. Each cabin allows for one spectator at a time to recline on a large white cushion and gaze at the square of sky. This installation is designed to provide the spectator with a space and moment of calm and

[28] The Tunis-based Collectif Wanda was created in 2006. As we are told in the WordPress text accompanying the 2013 festival in Marseille, the collective is an interdisciplinary platform for debate uniting mainly architects, including three permanent members (Lejri, Blaïch and Jrad) (Dream City, 2013).

contemplation, an escape from the noise and bustle of the Medina. Collectif Wanda's objective, in keeping with their aim to question perceived architectural order and certainty by conceiving of architecture in alternative ways, was to 'redonner sens à l'architecture dans la vie de tous les jours' ('give meaning back to architecture in everyday life') (Dream City, 2013). Their project to reinvest architecture with new meanings, thereby questioning the principles by which it is conventionally governed, extends to the wider space: 'que faire pour désenclaver la m[é]dina? [F]aire des promenades alternatives sur les toits? Ré-inventer de nouveaux lieux de vie en prônant une mobilité alternative' ('what can be done to open up the Medina? [G]o on alternative walks on the roofs? Reinvent new living spaces by advocating an alternative mode of mobility') (Dream City, 2013). The group's emphasis on the everyday and on mobility as means of opening up the city is reminiscent of the 'promenades alternatives' in Karray's *Live* and Bahri's *Orientations* (see Chapter 2). By contrast, though, Collectif Wanda's work involves contingent exchanges at the stage of its exhibition and through the spectator's movements within a delineated yet open space.

The architecture of *Le Ciel est par-dessus le toit* avoids referring to particular local or external styles, making space for an alternative, rather, via a neutral blank canvas. The work does, though, reappropriate a specific French literary work. It borrows the title of Verlaine's poem, from *Sagesse* (Verlaine, 1942 [1880]). In its short presentation of Collectif Wanda's work, the festival guidebook cites the opening lines, which evoke the calm blue sky 'above the roof' and the gently swaying branch of a tree:

> Le ciel est, par-dessus le toit,
> Si bleu, si calme!
> Un arbre, par-dessus le toit,
> Berce sa palme.

The installation engages ambivalently with Verlaine's text, which is actually a poem of regret written from the author's prison cell (see, for example, Morris and Rothman, eds., 1995: 432). The open architectural spaces created in this contemporary post-revolutionary context resonate with the aspiration to freedom expressed in the poem. But the poem evokes the author's separation from the world outside – 'Mon Dieu, mon Dieu, la vie est là,' – and his sadness, for which he blames himself. Collectif Wanda's work, by contrast, encourages an experience of freedom and tranquillity. The space within each structure is limited. But this space, designed to accommodate one spectator, is connected to individuality and independence, both physically and intellectually. It offers a space, and an interval, in which the spectator may rest and regain their energy (Dream City, 2013). It is a space of openness and exchange: the spectator is free to enter and leave as they please; the 'door' is always open. The pervasive use of white, the thin walls and the shifting curtain also highlight the structures' ephemerality. This installation, then, appears to rework this poem by a canonical French author, perhaps in a similar revolutionary spirit to its simultaneous critique of architecture.

Indeed, the group follow Verlaine's first four lines with their own words, suggesting a new direction for the poem:

Et si on possédait un carré de ciel ... Et si les rues devenaient aériennes ... Et si nos pas se mêlaient au vol des hirondelles ... Et si nos mouvements ne succombaient plus aux rythmes mécaniques ... Et si le silence n'avait pour écho que le souffle de nous-mêmes ... Et si les bâtiments plaidaient leur agonie ... Et si les architectes abandonnaient leurs certitudes ... Et si la vie l'emportait sur la géométrie ... Et si la ville se diluait ... Et si une réalité alternative se révélait ... Et si la liberté était ... (Dream City, 2013)

(What if we possessed a square of sky ... If the streets were aerial ... If our footsteps joined the swallows' flight ... If our movements were no longer bound by mechanical rhythms ... If silence had for its only echo the murmurs of our soul ... If the buildings pleaded their agony ... If the architects abandoned their certainty ... If life overtook geometry ... If the city were dissolved ... If an alternative reality were revealed ... What if there were freedom ...?)[29]

Through these words, by contrast with the original poem, the artists look to the future rather than expressing regret over the past. They suggest the hope of, and real possibility for, freedom through images of contingent movement: flight, dilution or 'le souffle de nous-mêmes' ('the murmurs of our soul'). Their images of freedom from architectural order, geometry, the human body, and its mechanical rhythms can be seen as metaphors for political liberation. The repetition of 'Et si ...' clauses – and particularly the final line, 'Et si la liberté

[29] My translation, adapted from the festival booklet, *DREAM CITY 2013 – VOYAGE A L'ESTAQUE*.

était...' ('What if there were freedom...?') – suggests that the revolution is ongoing while also evoking hope for the emergence of 'une réalité alternative' ('an alternative reality'). The line 'Et si la vie l'emportait sur la géométrie...' ('If life took over geometry...') is reminiscent of the contingent explosion of the geometric Arabesque-Rotorelief in Nicène Kossentini's *Le Printemps arabe* and *Heaven or Hell*. In engaging with, and implicitly contesting, this French poem, Collectif Wanda's work might be seen to evoke a postcolonial critique, reminiscent of Kossentini's and Fatmi's ambivalent dialogues with Duchamp. Yet, also like these artists' works, it involves a more complex, multi-directional process in exploring liberty in relation to the recent dictatorship in Tunisia and to ongoing constraints.

Resistance to constraints – in society, as well as in art and architecture – emerges, in this case, through the diverse spectators' contingent interactions with the open structure, and via the shifting natural environment surrounding it. The fleeting images captured in the skylights depend on the cabin chosen by the spectator and the position they adopt. These images also rely on the time of viewing and the architectural *hors champ*, including unpredictable sounds and the organic phenomena of the shifting sky, as a result of the evolving light and/or weather. The white structures register movement through shadows, while their curtains shift in the wind or with the passage of spectators. This alternative architecture is shaped by, and therefore subordinate to, its contingent environment and the spectators' movements. Both emphasise the connection between – and give equal importance to – interior and exterior. The structures are situated high up on the rooftops and yet they provide a counterpoint to the panoramic view that has frequently been associated with domination and surveillance. They encourage contingent views and subjective, sensorial, embodied experiences. The structures constrain the spectators' vision through the use of skylights, reminiscent of the use of framing and dramatically low (or high) angles in video art, including Bahri's *Orientations* or Troudi's *Deux minutes de Tunis*, or in Ghozlani's photographic *Postcards of Tunisia*. Like many of Troudi's videos, these 'frames' are static and 'waiting', paradoxically, to capture contingency. They similarly question the power and authority embodied by architecture and urban space through the movements of (in this case, knowing) 'passers-by' and through organic phenomena which obey their own natural laws. The light white open structures might call to mind sculptural poetics of absence in Erruas's installation of white-on-white flags. Yet, closer to Filali's use of windows for *L'Angle mort*, they provide a liminal space of exchange in which contingent, provisional, fluid images appear. In this case, encounters occur in a three-dimensional space and the spectators' interaction becomes a means of democratising architecture and the wider environment. The use of white by Collectif Wanda is suggestive, in this post-2011 context, of neutrality and a tabula rasa. The dynamic exchange between inside and outside, control and contingency, evokes revolutionary freedom, as well as the ongoing revolutionary processes of transition, negotiation and openness.

In this site-specific installation the contingent encounter is physically anchored in context, appearing within the Medina it aims to 'désenclaver' ('open up'). A nearby minaret forms an alternative backdrop to Verlaine's evocation of a church: 'La cloche, dans le ciel qu'on voit, / Doucement tinte.' ('The bell, in the sky we see, / Softly rings.') The spatial and sonorous environment of the Tunis Medina was lost in the installation's transposition to L'Estaque, where it was shown on a raised platform overlooking the harbour, its curtain billowing in the coastal wind. Yet, like Kallel's *Tisser la médina*, this work continued to resonate with the context for which it was originally created, given the subtitle 'Voyage à l'Estaque de Tunis à Marseille' and the use of the same text referring to the group's mission to 'désenclaver la médina'. Positioned on the Mediterranean coast, moreover, the relocated structures appeared to 'look back' to their original location. In this context the work continued to forge an alternative to iconic visions of Tunisia – and to architectural and social order, more widely – while its exploration of porous boundaries between inside and outside could be seen, in this context, to evoke cultural interconnectedness and to encourage transnational solidarity.

In Collectif Wanda's *Le Ciel est par-dessus le toit* iconic spaces and structures are 'reordered' through the contingent, albeit provisional, interactions of spectators. Contingent encounters occur through an installation and at the stage of the work's exhibition. Such encounters are similarly produced between spectators and an installation in *Parti Facelook / Parti Facelike* (2012) and *The Watchtower of Happiness* (2012). In these two works, however, spectators are involved in making a tangible object, which endures beyond the exhibition either privately or on online platforms. The spectators of these works participate in image-making not (or not simply) by posing for the photographer but by choosing from a range of disguises or by becoming the photographer. The two works produce different parameters for the contingent encounter, giving the spectators different degrees of freedom. They also engage with distinct themes and contexts. Yet, both works are reminiscent of contemporary and enduring transnational practices, particularly the social media practice of making selfies for platforms such as Facebook or Instagram and touristic practices of sending postcards or taking snapshots. In both cases, these practices are combined and developed, and the contingent effects produced by the spectators' uses of them are harnessed to produce alternatives to iconic visual language and essentialising perspectives.

Wadi Mhiri and Mouna Jemal Siala's *Parti Facelook / Parti Facelike* (2012; Figure 3.4) encourages the spectators' involvement specifically in a process of rethinking Tunisian identity following Ben Ali's deposition. The work was produced in the months following the first 'post-revolutionary' election in Tunisia (October 2011). This election was for a Constituent Assembly which would decide on a new constitution for the country. *Parti Facelook / Parti Facelike* consists of two photo booths – one for men and one for women – in neighbouring rooms. The photo booth also functions as a voting booth, which is indicated by the mock political party names, 'Facelook' and 'Facelike', on the sides, together with rows of photographs of potential leaders. Each spectator sits individually inside a booth and is engaged by the artist who sits unseen behind the screen (Mouna Jemal Siala animates the booth for women and Wadi Mhiri the booth for men). The artist asks the spectator to select a 'look' in answer to the question: 'A quoi ressemble la Tunisie aujourd'hui?' ('What does Tunisia look like today?') By moving their hand over a light, they can scroll through, and see their face within, a range of portraits of men and women. The participants can reimagine 'Tunisia' – and themselves – by choosing from a range of costumes associated with urban glamour or rural tradition, universal everyday wear, smart business suits or diverse traditional attire, including multiple types of hijab, worn with conservative dress or make-up, jewellery or large sunglasses. These disguises are designed to create portraits of caricatures, from men with fake long beards or bushy moustaches to a woman posing, as if for a catwalk, wearing heavy eye shadow and a leopard print dress with matching headband. (The photographs of 'candidates' on the outside of the booths show the artists in the same disguises.) The artist asks the participant to make any necessary adjustments to their posture or hairstyle before taking their photograph. They leave with a copy of the image and a sticker showing a phrase, in Arabic (*ena twasart*), which has two meanings: 'I took a photo' and 'I imagined' (the artists appropriated the visuals used in real political campaigns and replaced the term '*ena sawat* [I voted]'; in the mock campaign poster in Figure 3.4 the phrase 'Tunisia votes' has become 'Dream City votes'. Images of the circular stickers can be seen in the bottom right-hand side of this poster). This installation was exhibited at the same 'Dream City' festival as the works by Collectif Wanda and Sonia Kallel (*Tisser la médina*) in Tunis, Sfax and L'Estaque. Any differences in the experience of the work would have depended solely, in this case, on the cultural context and spectators' background. The structure of the installation remained the same and the booths were positioned indoors. 'Candidate' posters outside the exhibition, though, revealed specific responses to this aspect of the work in Tunisia.

Parti Facelook / Parti Facelike innovates a unique mode of interaction between artists and spectators. The image emerges in this contingent encounter, which draws playfully on the practices of taking selfies and 'liking' selfies on Facebook, as well as those of taking formal identity photographs or voting. The process is reminiscent of the form of tourist amusement which consists of positioning your face over a hole within a cut-out figure to pose for a photograph. The practice of parodic disguising (the images hold in tension the amateur 'actor' and their adopted persona) also recalls comic performance. At the same time, in involving a dialogue with the artist, who is hidden behind a screen, the experience might recall Catholic confession (for participants familiar with this sacrament). This contingent encounter combines contrasting modes: formal and informal, serious and ludic, and private and public. Spectators, in all three contexts, are likely to be familiar with most of these modes, while they will be unfamiliar with the incongruous combination of these practices. This ambivalent game is designed to amuse the spectators to draw their attention to the serious question of Tunisia's political future.

The diversity of portraits is reminiscent of the emergence of multiple parties in the wake of the 2011 revolution and resonates, perhaps especially for Tunisian voters, with the proliferation of choices available in the elections to the Constituent Assembly. While the portraits are caricatures – which contribute to engaging and amusing the spectator – in their range they indicate the political, social and cultural diversity of Tunisia. In a contrasting way to Filali's sculpture, *Bourgeons* (see Chapter 2), this work raises the same question as to the uncertain future of Tunisia and the possibility of acknowledging all parts and persuasions of its heterogeneous society. The question posed by the artist to the spectator is reminiscent of Sonia Kallel's title for her ambivalent sculptural work *Which Dress for Tomorrow?*, while Mhiri and Jemal Siala's installation demands an answer (contingent and playful) from each spectator. The two booths of *Parti Facelook / Parti Facelike* are presented in different rooms and conventionally gendered by using blue or pink for the low-lighting, signage, portrait backgrounds and stickers. This might be seen as a critical reference to the concern provoked, in some, by the draft constitution's inclusion of an article stating that women would be seen as 'complementary', rather than 'equal', to men (see, for example, Allani, 2013; Charrad and Zarrugh, 2014; Labidi, 2014b). This reading is encouraged if the work is considered in the light of Jemal Siala's contemporaneous video engaging with debates surrounding the practice of veiling in Tunisia, *Le Sort* (2011–12), to which I referred in Chapter 1. The installation alludes to, yet undermines, binary perceptions of women and men. The selection of photographs in and on the sides of both booths includes an equal number of male and female 'candidates'. Also, in practice, participants could enter the booth designed for the opposite sex, if the queue for their booth was long. While, in reality, debates regarding Tunisia's future (within and beyond the country) demonstrated a tendency to polarise religious and secular viewpoints, this work highlights the complexity of Tunisia through its diverse portraits of men and women between these constructed poles.[30]

The 'looks' for Tunisia that are generated by this process are largely controlled by the artists. They provide the templates and guide the spectators as they construct the image, telling them how to select their

---

[30] The diversity of Tunisian society is similarly reflected in Mouna Jemal Siala's later photographic project, *Non à la division* (2014). This collection consisted of 217 portraits of diverse Tunisian people with a vertical line drawn down the centre of their face: a sign of protest, as well as a hyphen ('trait d'union'), signalling their shared refusal of the division and discrimination threatening their society and their values, as the artist states on her website (http://mounajemal.tn/portfolio-item/non-a-la-division-2014/).

'look', encouraging them to adjust their position and asking them if they are ready for the photograph to be taken. The spectators must answer the artists' question – 'A quoi ressemble la Tunisie aujourd'-hui?' – by choosing from among the images selected by the artists, though this provision of a set of choices reflects the electoral process. The spectators' kinaesthetic involvement and contribution to image-making encourages their awareness of their freedom to participate in deciding the future of their country, but perhaps also the limitations and the confusion that accompanies the process. The installation might resonate in this way for spectators from a range of democratic contexts, highlighting the convergences between voting in Tunisia and France, for example. At the same time, it recalls specifically the new experience of voting in Tunisia following the emergence of numerous candidates and political perspectives in 2011. The ironic comparison of the processes of voting and 'liking' on Facebook might promote a cynical reflection on whether the revolution has succeeded. The parameters imposed on the work might also be seen to reflect the persistence of constraints. The diverse spectators are, nevertheless, free to choose their disguise and also to combine their individual faces with the templates, which suggests the potential for greater inclusiveness. They are ambivalently passive yet active, and a voter yet also a potential candidate. The work engages with the voting process, while also playfully distorting and exceeding it in a way that highlights the freedom of the ordinary person (the regular Facebook user) to participate in a democratic process, contributing to their country's future.

The photographs made by the spectators were taken away by them as personal mementos of their experience and not shown in public, either in the street or online. But Mhiri and Jemal Siala's work extended beyond the installation through the presentation of the same rows of the mock candidate posters (the artists in disguise) in the streets beyond the exhibition. The reception of these posters in Tunis and Sfax might be viewed pessimistically. These posters were ripped from the walls, leaving only traces of the artists' mock portraits, as photographs on Wadi Mhiri's Facebook page dedicated to this work demonstrate.[31] The reasons behind this hostile response cannot be

---

[31] Photographs of the torn posters can be found at www.wadimhiri.com/portfolio/art-de-la-rue-wadi-mhiri/category/12-dream-city?limitstart=0 (last accessed August 2014). See also houdaghorbelwadimhiri.com/parti-faclook-partie-facelike/ (last accessed October 2018).

known for sure, though it might reflect heightened sensitivity to images at that time in Tunisia (as Mouna Jemal Siala has suggested).[32] It is reminiscent of the response to JR's *InsideOut* project in Tunis, where the posters of faces of ordinary people were also torn down. As the video of JR's intervention makes clear, it was felt by some members of the public that the city's walls should either display all Tunisians or none at all (see Chapter 4).[33] *Parti Facelook / Parti Facelike* generates a different kind of contingent encounter when it moves beyond the indoor installation. The images are completed, rather than being open to multiple possibilities. But the parameters are taken away, including the work's framing as art and as an ironic engagement with the voting process. These ripped posters, on the other hand, highlight freedom of expression in public, following the deposition of Ben Ali. While different kinds of censorship have emerged in the wake of the revolution of January 2011 (Machghoul, 2013), art can provide a space for this freedom. These traces – like the ambivalence between control and contingency, constraint and freedom, in the indoor installation – resonate with Dakhlia's and Khouri's emphasis on the inevitably gradual nature of the transition to democracy (Dakhlia, 2011; Khouri, 2014). They also resonate with Dakhlia's discussion of turbulence as inherent to democracy, within and beyond Tunisia, and of the irrevocable rupture with dictatorship, nonetheless (see Chapter 1). This work exceeds iconic languages of the revolution through the kinaesthetic and contingent involvement of the diverse spectators at two stages. The iconoclasm triggered by an unframed fragment of the work in the streets contrasts with the more subtle renegotiation of icons through the installation. There, contingent, shifting provisional images of 'Tunisia' emerge in the space created between spectators and artists, as well as between contrasting transnational visual practices. This work encompasses plural and conflicting views, and allows (outside the installation, at least) for a mode of participation that is uncontrolled by the artists; in

---

[32] The artist suggested this in our email exchange of June 2020.
[33] Some spectators of Fedhila's *Super-Tunisian* were similarly enraged, as the video of her public mock political campaign demonstrates. An edited recording of the two-hour performance, which took place in front of the Municipal Theatre on the Avenue Habib Bourguiba in central Tunis, can be found at https://www.youtube.com/watch?v=73Sx_FqALc (last accessed January 2019). Further details can be found ont the artist's website at https://moufidafedhila.com/super-tunisian-start (last accessed January 2019).

this case, participatory art is both political and oppositional. Febrik's *The Watchtower of Happiness* generates non-iconic images through an alternative form of contingent encounter and a different means of display beyond the exhibition of the installation. This work explores images of the uprisings themselves in the sites of Sidi Bouzid in Tunisia, Tahrir Square in Egypt and Daraa in Syria.

The Watchtower of Happiness was first exhibited in London at the Mosaic Rooms (2012) and, subsequently, at the Victoria and Albert Museum's 'Friday Late: Record, Reframe Resist' (30 November 2012). Consisting of a tall wooden structure with cameras attached, the installation encourages the spectator to take photographs or be photographed against a large screen showing an aerial view of multitudes of protesters, adopting the position of a revolutionary activist (see https://febrik.org/the-watchtower-of-happiness/).[34] Photographs taken with the cameras, or with the participants' personal mobile phones, are uploaded to a blog: http://thewatchtowerofhappiness.tumblr.com/.[35] The documentation accompanying the installation provides details of the work's connection to the artists' analysis of photographs of the initial stages of the protests. These photographs were taken on personal cameras or mobile phones and uploaded to social media sites that were not censored by the protester's government:

The camera and recording device's [sic] (such as smart phones) continued formal and informal records [and] allowed for a multiplicity of representation across many channels, finding loop holes [sic] of dissemination despite censorship. Mass demonstrators began to contribute to the story telling of the events, often from spaces not accessible by or represented by official press or the media. These diverse records and the physical mass participation of the people (more numbers than every [sic] before and representing all sectors of society) began to redefine the term 'activists' to include all demonstrators, any person taking part rather than noted by organized parties with long[-]term political agendas.[36]

The artists observed differences between the images produced in the three sites of resistance in terms of, for example, what was framed, the body language of the demonstrators, and signifiers of their attitudes towards the ruling governments, as well as inventions, props and spatial practices. They identified three site-specific perspectives.

---

[34] Last accessed June 2020. [35] Last accessed August 2014.
[36] This extract is from the documentation panel exhibited beside the structure.

Under the heading 'The Perspective of Defiance (the collective discovery in Tunisia)', selected images demonstrate the recurrence of the panoramic view of groups of protesters looking directly at the camera and brandishing fruit – in reference to the suicide of fruit-stall owner Bouazizi – to make their point. In footage of the protests in Tahrir Square, the artists discerned 'The Perspective of Liberation (the comic drama as portrait in Egypt)': they comment on the recurrence of the protesters' direct look at the camera, as well as their comical poses and props – including makeshift helmets – which they invented to be able to remain in the Square. They note the humour of the Egyptian demonstrators in dealing with the crisis, as well as their 'great happiness', 'liberated and excited by what is to come'. The third perspective – 'The Perspective of Censorship (the unexpected photographer in Syria)' – reveals the unforeseen limited vantage points produced by tentative recordings made from private balconies or from behind the backs of crowds. These images from Daraa focus on the masses, carefully hiding individual identities for fear of government arrests and torture. Alongside the text and photographs, a map of North Africa and the Middle East shows three straight lines linking the three places and three further lines, each labelled to indicate the three perspectives, beginning at the same points and converging close to the point marking Tahrir Square to form a long pyramid. The three lines of perspective are replicated on the floor below the installation. The backdrop, on wheels, can be moved to line up with one of the three perspectives, and the artists guide participants to further labels indicating the positions of photographer and photographed in each case. A further perspective – that of surveillance ('The Towering Perspective') – can be adopted by climbing steps to the top of the watchtower and spying, hidden, through small openings. The installation explores the role of the camera in narrating these perspectives.

The differences between these perspectives and the cultural specificity of the three ground-level viewpoints emerge clearly from the text and images accompanying the installation. Such differences can, potentially, be lost in the experience of the installation and in the resulting photographs, if the documentation is not read. The lines of perspective traced on the ground are labelled, as they are in the documentation, but without reference to the country to which they correspond. The shifts in perspective tend to result, moreover, in similar styles of photograph taken against the same backdrop. The points intended to correspond to the Syrian perspective of the 'unexpected photographer' do produce a vision that is to some extent limited, being partially obscured by the structure, but participants tend to adopt the perspectives identified as Tunisian or Egyptian.[37] Some pose as protesters with arms in the air and mouth open, appearing to shout, or smiling with makeshift helmets made of paper plates and plastic cups. Others simply grin or adopt a more serious (or mock-serious) pose. The blog presents together these multiple, often ludic, portraits produced between friends. The photographs are most reminiscent of 'The Perspective of Liberation (the comic drama as portrait in Egypt)' in their frequent use of comical poses and props. One reviewer comments derisively on the touristic mode encouraged by the artists: 'The idea seems strangely close to those painted boards you get at the seaside, where you stick your neck into a head-shaped hole above the painted curves of a buxom beach-babe or a knobble-kneed Victorian bather. "Imagine you took part in the Arab Spring! – Wish you were here!"' (Bathurst, 2012). The performances are seen, from this perspective, to make light of these events, which emerged in specific contexts of oppression and led to violent conflicts and, in Syria, a full-scale war. The photographs in which 'props' indicative of the London art event creep into the frame – glasses of wine, cups of takeaway coffee, or 'helmets' made of paper plates and plastic cups – seem particularly incongruous. These comical performances and photographs can, however, serve productively to highlight this incongruity.

The Watchtower of Happiness is comparable to Wadi Mhiri and Mouna Jemal Siala's *Parti Facelook / Parti Facelike* in involving artgoers in ludic practices reminiscent of social media and tourism and, subsequently, in transferring the results of this process to social media contexts. In this case, the work directly encourages the participants to make selfies or take photographs of each other, like touristic snapshots, and to upload them to the blog. The photographs might call to mind the 'wish you were here' mode, as Bathurst points out, though they are less comparable to the painted boards with a head-shaped hole that she describes than the images produced by Mhiri and Jemal Siala.

[37] The experience of the 'Towering Perspective' is more distinctive, though not many photographs are taken from this angle. The spectator's view of the screen is often obstructed or displaced by participants, though they can imagine the voyeuristic viewpoint, being able to spy, unseen, through the openings in the screen.

They similarly recall, though, the enduring tradition of portraiture (in this case, through props rather than costumes) and that of comic performance (in the nature of the props and the expressions adopted). While the images produced by Mhiri and Jemal Siala's installation are, in addition, reminiscent of a costume party, the images produced by Febrik's participants are visibly connected to an art event. This installation similarly combines contrasting formal and informal, serious and ludic modes. The risks run by Febrik come partly from the use of informal and ludic modes in relation to the revolutionary demonstrations and partly from the greater degree of freedom given to the participants, who make their own images and upload them to the blog. Yet, both works use modes with which the spectators will be familiar, in ways that will be unfamiliar, to provoke a rethinking of images of the revolutions. Contingent encounters evolve through the blog (by contrast with Jemal Siala and Mhiri's use of social media simply to *record* encounters in the installation and surrounding streets). In the London context of Febrik's work, the spectators' production of images of themselves and others, and the practice of uploading their photographs, encourages them to identify with the ordinary person who becomes a revolutionary activist (on the ground and online). At the same time, traces of the London art event might raise awareness – in viewing the collection of images, if not in taking them – of the discrepancy between reality and representation. This discrepancy is indicated by the work's ironic title, associating a mode of surveillance, dominance and power – of internal governments and, perhaps, the international media – with 'happiness'. Although engagements with the installation tend to focus on one type of interaction, the work does signal these ground-level visions as contingent, subversive alternatives to the aerial view, or indeed the view from across the Mediterranean. The experience of incongruities also highlights the discrepancy between the very early stages of the Uprisings and their developments.[38] As the artists claim, 'These first instances of confrontation were equally defiant and gentle, serious and playful' (Febrik, 2012). Their comments seem to refer to the photographs taken in Egypt and Tunisia, rather than in Syria. This work's involvement of spectators actively in an ambivalent process of constructing images provides a

---

[38] The 'wish you were here' subtext perhaps refers, albeit ambiguously, not to the protests but to the art event.

counterpoint to the icons circulated and consumed on social media. For the participants, moreover, viewing the collection of images after the event involves seeing themselves in images of the 'Arab Spring' and remembering the physical experience of making them.

The Watchtower of Happiness and *Parti Facelook / Parti Facelike* exceed iconic languages of revolution through the kinaesthetic and contingent involvement of the diverse spectators and through their ambivalent positioning. The same can be said of Collectif Wanda's installation in relation to its more subtle reimagining of architecture and space. Viewers of these works by Febrik, and Mhiri and Jemal Siala, participate directly. Yet, a more important difference, in relation to contingent encounters of resistance is that they shift between subject and object, photographer and photographed, activist and official (or candidate and voter), artist and social media user, participant and spectator. Their ambivalent position highlights the multiplicity, complexity and instability of narratives behind the reductive metaphor of the 'Arab Spring'.

Participating across Borders: From Textiles to Virtual 'Stitching'

These projects by Hamid, the Ouissis and Kallel, Collectif Wanda, Mhiri and Jemal Siala and Febrik involve others through practices inspired by local or transnational artistic or social means of exchange – participatory or interactive (as conventionally understood). They engage others directly or indirectly at the stage of production or exhibition, or indeed prior to or beyond these stages. A comparison with art across cultures, media and formats reveals the recurrence of distinctive types of participatory contingent encounter to explore diverse revolutionary conditions and trajectories. It also demonstrates the wide range of 'participatory' methods to generate contingency as a means of creating alternative aesthetics of revolution.

The direct involvement of others in fabricating the art object, which can be seen in Hamid's *Mohammed Bouazizi* – and in the embroidered map produced with Collectif Luna as part of the *Laaroussa* project – can also be found in a work exploring the distinct Syrian context by Hazar Bakbachi-Henriot. Bakbachi-Henriot's *Graveyard* (2012), a wall-hanging that displays an abstract arrangement of seated women and gravestones, explores the personal losses of women refugees in

Antakya near the Turkish–Syrian border. It similarly involved a group of women in hand-making an object, which might recall (in this case) textile traditions in Aleppo.[39] *Graveyard* is a collage of pieces of floral cotton fabric stuck to a thin white sheet and roughly sketched with black paint. Bakbachi-Henriot, however, employs contrasting participatory methods to Hamid. The wall-hanging was made by these women, who worked together and in the presence of the artist. The artist conceptualised and supervised the work but did not contribute directly to its fabrication.[40] She was, then, not a 'participant' (the role assumed by Hamid). A direct contribution by the artist could, though, in this work which was completed as a group and by members of the public, have modified the style of the piece and led to a visible distinction between 'professional' and 'amateur' contributions. Bakbachi-Henriot limited her control of the work after the production stage by allowing the wall-hanging to remain as composed by the women (even if, as in Hamid's work, they are not named).[41] In this case, the intimate kinaesthetic process triggered, as the artist has stated, a verbal exchange, allowing the seventeen women (aged fifteen to fifty) to tell their stories of lost loved ones and thereby participate in the '*revolution*' and its representation (Bakbachi-Henriot, cited by Bordier, 2013; emphasis in original). Traces of the women who made the work are reflected by the appearance of glue along certain edges and the roughly penned outlines, as well as by the composition, which also evokes the solidarity encouraged by the work's process: female figures, in black material with flowered headscarves, emerge from the edges of the sheet

---

[39] This artist based in Bordeaux is originally from Aleppo, which is known for its textile manufacturing (Mosaic Initiative, 2012). '[The artist's] aim was to get the women to tell their stories by making collective art that uses embroidery and tapestry as its medium' (Mosaic Initiative, 2012). The medium used is collage, though with cotton fabric which might recall these local traditions. The simple floral pattern contrasts with the often elaborate and gold-threaded patterns of traditional textiles in Aleppo, while it aptly reflects the basic living conditions in the refugee camp.

[40] For this work, the artist organised a two-week art workshop in October 2012 with women in refugee camps in Antakya (Antioche), approximately 30 km from the Turkish–Syrian border with the organisation Urgence Solidarité Syrie (Bordier, 2013).

[41] The artist states, '*j'ai la responsabilité de leur voix*' ('I'm responsible for their voices'), suggesting that she conceives of her role more as that of a facilitator or 'porte-parole' (Hazar Bakbachi-Henriot, cited by Bordier, 2013; emphasis in original).

in a circle.⁴² The particular participatory method selected by Bakbachi-Henriot is connected to the specific location and context of production. For the artist, the creation of this work 'was a means for them to participate in the revolution, so that the world would know they exist and so that we wouldn't see them as helpless victims' (Bakbachi-Henriot, cited by Bordier, 2013; my translation.) Despite crucial differences from Hamid's work in context, theme and method, this work similarly explores a textile-inspired contingent participatory process to evoke alternative, individual, human experiences of 'revolution' beyond iconic images.

The Ouissis and Kallel produce a contingent encounter by allowing the sounds, voices, images or gestures of artisans engaged in a local process, in some measure, indirectly to shape the work. The production of spontaneous, unedited footage can, as we have seen in Chapter 2, be found as a means to exceed icons and the authoritative language of urban planning in contrasting video work by Mouna Karray, Oussema Troudi and Halim Karabibene. The people who enter the frame, in these works – the 'stars' to whom Troudi refers – contribute to their visions of Tunisia, albeit unknowingly; they, too, can be seen to 'participate' in the work indirectly. The participants of *Laaroussa* and *Tisser la médina* contribute in a distinctive way: they are recorded during a directly participatory process, which, as I have argued, becomes an integral stage of the work; they know they are being recorded; they are artisans and the sounds used are those of their practice or of their voices as they communicate this practice through words. The use of people's gestures, by the Ouissis, to develop a choreographic language is, moreover, unique. Yet, in both types of video art, unedited contingent footage of people engaged in everyday creative activities is combined with the artist's parameters to produce a non-iconic representation of Tunisia. A comparable use is made of footage *produced* by people other than the artist to explore the contrasting contexts of the Egyptian and Syrian revolutions.

Khaled Hafez's three-screen *Video Diaries* (2011) combines footage of the demonstrations in Tahrir Square from news channels with that produced on mobile phones and his own video showing the portrait of

---

⁴² The connection between the women is also conveyed by the use of the same floral cloth to denote their headscarves and to surround their figures in the form of gravestones. As Rachel Dedman notes, 'This double use of the material is key to the work[']s impact, connecting human loss to maternal grief' (2013).

Ahmed Basioni, who was killed in the protests.[43] Hafez's simultaneous juxtaposition of plural perspectives of the Egyptian revolution – including both official and unofficial versions – highlights the subjectivity and contingency involved in the process of memory-making. Dia Batal's *Mourning Hall* (2012), by contrast, commemorates the deaths of thousands of Syrians – named and unnamed – in a site-specific installation at the Arab Hall of Leighton House in London.[44] Yet, she similarly commemorates those lost by incorporating found footage of a usually hidden aspect of 'revolution'. In this case, the artist 'excavates' from the internet audio footage of the mourning chants sung at forbidden funeral processions. As the curatorial note tells us, the artist's reinterpretation of the hall is a response to the lack of mourning spaces in Syria during the conflict. Burials and mourning rituals were denied for the families of those killed. People resorted to hurried midnight burials in orchards or public or private gardens to avoid revealing their connections to activists.[45] Batal's use of found footage transforms and re-historicises this room in which the walls are adorned with tiles collected in Syria, Turkey and Persia during the colonial era by the Victorian artist and orientalist Lord Frederick Leighton (completed in 1877). Batal also uses the names and dates of those lost in demonstrations, which she similarly found on the Internet. Over each of the fifteenth- to seventeenth-century hand-painted Damascene tiles covering the walls surrounding the fountain in the centre of the hall, she layers black vinyl in which (in many cases) the name of a man, woman or child is stencilled in Arabic calligraphy. Each name is shown with the dates of the victim's birth and death, when this could be found by the artist.[46] Batal uses a palimpsestic process in dialogue with a 'found' site. Reminiscent of Safadi's *Promises*, we become emotionally involved as we walk around the hall, hearing the mourning chants

---

[43] The mobile phone footage, recorded by a hidden observer, appears to expose an individual shot by the police.

[44] This installation was exhibited as part of the Nour Festival in 2012.

[45] As the curatorial note also tells us, '[a]cts of mourning would turn into protests, and funerals resulted in more funerals'. *Mourning Hall* is informed by the emergence of what the artist has called these 'new collective, spatial, and visual practices' (2012).

[46] A number of tiles show no name – only a poignant series of holes, accompanied by their dates, some of which commemorate the unidentified bodies of children as young as two years old. Others display only a row of three holes, like an ellipsis.

competing with the usually calming sounds of water flowing from the fountain in the centre and physically approaching the partially shrouded tiles. This installation holds in tension discrepant historical moments of external and internal repression in Syria, and incorporates the voices, names and experiences of ordinary people, which creates a space for commemoration and encourages an understanding of the conflict in ways that exceed today's iconic and exoticist visions.

Spectators – like those who contribute, knowingly or unknowingly, prior to the work's exhibition or production – are involved in contingent encounters of resistance, to different degrees. The works of Mhiri and Jemal Siala, and Febrik, are participatory in a conventional sense, given that they involve spectators in producing images, though they develop new (actual and virtual) modes of participation in responding to the revolutions in Tunisia, Egypt and Syria. In terms of contingent encounters, however, these works are continuous with interactive works, including installations and sculptural objects, such as Kossentini's *Heaven and Hell*, Filali's *L'Angle mort*, Safadi's *Promises* and Favaretto's *As If a Ruin* (see Chapters 1 and 2). The spectators alter these works' physical appearance via their movements through or around them. They are involved, however provisionally, in disrupting authoritative visual languages through their shadows or reflections, or via the air they exhale or the draughts they create as they walk. Their contingent movements resist forms associated with stability and order by disturbing the boundaries between subject and object. In the works of Kallel and Collectif Wanda this 'disturbance' through physical movement is extended to the surrounding space. Collectif Wanda's work can be compared, in some respects, to a contrasting piece by Raeda Saadeh, *Wishes Tree* (2012), which was shown at the same festival. As the artist stands in a sprawling white gown, spectators are invited to write their wishes on pieces of multicoloured cloth, which they tie up and throw onto the white fabric in the knowledge that these will be buried at a holy site in the West Bank.[47] *Wishes Tree* is a performance and a

---

[47] We learn this from the assistants who hand out the pieces of cloth and encourage the spectators to write and throw their wishes onto the artist's dress. Saadeh has compared the process to a tree in Turkey where people make their wishes and to the ritual of throwing a coin into the Fontana di Trevi in Italy and making a wish (Saadeh, 2013). In addition to forging these metaphorical connections, this piece is transnational in including a literal journey to the West Bank – a transversal journey when exhibited in Tunis and Sfax.

contextually wider work, and one that encourages spectators to leave a mark: the artist's white dress is gradually covered in their multicoloured wishes – as well as unintended traces such as children's footprints and ice cream. Yet, it similarly involves an encounter over a blank 'canvas' to imagine alternative futures.[48] Saadeh's contingent expression of freedom takes place beside the iconic Bab Al Bahr (also known as the Porte de France) and, therefore, also appears as an alternative counterpoint to architectural order – and particularly to this embodiment of past authoritarianisms in Tunisia. The last stage of this work is invisible, and its ending is indefinite, like that of Kallel's *Tisser la médina*. Such works reveal continuity between provisional and enduring external contributions, which converge in heightening contingency to open a space for alternative voices. The same can be said for certain works that involve spectators by encouraging their engagement with online formats.

Troudi's two-minute videos of 'peripheral' spaces in Tunis in *Deux minutes de Tunis*, to which I referred briefly in Chapter 2, remain open to multiple possibilities for selection and rearrangement, given their plurality and their dependence on online layouts and algorithms – particularly when viewed on Google (Shilton, 2016). Graham, as I stated above, has defined such modes of online engagement as 'interactive', as opposed to 'participatory'. The spectators of Troudi's work do not contribute to the content or form of the individual videos. Yet, in viewing the videos in a different order (encouraged by the algorithm's rearrangement of them), they contribute to the 'reordering' of space; the contingent encounter – and the work itself – continues to evolve at this stage. The contingent encounter in Mohammed Khayata's photographic series, *Stitching My Syria Back* (begun 2014), similarly evolves from the stage of production to that of its

---

[48] The performance might be seen to draw attention, particularly, to the status of women in Tunisia, or in France when presented in Marseilles. Indeed, it was first shown in 2011 at a central square of the Birzeit University at the exhibition 'Framed–Unframed: The Changing Representation of Women in Palestinian Visual Arts', Ethnographic and Art Museum, Birzeit University (see https://universes.art/en/nafas/articles/2011/framed-unframed/img/03-raeda-saadeh/; last accessed November 2018). The artist does not speak and wears a white gown, reminiscent of a bridal gown and symbolic of purity. Yet, she counters the secondary role frequently given to women: 'the idea I want to show is that you come to me, I am the God and you make your wish. I am powerful and strong, I am in the middle, I am the God here, and I have the power of making your wish come true' (Saadeh, 2013).

presentation on Facebook by eliciting the spectators' involvement. Khayata's multiple images show Syrian refugees wearing a patchwork cloak to which they each contributed a piece of material.[49] These participants, and other spectators, comment on the photographs on the Facebook page.[50] Their contingent responses, in this case, do leave a lasting trace, but they do not alter the photographs themselves. They fall between Graham's definitions of participation and interactivity. Indeed, similar to a work's titles or captions, these responses are integral to the works. They situate the images within a dialogue; the people photographed not only look but also *speak* back. These images become part of a wider multilingual and multimodal conversation (messages juxtapose Arabic, French and English, Arabic script and transliterated Arabic, standard and colloquial SMS-style language, words and emoticons or the non-verbal kinaesthetic modes of liking and sharing). Images of Syrian refugees in Lebanon appear, in this context, alongside more recent photographs of friends, curators and other artists based in (and originating from) diverse countries, as well as images of the photographs of refugees – and spectators – at gallery exhibitions, which elicits further commentary. Through this evolving cross-cultural conversation, and visual *mise-en-abyme* of formats and curatorial and cultural contexts, the encounter between artist and participants is extended in a way that forges connections and solidarity within and beyond the Syrian refugee community. Like Kallel's *Tisser la médina*, albeit in a different way and context, this artist employs stitching literally and metaphorically to incorporate marginalised people and build a community.

This wide-ranging artwork conveys and shares diverse 'revolutionary' experiences from loss, commemoration and exile to the precariousness of democratic transition. Yet, it converges in using participation, albeit to different degrees and at distinct stages of the work, in ways that encourage alternative, non-iconic perceptions of a culture – internally and externally – as it follows a distinct trajectory of revolution.

---

[49] People of diverse ages, in various poses against different backdrops, are connected by the leitmotif of the patchwork cloak they wear.
[50] Like the artisans in Kallel's work, many of Khayata's participants become spectator-participants at the stage of the work's exhibition, alongside 'new' spectator-participants.

Conclusion

In these works, as in those explored in Chapter 2, an alternative to iconic faces, spaces or structures is produced in the encounter between the artist and elements that are, to different degrees, beyond the artist's control. Yet, contingency, in these works, is generated through the involvement of others. Many works cross the boundaries established conventionally between definitions of participatory and interactive art, and/or between object and process. This work frequently evolves and shifts between formats and contexts, including private and public, inside and outside, or actual and virtual spaces. Alternatively, it allows participants to assume different roles – successively or simultaneously. Contingent encounters often call for a distinction between, and hold in tension, various stages of the work – from an exchange that precedes the object to a post-exhibition conversation that frames it – and different types and levels of involvement: direct and indirect, knowing and unknowing, provisional or enduring. The participants' impact can be structural – producing, or modifying the composition of, individual parts – or additive – intervening in the work's 'negative' space (that is, the physical or virtual space surrounding the parts) by writing or leaving other traces, rearranging the parts, or moving and thereby highlighting imaginary routes or connections.[51]

This work develops new forms of contingent encounter – and, indeed, participatory art – by harnessing and heightening the unpredictable effects of existing practices, from local textile traditions to transnational forms of exchange particular to social media. Alternatively, it involves others through unedited or found footage, or by using their contingent gestures as the basis for a new corporeal language. All these works involve others specifically as a means of resisting essentialising perspectives of the revolutions in North Africa and the Eastern Mediterranean and the cultures emerging from, or still undergoing, them. The spectators', or other participants', contingent contributions are localised through content, form, material and/or via the particular site – iconic or marginal – in which they emerge.

Participatory art produced in this context tends to be more explicitly political than works exploring primarily other forms of contingent

---

[51] The term 'negative space' is used in art practice to refer to the space around a body or object rendered by the artist.

encounter or evoking an infra-thin critique, even while it avoids straightforward activist statements. A consideration of this art points to the unavoidable implications of balancing control and contingency in participatory art produced in such a politically charged context. This art can run the risk of marginalising its co-producers in the search for new aesthetics, though the hierarchy between artists and this type of participant can be mitigated in the framing and presentation of the work. It might be said, conversely, that works involving participants – particularly spectators – can run the risk of giving them 'too much' freedom, potentially allowing for misinterpretation and hostility, and extreme or extremist views. The spectators' responses are unpredictable, though the meaning of the open work depends, too, to some extent, on the parameters established by the artists and on the context in which the work is presented. The loosening of parameters – including the extension of a work in time or space (physical or virtual) – can, though, allow democratically for plural and conflicting perspectives, as I explore further in the next chapter. Taking such risks tends to be a deliberate and effective means of generating unpredictable responses and exposing wide-ranging views and of gauging and recording uneven public sentiment at a particular moment of a still unfolding revolution. The potential to marginalise artisans or other co-producers is more problematic. Some measure of risk, though, might be explained partly by the necessity to experiment with various forms of participation to forge a way between European or North American aesthetics and (different degrees of) internal constraint on visual expression.

Participatory art creatively explores contingent encounters to allow for alternative voices and visions of revolution. It subtly contributes to shifting perceptions of space and culture in Tunisia, Egypt or Syria and fosters connections within, and frequently far beyond, countries experiencing a revolution. In Chapter 4, I pursue further the idea of encounters as means to exceed iconic sites, and particularly what Marwan Kraidy has called 'spectacular bodies', while focusing on the use of the interface between spectators and the work of art to evoke revolutionary dynamics of liberation and fragility, victimhood and agency.

4 Corporeal Resistance and Aesthetics of the Interface

Diverse manifestations of the Arab Uprisings have frequently been conveyed – in journalism and art – through iconic images of the body, including shouting protesters with raised fists and 'spectacular body acts', from self-immolation to 'nude activism' (see Kraidy, 2016). A particularly complex web of icons surrounds women's participation in the revolutions. Contrasting examples can be found in Samuel Aranda's award-winning World Press photograph of a fully veiled Yemeni woman holding her injured son, the media image of a demonstrator subject to police brutality in Tahrir Square, which became known as 'The Girl in a Blue Bra', and the controversial naked selfie posted on social media by nineteen-year-old Egyptian student Aliaa Al Mahdy (2011).[1]

These images reveal, in divergent ways, the tendency of revolutionary imagery to portray women as victims and/or heroines. Aranda's photograph presents an anonymous woman as a passive victim of the events. His image calls to mind the Madonna-and-child composition, which can be found in works such as Michelangelo's *Pietà* (1498–1500), problematically absorbing the complex and uneven Arab Uprisings into Christian frames of reference. 'The Girl in a Blue Bra' was an active participant, though she similarly becomes an anonymous type – a martyr and a heroine – through the making and remaking of this icon.[2] The photograph of Aliaa Al Mahdy, who confronts the camera wearing nothing but a red flower and red shoes, is distinct in portraying not a victim of physical violence but an individualised act of resistance to the marginalisation of women, more

---

[1] Aliaa Al Mahdy's photograph appeared on her blog *A Rebel's Diary* on 23 October 2011. It was followed by Tunisian Amina Sboui's posting of a naked photograph of herself on Facebook, her torso displaying the words 'My body belongs to me, and is not related to anyone's honor', on 11 March 2013.
[2] On this photograph and its reworkings, see Hafez (2014) and Kraidy (2016: 177–81).

widely, which was recorded and disseminated by the performer herself. This image, though, similarly used the female body to convey an ideological message. While some perceived this naked, sexually provocative body as heroic and revolutionary, many saw it as traitorous, anti-revolutionary and anti-Egyptian.[3] (The response to the Tunisian Amina Sboui's naked selfies was similarly fractured (see Kraidy, 2016).) The denunciations and death threats Al Mahdy received drove her to seek asylum in Sweden (see Hafez, 2014). As Sherine Hafez asserts, 'It is essential not to discount her attempt to confront this oppressive structure in the most stark way possible, yet her attempts at challenging the growing misogyny in Egypt employed the very same techniques of gender ideology, her body. Hence, Aliaa reaffirmed the centrality of women's bodies as a terrain of conflict rather than escaped the terms of its discourse' (2014: 183). This body came, in fact, we might say, to represent a victim of the revolution, reflecting the perceived need to define the nation in uncertain times.

While all three images call to mind Hariman and Lucaites's emphasis on the ideological uses of icons, Al Mahdy's photograph is particularly illustrative of the way in which an image 'exceeds any code' and can, therefore, lend itself to alternative ideological uses.[4] Such images highlight the difficulty of depicting the body – especially the female body –

---

[3] As Hafez details, those opposed to the photographs included liberals and feminist groups, who felt that their demands for gender equality might be 'parochialised' and the complexity of women's struggle in Egypt be 'reduced ... to the superficial issue of dress/undress' (2014: 183). The controversy was exacerbated by Al Mahdy's association with *Femen*, a Russia-based group which has been criticised for their reductive brand of feminism, including their simplistic view of veiling as oppressive (Hafez, 2014: 183). As Kraidy states, 'This was the argument: al-Mahdy's act was Western in spirit, hence inauthentic', though, as he indicates, following other critics, 'the female body has a long history of being sexualised in the Arab world and particularly in Egypt' and, moreover, 'no one directed the same argument about political and cultural inauthenticity at Mohamed Bouazizi' (Kraidy, 2016: 162). As Kraidy argues, the controversy triggered by Al Mahdy's photograph was also due to its explosive mix of politics and sexuality and its aesthetic equivocality ('she was at once creator, model, raw material, creation ..., promoter and publicist' (167)). On this photograph, and comparisons to that of Amina Sboui, the case of Samira Ibrahim Mohamed, and the 'Blue Bra Girl' icon, see Kraidy (2016: 157–200).

[4] As Hariman and Lucaites state, 'Because an image both exceeds any code and remains relatively inarticulate, it can become a site not only for the ideological relay but also for depicting the dynamic negotiations that are the rich, embodied play of societal power relations in everyday life' (2007: 9).

without encouraging binary perceptions of the revolutions, while they also reveal the particular risks involved in uncovering women's bodies in contexts such as that of Egypt or Tunisia.[5] Yet, a range of alternative corporeal means of exploring the revolutions exists. This chapter explores works that encourage a rethinking of icons or iconic spaces by displaying ambivalent performances between concealing and revealing in ways that allow for a renegotiation of this familiar trope of Orientalism and counter-Orientalism. These performances – by women or men – are imaged in photography or video. The works are exhibited in galleries or online. Some display performances in studios or outdoors; others capture live interventions in the street, using graffiti, photography or dance (see, for example, 'Je danserai malgré tout 3', at www.youtube.com/watch?v=4OfWQ2GaVHg). While some performances dialogue allusively with a transnational range of enduring icons, others rework a physically present national flag or intervene at a local public site. Yet, I argue, they converge in displaying both body and icon as part of a multi-layered interface that interpolates yet distances their diversely located (and travelled) spectators to convey ongoing revolutions between constraint and resistance.

My use of the term 'interface' is inspired by Meriem Bouderbala's comment on this as: 'ce qui sépare le corps de chair de ce qui l'offre au regard: la peau, les enveloppes et les étoffes' ('that which separates the body from that which offers it to the gaze: skin, coverings and fabrics') (2012). Bouderbala compares this interface to an Islamic tradition, in which marks on the skin or folds of fabric both beautify and hide the body: 'Les marques sur la peau l'embellissent autant qu'elles la masquent; le drapé des étoffes dissimule autant le corps qu'il l'exalte dans son mystère' ('The markings on the skin beautify as much as they mask it; the folds of the fabrics conceal the body just as much as they exalt it in its mystery') (Bouderbala, 2012). But works exploring the revolutions tend to conceal or reveal specifically to convey revolutionary dynamics of constraint yet agency, censorship yet freedom of expression, or resistance yet fragility and uncertainty with regard to the future. Bouderbala refers to the ambiguities she explores in her own work: 'Parfois j'expose des fragments cutanés marqués de signes, de

---

[5] Kraidy compares Al Mahdy's photograph to Delacroix's partially nude Marianne in *La Liberté guidant le peuple* (1830) and to reappropriations of this revolutionary image (see Kraidy, 2016: 162–69).

scarifications, de blessures; parfois je m'arrête au tissu qui couvre le corps et l'enveloppe comme une chrysalide fragile ou comme une carapace hostile' ('Sometimes I expose the cutaneous fragments marked with signs, with scarifications, with wounds; sometimes I stop at the material that covers the body and envelops it like a fragile chrysalis or like a hostile carapace') (2012).[6] Yet, the work I address in this chapter tends to mark or cover the skin, or obscure the body almost entirely, through alternative uses of fabric – or other materials – and/or via framing, editing or camerawork. I consider shifts between concealing and revealing more widely, moreover, to encompass images of performance between work of art and *hors champ*, clandestine act and public intervention, and between spaces: physical and virtual, local and transnational. I show how the extension of the process of obscuring and exposing created by presenting the performance on screen – and, frequently, online – constructs a 'multi-layered interface' between the spectators and what is presented.

In maintaining a gap and point of tension between object and subject these works also resonate, to some extent, with Amelia Jones's argument that certain images of the body immerse the spectator but 'retain rather than attempting to resolve or disavow [the] tension between the subjective and objective world' (2013: 370). In her wide-ranging chapter Jones theorises how such images of the body exceed the oppositional models of signification constructed by Renaissance painting and perpetuated by the media of photography and cinema. Her focus is on work that breaks with enduring 'Euro-American' perceptions of self and image that suggest these entities are coincident or radically opposed. Jones argues that such models are exceeded in images of the body through the embodiment of the spectators by haptic or auditory elements. She draws on the work of critics, including Laura U. Marks, on film that provokes a tactile mode of seeing.[7] She also highlights, citing technotheorist Lev Manovich, how spectators are immersed in images in the digital era through the two-way communication that these images promote: 'computer representation makes

---

[6] Examples of the 'scarifications' and 'blessures' to which she alludes can be found in her series of ink and wash paintings exploring martyrs of the Tunisian revolution, to which I referred in Chapter 1 (*The Awakened*, 2011; see VIII and VIX).

[7] Jones engages with a complex range of work, including uses of Merleau-Ponty by Marks and Sobchack, Copjec's use of Lacan, and Derrida's critique of Kantian aesthetics.

every image inherently mutable – creating signs that are no longer just mobile but also forever modifiable' (Manovich, 2001: 174, cited by Jones, 2013: 377). She suggests that the tension between subjective and objective worlds is nonetheless maintained through the spectators' inevitable critical distance from the work; that is, their understanding of it as an image. The works I explore here also use photography or video in ways that exceed the oppositional models on which these media were originally based. But they do so partly by drawing on local or regional corporeal practices, which they similarly contest and develop. They interpolate the spectators through sensorial elements, resonating with Jones's argument. Yet, they produce a multi-layered interface specifically by partially obscuring, distorting or reworking the bodies and icons or iconic spaces they display through material, medial and cultural elements. They tend to show the body interacting with visual icons, verbal languages or specific sites.

These works can familiarise and alienate diverse internal and external spectators in ways that depend on their location and knowledge. The gap between object and subject can also be heightened through the use of contingent materials, the peripatetic mode or the involvement of others, or the dialectic between presence and absence. These images of performance resonate, in these ways, with the works I considered in the first three chapters, while they show such materials and processes interacting with a disruptive contingent body. A comparable gap between object and subject can be discerned in all the works in this study, in which such means can be seen diversely to protect opacity and resist definitions of the revolutions as stable and complete. The concept of the 'multi-layered interface' can encompass works that ambivalently interpolate spectators by immersing them while simultaneously distorting or constraining their view of a potentially iconic body, object or scene. I return to the potential extension of this idea in the conclusion to this book. In the meantime, this chapter focuses specifically on the construction of this interface and its development through the interconnected processes of imaging and performing the body.

I begin by examining works that allude critically to a range of icons of European or Arabic and Persian origins to evoke women's participation in the Arab Uprisings and pose questions regarding their future. Such references are combined with alternative uses of photography and Arabic calligraphy in *Bullets* and *Bullets Revisited* (2012–13) by Lalla Essaydi (who works between Morocco and the United States) and

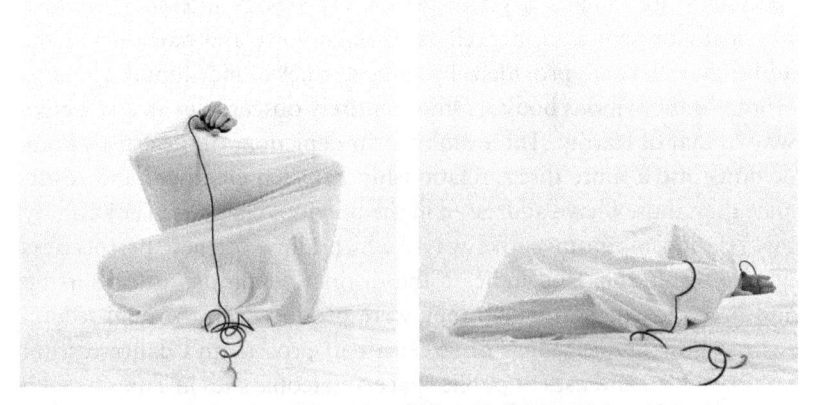

Figure 4.1 Mouna Karray, *Noir#4* and *Noir#8* (2013; 126 × 126 cm).
© Mouna Karray and ADAGP, Paris and DACS, London 2020

Liberté, j'écrirai ton nom (2012) by Majida Khattari (based in Paris). I consider the extent to which their aesthetics of concealing and revealing, and their dialogues with European images, question 'icons of revolutionary exoticism'. Contrasting performances of 'revolution' can be found in some works that respond to the specific contexts of Tunisia, Libya and Syria – from within or beyond these countries (there is not a neat division between 'diaspora' and 'local' works). In the second section I address how such works reveal new means of partially obscuring the body which confront more directly the revolutionary dynamics of constraint and liberation, but also fragility and uncertainty. I show how Tunis-based Mouna Karray's photographic series *Noir* (2013; Figure 4.1), inspired by the oppression experienced under Ben Ali, interpolates spectators by displaying the artist in white fabric against a white background, her body constricted and entirely concealed with the exception of her hand clasping the end of the shutter cord.

Comparable revolutionary dynamics can be produced in art exploring divergent contexts and through the medium of video. UK-based Naziha Arebi's *Granny's Flags* (2012) focuses on her grandmother sewing the flag of opposition to Gaddafi's regime in Tripoli. *LIBERTé* (2011), by Philip Horani (a pseudonym), screens the artist's own (partially hidden) performance as he paints the Syrian flag, superimposed by footage of demonstrations.[8] Through both works,

---

[8] The footage, according to the credits, was produced in Syria.

spectators are immersed yet distanced via a body interacting with a physically present icon, as well as through voice and narrative or the additional 'layers' provided by music tracks and found footage. Horani's anonymous body is almost entirely obscured in an alternative way to that of Karray. These ambivalent depictions of the artist's body demonstrate a more direct relationship between creativity and resistance than those I have addressed in the previous chapters. They convey this relationship in inventive ways, which allow for new perspectives on the revolutions and indicate the distinct conditions of censorship and precariousness in which they were produced. In the final section I show how online videos of street art in process and dance disrupt familiar views and uses of public space and iconic sites in Tunisia. Such videos display diverse interventions, including the 'calligraffiti' of El Seed (who currently lives in Dubai), the slogans and stencils of Tunis-based Ahl Al Kahf, a participatory photographic street art project led by Paris-based 'JR' (*InsideOut*, 'Part 1 – Tunis', 2011) and a series of dances by Tunis-based Art Solution (*Je danserai malgré tout*, 2011–13). I argue that these videos interpolate their diverse global audience in ways that compare with Horani's creation of a multi-layered multisensorial interface, while increasing its complexity by extending the performance in time and space.

Concealing and Revealing: Beyond Revolutionary Exoticism?

Lalla Essaydi's *Bullets* and *Bullets Revisited* (2012–13) and Majida Khattari's *Liberté, j'écrirai ton nom* (2012) focus on women's participation in the diverse revolutions and ask questions regarding the treatment and perceptions of women since the beginning of 2011. These artists' dialogue with Orientalist (and other clichéd) images to explore women and the Arab Uprisings runs the risk of reifying such images. Yet, they each construct a complex interface which encourages a rethinking of simplistic narratives of revolution. Both evoke women between constraint and liberation, victimhood and revolutionary heroism.

The shimmering golden photographs of women within opulent interiors in Lalla Essaydi's collections, *Bullets* and *Bullets Revisited*, might remind us of Orientalist paintings (see http://lallaessaydi.com/11.html and http://lallaessaydi.com/13.html). These paintings often portrayed timeless exotic, erotic harem scenes in which women lounged idly, as if unaware of the male painter's presence (see, for example, Ingres's *Grande Odalisque* (1814) or Delacroix's *Femmes d'Alger dans leur appartement* (Women of Algiers in their Apartment) (1834)). Yet, Essaydi's photographs aim to discourage the experience of voyeurism and passive contemplation. Since the mid-1990s this artist has been reworking Orientalist paintings by French, British and American artists, including Delacroix, Ingres, Sargent and Leighton – at times, explicitly, as in *Grande Odalisque 2* (*Les Femmes du Maroc* (The Women of Morocco), 2008). She replaces their mysterious, often passive, languorous and sexually available odalisques with clothed women, whose hair is modestly covered, and who confront the camera. The exposed parts of the women's skin – and the fabric they wear – are covered in Arabic handwriting. This language, like the images, is distorted and illegible even to those who read Arabic. The artist subversively writes (traditionally a practice restricted to men) in henna, which is used in the Maghreb to decorate women's skin for marriage ceremonies and other celebrations. The images are framed by irregular Kodak borders, recalling photographic negatives, to draw attention to the constructed nature of images. These practices contest Orientalist clichés, while simultaneously defying the boundaries that separate men and women in Moroccan society.

The work Essaydi has produced since 2011 differs most obviously in its use of golden bullet casings for the interiors and detail of the women's costumes to anchor the scene in the context of the Arab Uprisings. The artist states of her *Bullets* series:

The body of work evolved as a response to the developments in Morocco and the rest of the Arab world. This new work references fear about growing restrictions on women in the new, post-revolutionary era that followed demonstrations in the Arab world. / This new series is much more openly confrontational since the visual vocabulary I chose alludes directly to violence and violence projected on women. Women have been at the forefront of the uprisings in the Arab world, and as soon as these new regimes took hold, women were subordinated anew. It alludes to women's active role in the Arab Spring, but also to their subordination since then. (Essaydi, in interview with Esman, 2013: 6–7)

These works might be seen to refer to women's participation in the Moroccan February 20th Movement or in revolutions such as that in neighbouring Tunisia or Egypt, and the violence against women demonstrators in squares such as Cairo's Tahrir Square (Essaydi, in interview with Kippelen, 2017; on this violence, see, for example, Hafez, 2014). Essaydi's reference to women's subordination post-revolution might refer to the controversy in Tunisia provoked by the draft constitution (released in August 2012) in which women's role would be 'complementary' rather than 'equal' to that of men (as I noted in Chapters 1 and 3). But she avoids reducing a complex range of perspectives to binary perceptions of secularism and religion: she also states that women's 'subordination' 'is about ... preventing them from fully exercising the rights Islam grants them' (Essaydi, in interview with Esman, 2013: 7). The artist's reference to 'violence projected on women' can be taken to include enduring Orientalist clichés.

The bullets in these series are troubling in seeming to aestheticise violence. They heighten the ambiguity that is already present in Essaydi's parody of Orientalist paintings, which hovers between critique and homage, and her use of models who conform to conventional notions of beauty.[9] These photographs run the risk of being misinterpreted and reifying the clichés they were intended to contest, particularly if they are viewed in isolation. Yet, it is their aesthetic qualities that, arguably, draw spectators in, only to make them reassess expectations they might have had. Essaydi's *Bullets* and *Bullets Revisited* can draw attention to the violence experienced by women, while also signalling their agency. They do so by developing an ambivalent interface through the use of bullet casings and writing in henna, in conjunction with means of framing and positioning the body.

The bullet casings contribute to immersing the spectators sensorially in the work. The shimmering surface encourages them to move physically towards it. Yet, they are then unsettled when they recognise the objects as bullets. In addition, while the bullet casings push the women forward, they contribute to diminishing their space. The use of the same material for the back, middle and (parts of the) foreground seems to absorb the women within the décor. Space is also restricted by the framing of the image closely to the women. Some photographs – *Bullet#2*, for example – are presented from above, eliminating a

---

[9] While wishing to undermine these paintings the artist admits that she is also fascinated by them and, in turn, wants to produce beautiful objects. The artist reiterated this at a talk on the occasion of her exhibition of works from the *Bullets* and *Bullets Revisited* series at Kashya Hildebrand, London, 2013, when a spectator questioned her as to the potential for her photographs to reinforce Orientalist clichés.

'middle ground'. Gloria Wiley perceives a possible reference, in Essaydi's use of 'all-encompassing gold patterns', to Klimt's work (Wiley, 2013: 7). Wiley makes this point in relation to *Bullets Revisited#3* (2012), while the association to Klimt is perhaps even stronger in those photographs taken from above, which produces a more extreme effect of spatial flattening.[10] In these ways, the use of bullet casings appears to signal the violence experienced by women.[11] Yet, it is the bullet casings that remind us of women's active participation in the Uprisings.

The spectators are also ambivalently interpolated by the Arabic writing on the women's bodies. The use of henna both hides and beautifies the women, reminiscent of Bouderbala's words regarding Islamic tradition. Yet, the use of henna to write on the body produces a more complex interface. Presented together with bullet casings, the text – evidencing a traditionally male practice – might appear simply to provide a further symbol of power and to reinforce the impression of patriarchal domination. Yet, the text belongs to a woman. It consists of fragments from the artist's personal diaries.[12] It is intended to empower the women before us by giving them a voice. The practice of writing over the female body achieves a similar ambivalent effect to that in Shirin Neshat's photographs in her series *Women of Allah* (1993–97), though Neshat uses female-authored Persian poetry. The use of Arabic serves in Essaydi's work to protect women from definition; it is intended to alienate most Western viewers.[13] Yet, in the work of Essaydi, calligraphy can also be seen to protect women from *internal* attempts to define and subordinate them, since it is, for the most part, illegible also to those who read Arabic.[14] Certain individual

---

[10] The image embedded in Wiley's article is Klimt's *Portrait of Adele Bloch-Bauer I* (1907).

[11] Violence is also signalled ambivalently in the fragmentation of women's bodies via the use of diptychs and triptychs, which are reminiscent of Christian alterpieces.

[12] This is not actually known at the exhibition (as seen at *Beyond Beauty*, an exhibition focusing on five bodies of work by Essaydi produced between 2003 to 2012; Kashya Hildebrand Gallery, London, 24 October–8 December 2013). It has been stated by reviewers and by the artist herself at her talk at the Kashya Hildebrand Gallery (2013).

[13] The use of Arabic for this purpose can be found in Mona Hatoum's video installation *Measures of Distance* (1988) and a 'dress-sculpture' performed at Majida Khattari's *Défilé-Performance 1* ('Mahjouba', 1996, ENSBA, Paris).

[14] This was also intended by the artist.

letters and words are legible. Occasionally, it is possible to discern nouns (in one work, for example, the words for 'the people' (الناس) and 'the world' (العالم) can be found in one photograph), but, usually, only certain prepositions can be identified. There are no sentences. The writing, like the women, resists understanding. Essaydi's use of writing also differs from that of Neshat in that she marks the skin directly. The lines of unpunctuated writing are fragmented because they follow the contours of the body, winding around and behind the arms, hands, feet or face, or sinking into the obscurity of a partially closed fist. When arms are raised or bodies are horizontal, the text appears on a diagonal or upside down. Writing, in a reversal of the usual dynamic, is subordinated to the movements of the body. The same can be said of photography: its static, single perspective – which is associated with power and possession in colonial studio portraits – emerges here as limited, as indicative merely of a contingent and partial viewpoint. In Essaydi's images the body is, to some extent, controlled through photographic features such as framing, camera angle or level of focus. Yet the same devices are employed – in conjunction with ambiguous materials or contingent processes – to allow the body, in some measure, to escape the artist's control and the spectators' gaze. The writing curves away from us or appears to blur through the effect of foreshortening. Written on the elastic surface of the skin, the letters do not always succeed each other in a straight line; the dots (which are crucial to differentiating many letters in Arabic) can appear out of place.

Critics have commented on the subversive use of henna, given its associations with the female body. But henna is also subversive because it is an organic product that fades with time, and more rapidly in areas where the skin naturally folds, stretches or becomes moist. Certain areas of the text in the photographs have faded to a light orange colour. This contributes to the illegibility of the writing. Language is subject to the natural laws of a fluid, ephemeral material. Writing emerges, then, between communication and decoration, presence and absence. The organic material works in conjunction with the uneven, organic surface of the living body. In Essaydi's work the translatable, transparent languages of calligraphy and photography, associated originally with 'Eastern' and 'Western' ways of seeing, are reused to retain the gap between object and subject to protect opacity.

A further factor lends the women in the photographs agency and the power to resist simplistic views. This is the models' involvement in the process of making the photograph. Prior to taking the photograph, the artist discusses with the women the poses she would like them to adopt and asks if they agree.[15] Therefore, the bodies' positions emerge, at least to some extent, in the dialogue between artist and models; that is, between control and contingency. In Essaydi's earlier collections the models were involved to a greater extent by writing on the fabric and furnishings to be photographed. In certain photographs for Essaydi's *Les Femmes du Maroc*, we see the women writing on the fabric. We learn, in relation to the series *Converging Territories* (2004), that the artist considers her work 'a collaborative endeavour' produced with the women who pose for her photographs (we also learn that these women are of Moroccan heritage); her photographs 'are not uniquely personal; they also represent a narrative shared by women with similar understanding of Islamic heritage, cultural mobility, and gender identity' (Nasser-Khadivi and Rafif, eds., 2015: 112). The photographs are taken following hours of preparation during which the women (including the artist) exchange memories and experiences (Nasser-Khadivi and Rafif, eds., 2015: 112). This work departs from the definition of 'collaboration' and the greater degrees of participation I discussed in Chapter 3, but the women do contribute, to some extent, to the works of art. In the *Bullets* series, the women did not actually contribute to the process of writing, but the inscribed fabric worn by some echoes that produced by the women for the earlier series. The inclusion of images from the earlier series at exhibitions of *Bullets* encourages us to see the more recent works as a continuation of this conversation (as at Kashya Hildebrand Gallery, London, 2013). Essaydi's aesthetic of the interface is complicated further by references to a range of icons and apparently stable visual languages.

In *Bullet#19* the woman's pose is reminiscent of that of women in certain Orientalist paintings, such Benjamin Constant's *Reclining Odalisque* (*c.*1870). Yet, it is also reminiscent of an icon of the French Revolution, which depicts the assassinated revolutionary leader Jean-Paul Marat (*La Mort de Marat*, Jacques-Louis David, 1793). In Essaydi's image, the pose is reversed, and a living woman takes the place of the iconic assassinated male revolutionary, turning to confront

---

[15] Lalla Essaydi provided this information in response to my question at the artist's talk related to her exhibition 'Beyond Beauty', Kashya Hildebrand, London, 2013.

the spectator. It seems to allude to violence against women, and to the death of many women who participated in the demonstrations, but it also emphasises life and women's agency. This image is situated between past and future, appearing to commemorate the female martyrs while critiquing subsequent attempts to limit women's freedom and rights, and signalling that the revolutions are ongoing. It might be taken to indicate that the 'revolution' in Morocco is merely dormant, or that the fight for women's rights in Tunisia or Egypt continues. Essaydi's works counter the tendency to compare diverse manifestations of the Arab Uprisings to the French Revolution. A similarly ambivalent message is conveyed by *Bullets Revisited#3*, which, as Wiley notes, reworks Hans Holbein the Younger's *Dead Christ* (Wiley, 2013). Essaydi's photograph of a reclining woman with an elongated hanging arm is also reminiscent of Michelangelo's *Pietà* (1498–1500), to which David's painting of Marat has frequently been compared.[16] In Essaydi's reference to the *Pietà* – and perhaps also in her reworking of the *Dead Christ* – we might discern a parody of the use of Western Christian iconography to comment on complex events in the MENA region. Aranda's icon of the 'Arab Spring' resonates with sculptures and images of the Madonna and Child (like Hocine Zarouar's award-winning World Press photograph, *La Madone de Bentalha* (1997), which became an icon of the Algerian Civil War of the 1990s).

Essaydi's photographs allude ambiguously to other icons and practices that involve the female body, and which would be more universally recognisable. In *Bullet#15* she reworks the Roman goddess and symbol of justice. The dove, symbol of peace, is outweighed and the woman lacks the blindfold that signals objective judgement. This image appears to indicate the lack of justice for women following the Uprisings. The photograph can perhaps also be interpreted as an ironic reference to the enduring tendency to reduce women to symbols in Western art and wider visual culture, which is at odds with certain 'feminist' views of the perceived oppressed 'Arab woman'. We might interpret in a similar way Essaydi's engagement with contemporary practices of fashion photography, which is frequently associated with

---

[16] When Gloria Wiley compares Essaydi's work to that of Klimt (see above), she refers to the 'Byzantine aura' of his intricate gold patterns (2013: 7), suggesting a further possible connection to Christian imagery.

objectification (this can be seen, for example, in the poses and the emphasis given to the fabric in *Bullets Revisited #20* and *#23*). In adopting subtly different poses and positions, and in staring towards the viewer, the women photographed by Essaydi seem to refuse to be assimilated into pre-existing iconographies and frames of reference.

In seeking to convey the uncertainty for women in North Africa today, this artist's photographs develop an ambivalent interface. The women's hennaed skin might remind us of Bouderbala's words regarding the ambivalent marking of women's skin in Islamic tradition. But, in this case, henna is used to write, which produces further ambiguities. The emphasis on the surface of the skin – and the women's engagement of the viewer with their gaze – resonates with the immersive imaged bodies analysed by Amelia Jones. Yet, the gap is maintained through framing, camera angle and composition, as well as the introduction of unfamiliar elements (linguistic, material or corporeal). Essaydi develops a more complex interface. She photographs the female body, but presents ambivalent bodies between concealing and revealing, control and contingency, and between shifting degrees of familiarity and unfamiliarity, fascination and uneasiness, depending on who is viewing. Essaydi's dialogue with Orientalism is unsettling, even when framed within an exhibition. Yet, her *Bullets* series can be appreciated as a subtle parody. The bodies emerge from the opulent décor, and yet escape our gaze, protecting opacity between and within cultures and communities. The ambivalent dynamics in this artwork evoke constraint yet agency, stasis yet dynamism. 'Revolution' emerges not as a closed chapter – as a success or a failure – but as an ongoing process. This work evokes both past and future; it commemorates while looking forwards; it communicates uncertainty yet also possibility. A similar interface can be found in Majida Khattari's contemporaneous collection of photo-tableaux, while her work reveals distinctive photographic aesthetics of concealing and revealing the body and allowing it to shift between stability and instability.

Khattari's collection, *Liberté, j'écrirai ton nom* (exhibited at L'Institut des Cultures d'Islam, Paris, in the context of the festival '#Libertés!', 2012), comprises three interconnected photographs. Each presents ensembles of women and men, veiled or in different states of undress, sitting, standing or reclining among swathes of luxurious fabric. The collection crosses references to painting, photography and literature from diverse regions and countries, which are provided for spectators in a text presenting the work. *Majnoun* (meaning Madman – or the Mad one), presented on the left-hand side of the room, is intended to evoke the tragic ancient love story of *Majnoun and Leïla*, known across the Middle East and North Africa, as well as Michelangelo's *Pietà* and Aranda's World Press photograph of a Yemeni woman and her son. The work in the centre, on the back wall, is *Noeud Gordien*, intended to allude to Ingres's Orientalist *Bain turc* (1852–59, modified 1862). The photograph on the right takes the same title as Delacroix's painting of the French revolution of 1830, *La Liberté guidant le peuple*, while the central figure in this reworking, a woman veiled in black, looks towards us with the imperative 'Read' ('اقرأ') written across the fabric covering her head. The photographs in the entrance hall each depict a woman, partially covered in fabric, sprawling on the ground as if she has fallen: the fall of the female body is used as a metaphor for the fall of dictatorships. These photographs are collectively entitled *Clinamen*. In Epicurean philosophy the 'clinamen' is the unpredictable swerve of falling atoms).[17]

Khattari's photographic series is exhibited alongside her installation *Hymne à la vie*, which alludes, unambiguously, to the irrepressible voices of revolution – particularly, the Tunisian revolution. This piece, which fills the adjoining room, encourages spectators to follow a path through multiple ceramic 'shoots' springing from a bed of charcoal and painted with jasmine and the words of the Tunisian national anthem. These icons are exceeded via the suggestion of contingent organic growth, reminiscent of Filali's *Bourgeons* (see Chapter 2).[18] In addition, spectators are encouraged to participate by writing their own slogans on the surrounding walls, mimicking this act of resistance in the public spaces of countries undergoing a revolution. The photographic series, by contrast, might seem to convey a pessimistic view of the Arab Uprisings through fallen bodies enveloped in darkness. The use of the trope of veiling and unveiling is troubling in recalling Orientalist images. Yet, a closer consideration of the series reveals that it also contains a subtle

---

[17] The sources of inspiration for Khattari's works were noted in the sheet accompanying the exhibition by curator Véronique Rieffel. This was entitled: 'Liberté, j'écrirai ton nom' (which modifies the refrain of Eluard's poem of resistance to the occupation of France by shifting the verb 'écrire' into the future tense; Paul Eluard, 'Liberté', *Poésie et Vérité*, 1942 and *Au rendez-vous allemand*, 1945).

[18] I have discussed an earlier version of Majida Khattari's *Hymne à la vie* in Shilton 2013b.

critique of reductive perceptions of the revolutions and the societies in which they emerged. It conveys the uncertainty of 'revolution' and asks questions about the future of countries in transition.

In an online video interview about this work, Khattari emphasises the ongoing nature of the Uprisings, which, she says, are just beginning. Her words – like her collection – resonate with Essaydi's work, and with many works exploring the revolutions, in indicating the need to think beyond the binaries of success or failure, or indeed Western democracy and radical Islamism:

[C]'est vrai qu'on parle déjà d'hiver et on parle de révoltes ratées ... Je ne suis pas d'accord du tout avec tout ça parce que ça ne fait que commencer. On a besoin de temps, on a besoin d'éducation, on a besoin d'information. On a besoin d'énormément de choses pour évoluer et on ne peut pas juste du jour au lendemain avoir une démocratie, et en plus avoir une démocratie à la manière de tel pays ou tel autre ... On a surtout besoin de temps et de travail et de réflexion – et pas de censure. J'ai voulu répondre à ce qui se passe dans le monde arabe et je voulais évoquer cette notion de liberté qui est en ce moment vue et entendue différemment. (Khattari, in interview with Mondomix, 2012)

([I]t's true that we're already speaking about winter and we speak about failed revolts ... I don't agree at all with all that because it's only just beginning. We need time, we need education, we need information. We need so many things to be able to evolve and we can't just, from one day to the next, have a democracy, and, in addition, have a democracy in the style of such and such a country or another ... We particularly need time and work and reflection – and no censorship. I wanted to respond to what's happening in the Arab world and I wanted to evoke this notion of freedom which is, at this moment in time, seen and understood differently.)

Khattari's words anticipate Khouri's call for patience and humility in attempting to understand the complex revolutions (Khouri, 2014: 14). Her insistence on the need for an absence of censorship is reflected in her choice to explore the idea of freedom through the body, particularly the female body, which has long been used to evoke freedom in the history of painting: 'Je voulais cette liberté dans mes images: voilées, pas voilées, habillées, déshabillées' ('I wanted this freedom in my images: veiled, not veiled, dressed, undressed') (Khattari, in interview with Mondomix, 2012).[19]

---

[19] This ambivalence between veiling and unveiling is reminiscent of Khattari's aesthetics in her live *défilés-performances* (catwalk-performances), in which she has sought a 'third way' between arguments for or against veiling in France since 1996. She adapts her aesthetics in this photographic work.

While very different in appearance to Essaydi's photographs, those by Khattari convey uncertainty, maintaining the tension between embodied subjects – viewed and viewing – via a number of comparable manoeuvres. In these photographs, it is the use of lighting, and sometimes of close-up shots, which draws attention to the surfaces of both skin and luxurious textured or shining silk fabric. At the same time, the bodies are partially obscured from the spectators. They similarly occupy an ambivalent location between foreground and background. Yet, contrasting with the impression of entrapment within a compressed, airless vault, some of Khattari's photographs evoke uncontrolled movement through boundless space. The ambivalent location is heightened through dramatic contrasts between light and darkness. The figures appear to emerge from a black background evacuated of spatial or dimensional cues. The women in the *Clinamen* series appear as fallen or, in the absence of a visible base, as still falling through the void. There is a possible reference, here, to images of the Fall of Icarus, which would suggest, pessimistically, that the revolutions were over-ambitious. Yet, the Epicurean idea of an unpredictable swerve that inspired the artist is more ambiguous, suggesting freedom from dictatorship and convention but also chaos, an inevitable evolution but without a clear sense of direction. The sense of transition, of revolutions that have resulted in a decisive shift but cannot yet be viewed as complete, is echoed in the use of fragments of frames, which pin down only two opposite corners of each of the three principal works.[20] These are reminiscent of the unfinished appearance given to the borders of Essaydi's images, which similarly conveys the revolutions – and women's identities – in process. The traditionally single viewpoint is multiplied through the shifting angles and levels of focus, which are combined via the triptych (also used by Essaydi).

Comparable to Essaydi's work, the bodies' poses and arrangements allude to – yet ambiguously rework – icons and practices from distinct cultural traditions. Spectators are similarly interpolated and distanced via a complex imbrication of physical and metaphorical elements. The central photograph undermines the hierarchies between cultures and genders constructed by paintings such as *Bain turc*, by presenting

---

[20] Rieffel refers to this allusion to a still ongoing revolution in terms of an 'esthétique de l'inachevé' (see note 17 for source).

partially covered women and men.[21] In presenting male bodies, Khattari questions the feminisation of the Orient and the sexualisation of the colonial relationship in Orientalist painting. We might also compare this image to Delacroix's *La Mort de Sardanapale* (1827) in its arrangement of partially nude women and men, though the men in Khattari's photograph lie draped in fabric like the women.[22] The complicity established between viewers and viewed through Orientalist painting is also disrupted by the juxtaposition of three images. The circular frame given to *Bain turc*, which encourages the voyeur to spy through a hole in the wall is, in addition, replaced here by the incompletely framed photograph. The title of this work alludes to the legend of the 'Gordian Knot', which Alexander the Great is said to have simplistically resolved by slicing through it with his sword. This title encourages us to consider the Arab revolutions in terms that go beyond the tendency to judge them reductively against a Western notion of democracy. The spectator is discouraged from perceiving the revolutions in binary terms of spring or winter, democracy or extremism – and of repeating the neo-colonial manoeuvre of aligning these oppositions with unveiled and veiled women. While the ambiguously liberated women in *Noeud Gordien* are partially exposed, 'Liberty' in the reworking of Delacroix's revolutionary painting wears a full black veil in reference to the Yemeni women at the forefront of the revolutions. Khattari, like Essaydi, emphasises women's participation in the Uprisings, pointing to the contrast with their current situation, but also emphasising that the process is not yet complete (Khattari, in interview with Mondomix, 2012). These ideas are conveyed sensorially via the instability between stasis and dynamism; that is, by the women (across the collection) who have fallen yet appear still to be falling, who lie still but with eyes open, like the reclining women presented by Essaydi. Bearing further comparison with *Bullets*, the standing veiled woman – the Yemeni 'Marianne' – confronts spectators and speaks to them through the writing on her veil. She demands that they 'Read', perhaps

---

[21] This is reminiscent of Khattari's *défilé-performance* of 2008 (Hôtel de la Monnaie, Paris, Parcours St Germain), in which she began to present veiling and unveiling women – or women and men – in groups, pluralising simultaneously the possible meanings which can be attributed to the perceived immutable symbol of 'the veil'.
[22] They contrast with Delacroix's association of Eastern men with violence and despotism.

encouraging the mainly non-Arabophone Parisian public to move beyond Orientalising or universalising discourse on Arab countries. Ironically, the word cannot be read by such spectators, though a translation is provided in the curator's panel beside the entrance to the room. This imperative might resonate differently with speakers of Arabic as, many will know, it is the first word of the Qur'an. It might be seen as a call for religion to have a role in post-revolutionary states, while it also conveys the importance of listening to women's voices. Yet, spectators able to read Arabic are also alienated: beyond this injunction, which appears again on the woman's shoulder, very few of the isolated Arabic words on the woman's veil can be read, since they disappear within the folds of fabric. The words which can be read – or guessed at – cannot be interrelated clearly. One of the few clear words is 'سافر', the verb 'to travel': it is tempting to relate this to women's inevitable movement and agency despite current constraints and reductive perceptions. As in Essaydi's work, the use of illegible Arabic protects the woman from definition.

This photograph explicitly reworks Delacroix's painting of uprising against Charles X. It replaces the Marianne and the armed male protesters painted by Delacroix by the Yemeni woman with two men positioned on each side and a veiled figure further behind. The central work in the room (*Noeud Gordien*), if viewed in connection with this photograph, seems to refer implicitly to the same image of French revolution. While Khattari's *Liberté* reworks the upper part of Delacroix's painting, this work resonates with the lower half of the painting. In particular, the partially exposed male figure lying dead on the left-hand side with his legs on the pile of bodies is echoed in the left third of Khattari's central photograph. This figure, in Delacroix's painting, recalls a figure among the pile of dead bodies in Géricault's *Le Radeau de la Méduse* (1819).[23] In Delacroix's painting this figure has shifted from the right to the left, adopting a similar position in reverse. In Khattari's photograph the figure appears further back on the left and is presented from behind, a third perspective: this is the same position as in this photograph displayed in the hall. In a more dramatic reversal, the figure of the revolutionary protester becomes a woman.

[23] On the influence of Géricault's painting on Delacroix, see, for example, Musée du Louvre (n.d.).

The nude female torso of the figure in *Noeud Gordien*, with arms hanging by the sides and above the head, is echoed in *Majnoun*, while the pose here explicitly alludes to that of Christ in Michelangelo's *Pietà*. In this further gender reversal, a man takes the place of Mary, while his head rests on the woman's dead body. This also reverses the roles of the woman and man in Aranda's photograph. The roles of the two figures correspond more closely to those of Majnoun and Leïla, while the exposure of the female figure also contests the iconic image of the 'madman' (Majnoun) lying on his lover's tomb. *Majnoun and Leïla* is a story about tradition and convention preventing freedom and love. Khattari's reference to the ancient work suggests its relevance to contemporary society, particularly given the constraints that continue to be imposed on women's freedom in some post-revolutionary contexts.[24] The simultaneous allusion to the Aranda photograph, and the reversal of roles, laments the martyrdom of women, while it reminds us of their active participation in the revolutions. It is positioned directly opposite the photograph of the Yemeni 'Marianne', the embodiment of 'Liberty', 'leading the people'. Khattari, like Essaydi, discourages us from seeing women simply as victims. Reminiscent of Essaydi's reworking of Lady Justice, the allusion to Delacroix's Marianne also stands as a reminder of the history of reducing women to symbols in European art and, the artist suggests, of women's oppression in all civilisations (Khattari, in interview with Mondomix, 2012).

While Essaydi's series portrays the revolutions solely with reference to European images and frames of reference, albeit critically, Khattari's collection includes references to Middle Eastern texts. Khattari's presentation of men alongside women also contrasts with clichés of despotic or depraved male characters in some Orientalist painting. The dialogue with Orientalist images still runs the risk of reifying clichés.[25] It is perhaps most effective when viewed with the verbal explanations supplied in the televised interview. Khattari's and Essaydi's photographic series are densely layered intertextual works. Yet, both artists include references to some icons that are likely to be known by their

---

[24] This photograph might also be seen to refer to Louis Aragon's reworking of *Majnoun and Leïla* in his poem *Le Fou d'Elsa* (1963); I am very grateful to Dora Latiri for alerting me to this connection.
[25] Comparable to Essaydi's photographs, Khattari's collection might also be seen to reinforce conventional notions of beauty.

various audiences, including the *Pietà* or Lady Justice, and practices with which they will be familiar, such as the use of henna or fashion photography. The works' intertextuality adds to spectators' uneven experiences of familiarisation and defamiliarisation. Spectators are diversely interpolated and distanced through the ambivalence between the visual and the haptic, the visible and the invisible, the recognisable and the unrecognisable, control and contingency.

Khattari's and Essaydi's work is reminiscent of Bouderbala's words in exploring the interface between the body and that which offers it to the spectator's gaze: the body's shifting contingent surfaces are emphasised by uses of fabric, or henna, or the use of light and shadow. This artwork also resonates with Amelia Jones's argument that certain images of the body in contemporary art immerse the spectator yet retain a gap between object and subject. But these works develop a more complex, ambivalent interface. Specifically, they generate a dynamic between stability and instability by combining corporeal language with materials and photographic devices which paradoxically constrain and liberate the women. Photography comes to be aligned with uncertainty, as in the work of Lamine and in Bouderbala's *Flag Nymphéas* (Chapter 2), but through its connections to bodies between concealing and revealing, and between cultures.

A range of work exploring distinct revolutionary contexts converges with these series in interpolating yet distancing spectators through corporeal language in interaction with other sensorial, medial and cultural elements. Yet, it develops aesthetics of the interface through alternative uses of photography or video and by concealing and revealing the body in radically different ways.

Performing Revolution: Constraint and Liberation in Tunisia, Libya and Syria

As I suggested at the outset, there is not a neat division between works exploring the Arab Uprisings from external and internal perspectives (and many of the artists of these works tend to read through shifting local, regional and global lenses; see Chapter 2). Tendencies can, though, be identified in some work that is commissioned and produced, at least initially, for audiences in countries such as the USA, France or the UK. The allusion to specific (predominantly Orientalist and other iconic European) images, which we find in the work of

Essaydi and Khattari, appears to be designed for viewers in diaspora spaces. Their dialogues with Orientalism can be explained by the fact that they adapt the aesthetics in their previous work responding to 'Western' perceptions of Arabo-Muslim cultures. Khattari's *Hymne à la vie*, though, eschews this dialogue. Work exploring the Tunisian revolution through the trope of veiling and unveiling can, moreover, be found in locally produced art. Mouna Jemal Siala's video *Le Sort* displays a performance by the artist in which her face is gradually covered and uncovered in black paint in a series of stills played on a loop. Yet, this trope is used here primarily to explore tensions particular to Tunisia since the revolution. It conjures the debates in Tunisia in 2011 regarding the religious or secular future of the country, and the controversy over the constitution drafted by Ennahda, while it blurs the boundaries between these apparently polar positions. Works produced locally – whether by artists based largely in the country or not – allude more frequently to a specific context than works produced externally, though again there is not a clear division.[26] Yet, this piece by Jemal Siala, reminiscent of Essaydi's and Khattari's collections, displays an ambivalent body between concealing and revealing to interpolate spectators while highlighting the complexity of debates and (in this case) the range of possible outcomes of the Tunisian revolution.[27] Other works explore the Tunisian revolution, or other specific revolutionary contexts, through contrasting depictions of the body.

Some works focus on an artist's body that is hidden to the extent of being unrecognisable or unidentifiable. Other works capture an identifiable body – that of the artist or a participant – physically interacting with and reworking icons, or iconic spaces, of revolution or nation, by contrast with the allusive intertextual dialogues in work by Essaydi and Khattari. These works frequently refer, though, like Essaydi's and Khattari's collections, to local and national or transnational cultural spaces. Yet, they do so in ways that range from minimalist aesthetics to

---

[26] This is demonstrated by examples including Khattari's *Hymne à la vie*, produced in Paris, and Majd Abdel Hamid's *Mohammad Bouazizi*, created in Ramallah.

[27] The use of the French composer Erik Satie's 'Lent et douloureux' (Paris, 1888) could be taken to indicate the 'slow and painful' process of an ongoing revolution, though it appears ironic, given that Satie might have been inspired by Flaubert's *Salammbô* (1863 [1862]), an Orientalist depiction of Carthage and its women (on Satie's possible sources of inspiration, see Davis, 2007).

multi-layered works combining different media and incorporating footage produced by others. Some of these works are commissioned for galleries, while others are produced independently for online circulation. The online video is frequently a way of making public a work that had to be clandestine in its live form. This medium and context for display tend also, or alternatively, to be selected as a means of turning a spontaneous and ephemeral intervention in public space into a more durable and pervasive act of resistance.

Mouna Karray's *Noir* (2013), a photographic, gallery-based work, exemplifies a minimalist interface and depicts, yet conceals, the artist's own body (Figure 4.1). The series comprises eight photographs, which show a performance in white fabric against a white background. The images display an unrecognisable body almost entirely enveloped in opaque white fabric. Only a hand emerges from each contorted form, holding the air release, a remote control shutter release which makes it possible to take the photograph at a distance. Most of the images depict a tightly compressed body, the form of which shifts subtly from one image to another, while the photograph on the far right-hand side presents a limp figure, lying with hand open around the shutter trigger.

Karray's series evokes ongoing tensions in Tunisia. The pervasive use of white, together with the impression of confinement and suffocation in all the images, suggests that oppression continues despite the deposition of Ben Ali. Bernard Collet likens the white material worn by the performer to a liminal shroud (Collet, 2013: 122; trans. Ken Berri, 124). Karray's performance in such a shroud is reminiscent of Erruas's mourning through the process of weaving in white in *Les Drapeaux*. The tightly bound body suggests a person buried alive. At the same time, the artist's emerging hand, which firmly grips the end of the shutter cord, and the palpable tension of the dynamic body, signals activity, creativity and the persistence of life.[28] As the artist herself states, 'Mon corps est emprisonné, contraint, mais créateur' ('My body is imprisoned, constrained, yet creative') (cited by Mercier, 2014: 1). Through images of a captive body, Karray explores the ideas of imprisonment and oppression, of women and men, yet also resistance: 'These

---

[28] See Garance Malivel, who points to the convergence of violence and hope via this symbol (Malivel, 2013: 63).

ideas have always haunted me and continue since Ben Ali's regime and his repressive system. ... The series represents a struggle and resistance against repression, deprivation of movement and lack of freedom of expression' (Bowcock, 2016: 47). Karray's photographs, and her words, suggest that oppression cannot be without resistance: 'C'est dans l'enfermement et dans les tensions qu'on résiste et s'agite ...' ('It is in situations of confinement and tension that we resist and become agitated ...') (cited by Mercier, 2014: 1). The title, *Noir*, reflects this idea: 'c'est dans le noir qu'on commence à voir ...' ('it is in the dark that we begin to see') (cited by Mercier, 2014: 1).

Karray's work presents a body between concealing and revealing to highlight the revolutionary dynamic of constraint yet agency, reminiscent of the photographic series of Essaydi and Khattari. Yet, contrasting with their complex multidirectional palimpsests, this work explores the artist's own body between presence and absence. Karray's work can, in fact, be connected to various spaces, while it avoids the dialogue with France and Europe that tends to be central to counter-Orientalist work. Her minimalist approach was influenced by her training in Japan, while the square format she adopts is inspired by that which is frequently present in Islamic architecture.[29] The particular tense contorted forms created by enclosing the artist's body in fabric were inspired by a personal memory of her adolescence in Sfax. She describes seeing a cockerel struggling in a plastic bag, as it was being taken home by the man who had bought it (see Mercier, 2014: 1). It was this incident that inspired the artist's realisation that 'C'est dans l'enfermement et dans les tensions qu'on résiste et s'agite' (as cited above).

Noir interpolates spectators by tightly framing a body that merges with its background. It draws attention to the shifting folds and shadows of tight white fabric in contact with a visibly absent yet dynamic body. The black shutter cord explicitly joins the body to the photographic surface. It indicates the artist's status as both object and subject of the image. This wire unravels towards the spectators, involving them in a reciprocal exchange with the work. At the same time, the spectators are distanced. The body is inscrutable. Only the artist's hand

---

[29] As Karray states, 'the square is a fundamental element of Islamic architecture. The sleek style of North African mosques has been as much of an influence on me as Japanese minimalism' (Karray in interview with Morgan, 2016: 2).

identifies this corporeal form as female and its action signals that the body we see is that of the artist. Contrasting with presentations of bodies between exposure and concealment by artists such as Essaydi, Khattari, Bouderbala and Jemal Siala, Karray's forms are shrouded to the extent of being almost unrecognisable as female. Through her hidden body, Karray more dramatically flouts the conventions of portraiture and refuses definition. The gap between inscrutable corporeal forms and embodied spectators is reinforced via the ambiguous figure in the photograph at the right-hand end of the collection. The tension palpable in the other images is lost in this one. We might perceive this body as a lifeless figure which has lost the will to fight. Karray's work might, through this photograph, appear to point to the potential failure of the revolution. Yet, this 'collapsed' figure might, alternatively, be taken to convey relief and an ability finally to be able to breathe and to express oneself, following years of censorship. It resonates with the loss of air pressure involved in the liberatory act of taking this photograph with the air release device, as the artist has suggested.[30] It might, though – given the emergence of alternative forms of censorship after the revolution – be taken to evoke the continuing need to resist, while alluding to the real dangers involved in resistance – including resistance through art.[31]

Noir offers an alternative way of presenting the Tunisian revolution between success and failure, and as an ongoing process. The artist's images of constrained yet tense, dynamic bodies are reminiscent of Aïcha Filali's use of branches that grow despite the restraints imposed on them in *Bourgeons* (see Chapter 2) and of Benjelloun's verbal image of inevitable resistance: 'le vase devait finir par déborder' ('the vase had eventually to overflow') (2011: 12). The ambivalent covered bodies of

---

[30] I am very grateful to Mouna Karray for our conversation about her work in June 2020 (while emphasising the openness of the work, she signalled the possible evocation of relief in the right-hand figure in *Noir* and its potential connection with the air release device).

[31] Karray's disturbing figures take on new meaning when transposed outdoors and depicted in beautiful southern Tunisian landscapes in her series *Personne ne parlera de nous* (Nobody Will Talk about Us) (2012–15). In this work, which the artist began before the revolution, anonymous enclosed yet dynamic figures symbolise 'the disinherited Tunisian south' and southern resistance (Karray in interview with Morgan, 2016: 1). Photographs from this series were shown on advertising boards in the street during Dream City in Tunis, 2012, thereby bringing images of this marginalised rural region to the capital.

Noir resonate with both images evoked by Bouderbala, the fabric enveloping them 'comme une chrysalide fragile ou comme une carapace hostile' ('like a fragile chrysalis or like a hostile carapace').[32] The photographs distance spectators through their particular use of white fabric to evoke fragility yet also hostility and to conceal the artist's body to the extent of rendering it unrecognisable, even while her gesture means she can be identified. The fabric reveals the constrained movements of the body without exposing its shape. 'Revealing' is, otherwise, limited to the artist's hand and the creative act. Through this use of concealing and revealing the images are anchored in the context of continuing tensions and constraints on freedom of expression in Tunisia.

Naziha Arebi's *Granny's Flags* and Philip Horani's *LIBERTé* also present alternative aesthetics of concealing and revealing the performing body. Each uses video to draw attention to the surface of the skin but also of a flag. In contrasting ways, an icon is incorporated and renegotiated through its alignment with a shifting, contingent body. In Horani's work the artist's hidden body hints at the risks involved in creating, in alternative ways to Karray, which are particular to the distinct context of revolution and conflict in Syria. The interface is also developed further in both video works through the uses of literal movement, multiple media and/or the more elaborate interventions in time for which this medium allows.

Naziha Arebi's four-minute film, *Tripoli Stories – Granny's Flags* (2012; 4'13), focuses on the artist's grandmother in Tripoli, a few months after the overthrow of Muammar Gaddafi in August 2011, sewing the red, black and green flag of Libya, with a white crescent and star in the centre, and recounting how she sewed these flags in hiding, during the recent civil war.[33] This flag, which was established in 1949 and used by the Kingdom of Libya between 1951 and 1969, was reinstated as the national flag in August 2011, replacing the green flag introduced by Gaddafi in 1977 as a symbol of the 'Green Revolution'.[34] During the civil war, the striped flag – or a variation

---

[32] Malivel comments on the ambiguity of the white fabric used by Karray as simultaneously 'voile, linceul, camisole ou chrysalide' (2013: 63).

[33] This video was made during a Scottish Documentary Institute workshop in Libya, organised by the British Council. See www.scottishdocinstitute.com/films/tripoli-stories-grannys-flags/.

[34] See www.britannica.com/topic/flag-of-Libya.

consisting of vertical bands and no star and crescent – was used by the Libyan opposition (Asad Hashim, 2011). The dynamic between oppression and resistance emerges, in this work, through oral narrative and the moving image, which record a woman's memory of fear but also active participation in the Libyan War. Arebi's video crosses the boundaries between private and public space and presents both body and icon through fragments and surfaces.

At first, we do not see the flag. The film alternates, initially, between tightly framed close-ups of the elderly woman's hands – sieving flour, kneading bread mixture, breaking cooked bread and eating it – and her face, against a patterned sofa and cushion. While we see these images, Haja Fatma tells her UK-born granddaughter, in Libyan Arabic, of her experience of the recent civil war and life under Gaddafi.[35] She recalls the four regimes she has experienced in Libya, alluding to the monarchy of King Idriss, the Italian occupation, the Franco-British condominium, and Gaddafi's dictatorship. Shots of the woman's face and shoulders, moving in the play of light and shadow from a nearby window, are interspersed with others, filmed in darkness, showing the wavering flame of a candle or her folded hands, as she recalls their extreme fear of anti-aircraft bullets during the recent civil war. She remembers how they spent the thirty nights of Ramadan doing nothing but bake bread between power cuts. A short break in the narrative, while the film shows the woman praying, before cutting to a shot of the night sky and moon, signals a shift in tone. The woman relaxes, smiling at first: 'We are happy that Muammar died. We got rid of him. He used to smother us. Right from the beginning he started hanging people. Hanging us, imprisoning us, killing us. Muammar. Gaddafi. Gaddafi. Gaddaaaafi'. She makes a sweeping gesture, as she repeats the dictator's name like a mother scolding her child. We then see her pull a large swathe of bright red material onto her knee and she begins to sew a flag. Close-ups of her hands sewing, her materials, or her eyes appear as she tells the story, laughing, of how she secretly made flags and passed them on to her grandchildren: 'These flags released the tension from our hearts. I had to sew in hiding. I didn't

---

[35] The video was subtitled in English at the Arab–British Centre, London ('The Libyan', curated by Noon Arts, 22–30 November 2012). The work has also been shown in film festivals in Tripoli, as well as in Jordan, Morocco, Canada and a range of European countries (see scottishdocinstitute.com, as above).

mention it to anyone. When people came over, I hid it. Once they left, I took it out again. If they knew, they could kill me.'

Reminiscent of Erruas's installation, *Les Drapeaux*, the painstaking process of sewing flags is associated with both catharsis and subversion. In this case, this process is the subject of the work, which is more reminiscent of Essaydi's photographs of women writing on their clothes in her earlier series, *Femmes du Maroc*. In Arebi's video the artist's grandmother recounts how she and others began to make the striped flags as a means of dealing with the experience of violent conflict, removing 'the pain from our hearts.' For the woman filmed, making flags was both purgative and a dangerous, clandestine revolutionary activity, an act of resistance to Gaddafi's regime. Resistance continues into the present. The film may seem celebratory, in its second half: the dictator is dead; Haja Fatma now laughs as she looks back on her subversive activity; violence and fear may seem to be experiences of the past. Yet, she continues to sew; national identity is still in the process of reconstruction. Directly after she recalls how her life was in danger, there is a brief pause in the narrative and in the woman's laughter, while the camera focuses on the nearby window, as if to leave space for us to consider whether the days of fear are really over. The final shot of the film shows the woman's eyes smiling at the camera, as we hear her final, poignant lines: 'Will you understand this later on? It would be a waste if you didn't understand me.' Her words are ambivalently directed at her grandchildren, continuing the conversation she remembers having with them, the artist (her granddaughter from the UK) and the spectators (first in Tripoli and then in places such as London). They seem to pose a wider question as to the future of Libya, and to intimate the need to build on what has already been achieved. Through narrative and image, this work connects past and present to highlight that Libya's revolution is ongoing (indeed, January–March 2012 would see clashes between former rebel forces in Benghazi which opposed the National Transitional Council).[36] This work, however, not only records a memory, and continuing practice, of resistance. *Granny's Flags* is itself a work of resistance. It counters iconic images of revolution and nation by presenting a personal story of domestic, everyday, gendered resistance and by aligning the revolutionary flag with the narrating woman's body.

[36] See 'Libya profile – Timeline' at: www.bbc.co.uk/news/world-africa-13755445.

Arebi's film – as prefigured by the title – shows a woman in possession of the political symbol of the flag, which is usually associated with and destined for the outside, public space. The interior, domestic space becomes a politically charged space of resistance. At the same time, the flags are domesticated: the woman makes flags as she makes bread. Arebi avoids representing the body as spectacle by focusing on everyday ordinary domestic activities, and on a member of her family. The flags and the woman's body exceed iconic visual representation. Both emerge in fragments. The woman is frequently filmed in such a way that the top of her head disappears beyond the edge of the frame. In other sequences the camera zooms so closely into the woman's skin or the texture of her woollen cardigan that her body moves out of focus.[37] These close-up shots, and the play of light from the window, highlight the haptic surface of the skin. The flag is subjected to the same process. The fragments presented highlight the unfinished quality and the materiality of the flag: its frayed edges and the texture of the fabric. The strip of red material – the one most in evidence – at one point fills the entire frame, shining or revealing shadow as it shifts in the light of the window. The red stripe, originally symbolic (when the flag originated during the monarchy of King Idris) of the blood shed by Libyan people under Italian fascist rule, comes to be identified, through the woman's story, with those who died in the recent civil war.[38] The flag comes to be associated with senses other than the visual, not only through shots of its shifting surface but also through the alternate sensuous images of sieving flour, kneading bread, eating, drinking and plates of food. The icon is also closely connected to the woman's movement and voice. The striped fabric is pulled and shaped by the woman's hands. It is also moulded to her body, shifting as the woman moves, and as she tells her story. The material shifts and folds as she works on it, so that we gain only a partial view of the icon. The flag loses the power with which it was associated under King Idriss and is reinvested with new meaning by an individual female subject. The process evokes women's continuing participation in the formation of the nation, and their inseparability from the country's future. Sewing comes to be associated with subversion, while it can also be seen as a

---

[37] This tactic is reminiscent of Agnès Varda's filming of her own ageing body at certain moments in *Les Glaneurs et la glaneuse* (2000).

[38] The black stripe shows no crescent and star, thus corresponding with many of the flags employed by the Libyan opposition to Gaddafi.

metaphor, 'entwining' the personal and the political, and the individual and the collective, as well as different generations and cultures.

The images we see of a woman sewing a flag in her home provide a counterpoint to images of the female demonstrator, often brandishing a flag, in the public space. They also contrast with sexualised female symbols of revolution and with images of the female victim of violence in revolutionary insurrections. Yet, Arebi's film also avoids simply providing an alternative symbol in which 'woman' and 'nation' are closely identified. The film resonates, to some extent, with classical paintings of women sewing flags, particularly in the context of the American Revolution. Numerous paintings and memorabilia commemorate the American Revolution with an image of Betsy Ross sewing the stars and stripes, including an oil painting by Edward Percy Moran, which shows the demure seated servant to her nation with George Washington standing beside her (*Then, Now, and Forever!* (*c*.1908)). The stars and stripes are clearly visible. Sewing is, in such works, identified with the commemoration of the Revolution (brought about by a group of male political figures) and the birth of a new and apparently cohesive nation. Arebi's film, in which sewing is connected to revolutionary activity and female agency, past and present, provides a marked contrast to paintings such as that of Moran and to the wider tradition of genre paintings of 'The Seamstress'. *Granny's Flags* resonates with numerous paintings depicting a woman sewing in her home by, or in the light of, a window, from Johannes Vermeer's *Lacemaker* (1669/70) to Joseph Rodefer DeCamp's *The Seamstress* (1916). Yet, it shows an image in motion of an elderly, individually named woman who is given a voice. This video is strikingly reminiscent of Katia Kameli's work on Algeria, particularly her alternative depiction in video of an elderly Algerian 'woman in her apartment' – *Aïcha* (2001) – which engages ironically with Vermeer's *Milkmaid* and resonates with genre paintings of 'The Laundress'.[39] Yet, Arebi specifically films her

[39] Both artists present North African women in ways that resist objectification and emphasise their contemporaneousness, though Arebi's strategy contrasts with Kameli's use of grainy accelerated footage and music (Khaled's *Raï* song, *Aïcha*). Arebi's focus on domestic activities, and on a member of her family, similarly resonates with Kameli's work on Algeria, particularly her short film *Bledi, a Possible Scenario* (2004), to which I referred in Chapter 2. The sequences in *Bledi* focusing on the hands of elderly women preparing food, interspersed with documentary-style fragments in which the women speak, anticipate those filmed by Arebi, while her work uses such aesthetics to illuminate a hidden, gendered dimension of the Libyan revolution.

grandmother's testimony to recent events in Libya in real time and exceeds iconic language through a combined use of framing, focus and editing.

Granny's Flags reveals new means (and meanings) of generating ambivalence through concealing and revealing in displaying potential icons – a female body and a flag in the making – that blur the boundaries between the domestic and the political, the site of refuge and the site of revolutionary action. In this work, by contrast with the three photographic series I have discussed above, the woman is not concealed or revealed by fabric but by fragmentary or restrictive framing, shifting levels of focus, and alternate scenes of analogous actions. While the shifting haptic surfaces of fabric and skin interpolate the embodied spectator in a similar way to those series, the fabric is here the icon itself, which also shifts in and out of view. Its power is undermined – or in the process of being redirected – by the emphasis on its fabrication by a woman, its materiality, and its alignment with female corporeality. Philip Horani similarly employs video and performance, and aligns body and icon, but in a strikingly different way, to evoke the particular context of the ongoing revolution and conflict in Syria.

The online video, *LIBERTé* (2011; 2′29; see http://vimeo.com/45661752) which, we are told in the closing shot, 'could be created by Philip Horani', recreates the Syrian flag through a 'painting-performance' in which we see the anonymous male artist's hand and arm as he works.[40] The image first shows the artist rapidly sketching, with dripping diluted oil paints, the figures of demonstrators in Syria over found footage of a demonstration. The layered scenes are accompanied by an instrumental excerpt of 'Believe', by the British electronic music duo the Chemical Brothers, as well as the sounds of a demonstration. The crowds chant the slogan (also chanted in Tunisia and Egypt in late 2010 and early 2011) 'the people wants the fall of the regime' (Bank, 2016). While the painting-performance moves at an accelerated pace, the footage and soundtracks are played in real time. As the artist paints a protestor's banner with the word 'حرية' ('Hourriya', freedom, which is subtitled in French), we hear demonstrators shout the same word. The demonstration rapidly turns to violence: we hear anguished cries, shooting and explosions, together with the intense music. This shift is

---

[40] Last accessed June 2020. This video originally appeared on Ibraaz.com. After the artist left Syria and moved to live in exile, first in Georgia and then in Belgium, he began to use his real name, Abdalla Omari (Bank, 2016), displaying this work on his website (see www.abdallaomari.com/).

echoed visually by the artist splashing his scene with red paint, which sprays, drips and runs down the canvas. The lower third of the scene is blocked out in bright red and the upper third in dripping black until the demonstration is no longer identifiable as such. The film fades to black and the noise turns to silence for a brief moment before the performance resumes, this time to the instrumental opening bars of a calm, melodic acoustic guitar song ('Raoui' (Storyteller)), by France-based Algerian singer Souad Massi (2007). The red and black blocks become recognisable as parts of the Syrian flag as the artist paints a row of palm trees across the central strip, before erasing most with white paint until two green marks resembling the flag's five-pointed stars remain. Finally, the artist rotates the painting, so that the flag is the right way up. The performance is followed by a statement affirming that 'All videos and sound effects (demonstrations, shooting, bombing and explosions ...) has [sic] been made in Syria ...' *LIBERTé* differs aesthetically from Arebi's use of video in incorporating footage of a public space, in using music and found footage, and in playing the film at an accelerated speed. It shows the artist as creator of the work, though it allows only parts of his body to enter the frame. We fleetingly glimpse the artist's hand, forearm, breast, bearded chin, and his head when he bends to reload his brush; at the end of the performance his upper arm and shoulder are revealed as he reaches to rotate the canvas. The videos converge, though, in their depiction of the repossession, and subjective renegotiation, of a national icon through a creative bodily performance.

Iconic visual language is similarly questioned through the production of contingency through corporeal movement and creative process, as well as the appeal to a range of senses. This piece, like that of Arebi, draws attention to the haptic surface of the flag, while it does so not through fabric that shifts with corporeal movement but by dripping, splashing paint, connected to the body's gestural actions. The performance is also overlaid with audiovisual footage and soundtracks. The brushstroke – like the stitch – is a mark of the creator's subjectivity, which disrupts the habitually uniform and monochromatic blocks of colour and the symmetrical geometric insignia. While Horani's work is performed by the artist, its incorporation of found footage and music tracks can be seen as a way of allowing others – including demonstrators – to contribute, albeit unknowingly, to the work: a participatory strategy I discussed in Chapter 3. (Arebi's video, by contrast, is shaped in part by the story of a knowing participant.) Horani's work avoids 'storytelling' in a documentary mode, while his use of the instrumental opening of Souad Massi's راوي ('Raoui', meaning 'Storyteller'), brings the theme of 'narrative' into *LIBERTé* in an allusive way. It seems to confer the role of storyteller on the artist, while he uses it to orchestrate various fragments evocative of possible narratives and perspectives. It is tempting to relate the use of Massi's song, which expresses nostalgia for a time gone by, to a desire to escape the unbearable situation in Syria: حكي لنسينا في هاد زمان ('narrate to make us forget these times'). This work, also reminiscent of Arebi's video, 'layers' discrepant time frames: Horani's painting over found footage commemorates those lost in the Syrian conflict, while indicating the ongoing reconstruction of identity. The layering of paint and change of music track, which transform the scene of violent conflict into a tranquil row of trees and then the stripes and stars of the flag, intimates the people's contribution to this process of reconstruction. The work's positive suggestion of organic growth, of new life emerging in the wake of violence and of a period of calm following the storm, seems to express hope for the future. Despite the distinct context of the ongoing war in Syria, *LIBERTé* converges with *Granny's Flags* in holding in tension the themes of remembering and resisting.

If Horani's work reveals striking parallels to Arebi's work, it also demonstrates an alternative approach to performance, and to the aesthetic of concealing and revealing the body. *LIBERTé* differs from the works considered thus far in this chapter in that the body at first appears peripheral to the subject of the work, receding literally to the edges of the frame. Horani's painting-performance is reminiscent of the photographs of Jackson Pollock performing his gestural drip paintings in the 1950s, which Amelia Jones shows to be a type of performance art (1998: 53–102). In Pollock's case, the exhibited work of art is the painting that resulted from his actions. The photographs function as documents of the preceding performance, while they encourage the spectator to understand the drips and marks on the canvas as visible traces of the artist's body and creative genius. In Horani's video the performance is, by contrast, central to the work displayed. We see the drips and splashes, as well as the gestures employed to produce them. The painting is intimately connected to corporeal movement. Yet, it is distanced from the artist, whose identity is not revealed by his body or by his name. The use of found footage and music tracks also detracts from the idea of the artist's centrality to the work.[41] In further distinction from North American Abstract Expressionist works, *LIBERTé* is firmly anchored in the real: the drips, splashes and blocks of colour are explicitly linked to violent conflict and, subsequently, to the flag. In relation to the painted flag, we might recall Jasper Johns's 1950s paintings of the American flag, which directly parodied Abstract Expressionist painting and critiqued post-war American politics. Horani's critique, though, through his anonymous multimedia performance, is anchored resolutely in contemporary Syria. Horani's performance diverges sharply in tone from Abstract Expressionism, which was marketed as a symbol of American freedom following the Cold War. This exploration of 'Liberté', by contrast, desperately cries for freedom, while eschewing any sense of national unity and cohesion. In its use of the French word for its title, the work might encourage comparison with Delacroix's revolutionary painting of *Liberté*. Yet, Horani's *LIBERTé*, in which 'revolution' is merely a hope, conveys a mass of protesters still in the throes of violent conflict. In this case, it is the artist who is 'leading the people' – not by facing towards us, Syrian flag in hand, but hidden from us, seemingly burying the martyrs under the national banner.[42] Karray's photographs of her hidden body signal the risk of free speech and free art in the Tunisian context, while the body and work of art are nonetheless identified as hers. In the Syrian context, this artist's concealment of his identity is crucial, since revealing it could lead to his assassination. Indeed, the dissimulation of the artist's body – and particularly his face – is itself indicative of the specific context of Syria, in which the 'revolution' is ongoing. The footage, the shift in music, and the evolving painting point to the past and future, while the partially hidden body signals the present moment of this performance in 2011. In *Granny's Flags* flag-making is remembered as a dangerous act of subversion; in *LIBERTé* the flag is made at a time when the danger and fear of reprisal is still acutely real. Displayed online, moreover, this dangerous clandestine act of subversion takes place in the public – and global – domain.

While the body, in *LIBERTé*, is marginalised visually, it plays a central role in anchoring the work in a specific Syrian context. The

---

[41] The artist is viewed as central to Abstract Expressionist paintings.
[42] The demonstrators, too, are hidden. We might recall Febrik's identification of the tendency to photograph demonstrators in Daraa en masse to mask their identity.

presence of this shifting body, concealed yet partially revealed, is also crucial in signalling the instability and contingency of the icon, and in interpolating the spectator. The contingent drips and splashes of paint are visibly linked to the unstable gestural language of the anonymous body. This moving body is also intimately connected to the evolving icon via the projected footage; the images of demonstrators flicker across both canvas and skin, joining their shifting uneven surfaces. The marginalised body contributes to the production, in this work, of a more complex ambivalent interface than that generated by Arebi's video, or the photographic works of Essaydi, Khattari or Karray. Horani's video engages the spectator, while refusing to allow a transparent and stable picture of a knowable icon, through a mobile palimpsest of paint (which is incessantly erased and repainted), skin (which shifts with the body's gestures) and the light, sound and images of audiovisual footage. The two music tracks add further evolving layers. The video connects, while maintaining tension between, the artist's body and the viewers via multiple images, surfaces and time frames – indicated by the discrepant speeds of the performance and the footage and music. Spectators of this online video are engaged in their specific global/local contexts via various medial and cultural elements. The work forges transnational (including transversal) connections and provisional or potential networks of solidarity between Syria and other countries in using the electronic music of the Chemical Brothers from the UK and the contrasting acoustic guitar piece by the France-based Algerian-born Souad Massi. The song chosen is in standard Arabic, connecting Arabic-speakers across the world, while the video includes only its instrumental opening, extending its global reach and affective potential.[43] This piece also unsettles and affects spectators through the use of the sounds of conflict and music together and by situating us behind the artist. We adopt his perspective, accompanying him as he paints. We are present with him, while he remains unrecognisable and unidentifiable, eluding attempts to connect the work to the artist – by external critics or by those, internal, who would use violence to silence oppositional voices.

---

[43] Massi's style draws on diverse influences, including Arabic, African and Western music, including rock, country or the Portuguese fado. She also sings in Algerian Arabic, French, Kabyle, and occasionally in English. (www.bbc.co.uk/music/artists/0f7a9866-5644-4a45-9781-b87e60eb3269; last accessed January 2019).

In alluding to the distinct contexts of revolution in Libya and Syria, and in using video, *Granny's Flags* and *LIBERTé* appear initially to diverge radically from representations of the body in photography by Essaydi, Khattari and Karray. In Horani's work, the body – male, in this case – is visibly marginalised. Both, in addition, literally incorporate the flag associated with the revolution in each context. Yet, striking parallels with these photographic series can be discerned in Arebi's and Horani's use of the body to signal the instability and contingency of seemingly static and monolithic iconic visions of revolution and nation. These works similarly produce an ambivalent sensorial interface. They mobilise the shifting surface of a partially obscured body to interpolate the spectator, while holding them at a distance. Allusions to other cultures and histories add further metaphorical layers. At the same time, these videos reveal alternative approaches to aesthetics of concealing and revealing the body, and indeed signal the range of possibilities for such aesthetics in this medium. Arebi uses personal testimony, discrepant narrative and image, light and shadow, restrictive framing and close-ups. Horani, by contrast, combines multiple media and superimposes accelerated and real-time footage or music tracks, incorporating perceptible connections to different times and spaces. Arebi films the domestic actions of her grandmother, sewing and making bread, while Horani displays his anonymous performing, painting body. Arebi allows the grandmother's story in some measure to shape the work. Horani uses found footage by, and depicting, unknowing and unknown 'participants'. Yet, these contrasting works converge in displaying the bodily recreation of an icon in process.

Horani's video can be compared to a proliferation of online videos of street art in process. His presentation of a painting-performance is distinctive in concealing the artist's identity and occurring in an indoor setting, the details of which are also hidden. In the online videos that I analyse below, the artists are visible and rework not a flag but an iconic space: they intervene in public space, symbolic of the previous regime's order and power and/or of more recent constraints. The iconic image, though, is similarly disrupted by the artists' corporeal performance and by the ambiguous process of loss and gain that is allowed by framing and editing. Both icon and body shift between concealing and revealing, order and disorder, and between different times and spaces. Yet, these videos, which are longer and made – at least, in part – outside and often while moving, heighten the potential for multiple layers and for contingent encounters, taking further our understanding of the interface in aesthetics of revolution.

Digitising Street Encounters: Tunisia in Graffiti, Photography and Dance

Videos of work by El Seed, Ahl Al Kahf, JR and Art Solution display diverse types of street art in Tunisian public space. A video by El Madinati (2012, 3'59; www.youtube.com/watch?v=NKNTkG5dr4A) shows the French-born El Seed spray-painting his distinctive intricate 'wildstyle' Arabic graffiti onto a façade of the Jara mosque in his Tunisian town of origin, Gabès.[44] Ridha Tlili's video of Tunis-based graffiti artists Zied and Mohammed Ali, who are part of the group of graffiti artists Ahl Al Kahf, portrays, by contrast, a clandestine intervention in a side street of the capital at night ('Ahl al-Kahf: Graffiti', 2011; Tlili, in cooperation with Al-Arabi Al-Hor; 2'26; www.middleeastdigest.com/pages/index/6058/ahl-al-kahf_graffiti).[45] Their intervention consists of spraying templates, writing slogans and throwing paint. The video *InsideOut*, 'Part 1 – Tunis' (March 2011; directed by Alastair Siddons and produced by Emile Abinal) screens the first part of JR's ongoing transnational participatory photographic project (www.insideoutproject.net/en/group-actions/tunis-tunisia).[46] The Parisian artist worked with Tunisian photographers Hela Ammar, Sophia Barakat, Wissal Dargueche, Rania Dourai, Hichem Driss and Aziz Tnani to produce multiple photographs of ordinary Tunisians. These images were enlarged and pasted primarily at sites where, previously, only portraits of the deposed leader could be found.

---

[44] Last accessed June 2020. Uploaded on 7 September 2012; also uploaded to Vimeo on 6 September 2012. The graffiti type known as 'wildstyle' consists of complex interwoven lettering which, as Janice Rahn has commented, resembles Celtic interlace (Rahn, 2002: 14).

[45] Last accessed January 2019. The video was uploaded to the multilingual ezine *Jadaliyya*, which addresses cultural, social and political issues in North Africa and the Middle East, in a short article by Al-Arabi Al-Hor in Arabic and English on 21 June 2012. It was also available on Vimeo.

[46] Last accessed June 2020. This 'global platform for people to share their untold stories and transform messages of personal identity into works of public art' has involved over 260,000 participants in 129 countries, at the time of writing: www.insideoutproject.net.

Je danserai malgré tout, a series of four videos by the Tunis-based street dance group Art Solution (2012–13), similarly captures interventions at key sites of the capital, including the Bab Al Bahr, the Ministry of the Interior and the National Theatre, and at times involves passers-by. 'Je danserai malgré tout 3', on which I focus below, portrays a dance in front of the Bab Al Bahr led by Bahri Maz, Chouaib Cheu, Nahed Dou Di, Ghada Dada and Adnen (2 February 2013; 10′57; see www.youtube.com/watch?v=4OfWQ2GaVHg).[47] These interventions in graffiti, photography or dance on the streets of Tunisia are displayed in video online, where they engage a wider and more diverse audience. It is via framing, editing, and the addition of elements including sound, text and/or found footage, that the contingent body emerges as a destabilising revolutionary force. In videos of graffiti, which show the artist/s working, the intervention becomes a form of performance. Graffiti is frequently created, particularly in these revolutionary contexts, to be disseminated and experienced through video. These graffiti-performances, like Horani's painting-performance, shift the emphasis of the work from the outcome to the process of production. They might, in this way, similarly call to mind what Amelia Jones has termed the '"Pollockian" performative' (1998). Yet, also comparable to Horani's work, they reveal a more complex type of performance, which relativises the artist's central position and control over the image. Videos of graffiti, photography and dance in Tunisia produce a gap between the work and the spectators not only by combining filming with an ambivalent contingent performance but also by incorporating the peripatetic mode and various forms of participation.

The video of El Seed's painting on the Jara mosque, by El Madinati (www.youtube.com/watch?v=NKNTkG5dr4A), is comparable to Horani's work in ambivalently interpolating and distancing its diverse spectators through multiple cultural references and layers. El Seed has painted 'calligraffiti' at sites across the world, including Paris, Rio, Cairo and Dubai. Through his cross-cultural style, which he developed originally to counter clichés of Arabs and Muslims in France, the artist responds to tensions between specific communities and aims to 'bridge cultural divides' (Zoghbi and Karl, in El Seed, 2011: 101).[48] El Seed's

---

[47] Montage by Bassem Hachani; filmed by Hazem Berrabah, Zied Litaiem and Mehdi Bouhlel; percussion by Aymen Ben Yahmed. The video was uploaded to YouTube by Bahri Ben Yahmed on 3 February 2013 (last accessed June 2020).

[48] I have detailed elsewhere the means and effects of combining graffiti and calligraphy, and of presenting the piece *in situ* and on video, primarily in El

calligraffiti evolves in interaction with each particular site. While he frequently translates lines from secular texts produced by the culture in which he works (for example, by Balzac, Baudelaire and Stendhal in Paris), his painting in Gabès is a citation from the Qur'an: 'O humankind, we have created you from a male and a female and made people and tribes so you may know each other' (translation by El Madinati). By painting this phrase on a mosque, in a style that draws on calligraphy and graffiti, he intends to connect communities that are often polarised by debates between religious and secular futures for the country.[49] The content of the phrase, taken from the Qur'an, coheres with the structure. The gestural lettering, however, departs from tradition. El Seed's large-scale writing, produced with his entire body, diverges from the rules of Arabic calligraphy to the extent of being illegible. This phrase can only be known *in situ* if such information is provided in advance (online or verbally) – even by those who are literate in Arabic. Even with knowledge of the phrase, moreover, the connection between it and the elaborate 'calligraffiti' on the mosque cannot easily be made. Yet, the cross-cultural style can still convey visually the coexistence of the religious and the secular, as the artist intends. In the video of the work, these incongruous aspects of his practice are emphasised. Shots of him spraying the structure, while standing on a cherry-picker lift, emphasise the corporeality and scale involved. They also highlight the contingency for which his movements and materials allow, by contrast with the precise writing in ink of the seated calligrapher whose gestures are regulated by their breathing. The cultural incongruity of El Seed's style at this site is heightened through the use of a hip hop track (an instrumental version of 'Rasgao Mi Corazon' by Mision de Los Escogidos) and the shifting speed of the film which, at times, repeats his gestures to the track's rhythm.[50] The video alternates between such manipulated non-verbal sequences and a real-time documentary mode in which the artist appears in interview against the backdrop of his intervention. Speaking in *Darija* (Tunisian

---

Seed's work in Paris. His translations of lines from canonical French writers in Paris, such as Balzac on the Pont des Arts, can be seen to indicate a diverse and evolving French identity (Shilton, 2018).

[49] His intervention, like works including Karray's *Noir*, occurred in the wake of the attack on 'Le Printemps des Arts'.

[50] The acceleration of his art process contrasts with his actual process, which is closer to calligraphy in its laboriousness.

Arabic) with English subtitles, El Seed communicates his return to his home town of Gabès, as well as his objective to inspire people from different backgrounds '[t]o come together, to bring love and to unite'. He also reveals the meaning of the painted phrase, citing classical Arabic. The written responses to the video, to which I return below, convey a predominantly positive reception of the mural.[51]

This video incorporates visual, verbal and auditory cultural references differently to Horani's video: through calligraphy and graffiti, the mosque and the Koranic phrase, the hip hop track, and the use of Classical Arabic, *Darija* and English subtitles.[52] These elements, though, will similarly resonate in distinctive ways for the diverse viewers. The juxtaposition of (here, oscillation between) various speeds and modes comparably heightens ambiguity – in this case, around a monument that is often associated with certainty and with a single vision of Tunisia. Yet, this video allows for further layers and incongruities, not only in using the documentary mode which, here, produces crossings between different languages – written, oral and visual – but also by extending the intervention in time and space.

The length of this film (3'59) allows it to switch between shots of the calligraffiti – completed or at different stages of the process – from close by, from afar and from various angles: low, high and aerial. This extension in time and space also allows for shots of the artist and/or his work to be interspersed with images of the wider environment. The video captures the surrounding streets, spice stalls, architecture and the society of Gabès. We see people engaged in diverse everyday activities and actions: sorting fish they have caught, eating fish, preparing couscous, dancing, playing in water, laughing, or simply passing by. Some are shown engaging with the filmmaker, talking to him, embracing him or, in one case, showing him a copy of the Qur'an. El Seed's intervention is, in this way, connected to its context and the communities it aims to bridge. This environment, like the sequences that show the artist working, shifts to the rhythm of the hip hop track, reinforcing

---

[51] In his TED Talk of 2015 El Seed suggests that the mural was received very positively by the imam he had approached and that it united the local community (available at: www.ted.com/talks/el_seed_street_art_with_a_message_of_hope_and_peace?language=en). Responses to the video online – from a diverse global audience – only rarely conflict with this picture, as I discuss below in comparison with the online portrayal of JR's intervention.

[52] The music track is originally in Spanish, which may be known by some viewers.

this connection. The video moves beyond the secular/religious binary. The diversity of the people of Gabès is emphasised through the video's use of multiple cultural references, from objects, costumes and written signs to local food and means of preparing it, but also via form: like the graffiti, the people appear in different lights, at shifting speeds and from multiple perspectives. The plurality of angles and the extent of the space filmed indicate the filmmaker's displacement around the site of El Seed's intervention.

The peripatetic mode heightens the potential for spontaneous encounters and footage that could not be foreseen entirely, as we have seen in relation to videos including Karray's *Live* and Bahri's *Orientations* in Chapter 2. This video has been carefully shot and edited, but it nonetheless uses footage that was determined to some extent by the people who entered the frame. These people become, to a degree, participants in the work. The work (the video) emerges between these people, or the surrounding landscape, and the filmmaker, extending beyond the ostensible artist and work: El Seed and his calligraffiti. The performance differs, therefore, from the Jackson Pollock–style performances discussed by Jones (1998), which are seen to originate from the artist's genius. But this video marginalises the artist in a contrasting way to Horani's work. El Seed is the main performer, but he shifts in and out of the frame, and others are allowed to shape the work to a greater extent than the producer of, and people shown in, the found footage in *LIBERTé*.[53] The people of Gabès are linked directly to the original intervention, moreover, by shots that show them gazing upwards at the graffitied minaret. Through such images, the reception of the calligraffiti, like its production, becomes an integral part of the work. Diverse spectators of the video online watch local spectators of the live intervention. The video could be seen, in this respect, to run the risk of objectifying them: the watchers become the watched, reminiscent of Edward Said's thesis in *Orientalism* and of Linda Nochlin's postcolonial analysis of spectators and spectacle in Jean-Léon Gérôme's *The Snake Charmer* (late 1860s) (Nochlin, 1991; Said, 1995: 103 [1978]).[54] Yet, the camera constantly shifts perspective as it shows a diverse and shifting group looking at a similarly ambiguous work. Tunisian and non-Tunisian spectators of the

---

[53] The video captures a mix of knowing and presumably unknowing participants.
[54] As Said stated, in *Orientalism*, '[t]he Orient is *watched* ... the European ... is a watcher' (1995: 103 [1978]).

video are reminded of *their* diversity by the plurality of cultural references. This video not only draws spectators' attention to an underrepresented Tunisian town. It also ties art to cultural and social diversity and daily life, which might encourage them to consider the revolution in ways that avoid reducing it to a debate between religion and secularism.

Ridha Tlili's video displays a distinct type of graffiti, by Ahl Al Kahf, and a contrasting means of filming the graffiti-performance, while it similarly encourages a rethinking of iconic space. This video displays a clandestine intervention in the capital, filmed at night, without music and in real time (www.middleeastdigest.com/pages/index/6058/ahl-al-kahf_graffiti). A handheld camera follows the artists as they prepare their materials in an apartment before finding a location and undertaking their intervention. Their conversation in *Darija*, like their writing on the wall, appears as subtitles in standard Arabic and English. Their templates, slogans and slung paint contrast with El Seed's elaborate 'wildstyle' and are closer to fast-paced 'throw-ups'. This style is appropriate to their illegal intervention which, while meticulously prepared, must be executed swiftly. The templates they spray are the faces of Ben Ali and the interim prime minister, Beji Caid Essebsi, who would become the president in 2014, as well as Banksy's *Radar Rat* (2004).[55] There is also the face of a person who is not known publicly, on the left, with the words 'Stop putting rubbish in our heads' written in Arabic above. With these methods they can produce a clear message. The meaning behind their evocation of governmental figures is unequivocal, given the juxtaposed principal slogan in Arabic, translated in the subtitles: 'Oh people, rebel against the traces of dictatorship.' By contrast with the video of El Seed's work, views of the space surrounding the intervention are constrained and the precise location remains visually unidentifiable. Its iconic value, though, is signalled verbally when we hear one of the artists signalling the nearby Ministry of the Interior. The words and images of Ahl Al Kahf's intervention are more explicit and more conventionally 'revolutionary' than those of El Seed. Yet, they – and the video – similarly convey the revolution as ongoing. Tlili's video also comparably focuses on the art process. In this case, the emphasis on the process reveals the

---

[55] The print of *Radar Rat* is dated 2004, while the graffiti was originally produced at Santa's Ghetto, Dragon Bar, Shoreditch, London, 2002 (artificialgallery.co.uk).

particular conditions of production; that is, the continuation of censorship and the constraints within which artists work.

This video, like the intervention it depicts, diverges from the multi-layered and formal complexity of El Madinati's video of El Seed. Yet, it still ambivalently interpolates its diverse audience through cultural and medial elements. The visual languages of the artists' intervention are iconic, but the local political figures and the transnational *Radar Rat* will be familiar to different degrees for their diverse audiences. These images are combined with verbal languages. We hear them discuss the interim government and their own activities in *Darija*, while we see standard Arabic and English – spoken and written, scrawled on the wall and as subtitles in the film. In this case, the video is embedded in an article in the multilingual magazine *Jadaliyya*, which contributes further layers.[56] The text, surrounding a photograph and video of the intervention, summarises the graffiti artists' point of view regarding the post-revolutionary transitional government. It also reveals the group's influence by artists and thinkers from Europe and the USA (Banksy, Ernest Pignon, Foucault, Deleuze and Negri), as well as their belief in their group as a 'universal movement beyond borders, breaking limits and opening up to the possibility of setting up a new world'.[57] These figures of resistance to authoritarianism in diverse contexts, like the characters depicted by Ahl Al Kahf, will be familiar to different degrees for their shifting audience. While this list consists of figures from 'the West', the video highlights reappropriative uses of the transnational by Tunisian artists and a Tunisian filmmaker at a local site in combination with local *Darija* alongside transnational Arabic and English. This negotiation between the local and the transnational might remind us of Rachida Triki's perception of 'transcultural resistance' in Tunisian art in 2009, which I discussed at the outset. At the same time, this video exemplifies the multidirectional complexity – extending to the surrounding text and its diverse online audience – and the direct confrontation with the iconic, which can often be found in post-2010 Tunisian art.

Tlili's video, like El Madinati's portrayal of El Seed and his intervention, also moves beyond the visual and verbal graffiti, giving more

[56] The full text can be found at www.middleeastdigest.com/pages/index/6058/ahl-al-kahf_graffiti (last accessed April 2019).
[57] Translation by *Jadaliyya* (I have altered the last word, which reads 'worked').

attention to the corporeal, haptic and auditory process. We see close-ups of the artists' faces and hands as they draw, apply dripping paint or peel apart templates in their apartment, and hear them whispering, shaking aerosol cans and spraying them as they work in the dark and rain. We watch the furtive gestures of their shadowy figures as they work, by contrast with El Seed, without permission. At the same time, the spectators' vision is restricted. Not only are the artists shown through close-ups and in fragments, reminiscent of Arebi's work, or in darkness, but the location and wider space are hidden by the filmmaker's exclusive focus on the artists. The gap between space and spectators is produced, as in the video of El Seed, not only through the multilingual and the multisensorial but also via a dynamic between control and contingency, the potential for which is heightened by the work's filming outside and in motion.

While El Madinati's video of El Seed connects sites through the editing of shots from multiple vantage points, conveying the filmmaker's movement implicitly, Tlili films the sequence outside as he walks. The shaking camera conveys the filmmaker's presence and his movement. The footage is, in this case, determined by the people followed, reminiscent of Katia Kameli's particular, postcolonial form of filming while walking in Algiers, to which I referred in Chapter 2. Yet, by contrast with Kameli's video and that of El Seed, Tlili's video, made in quiet streets at night, does not produce encounters with 'participants'. In this video, the relationship is reversed: the filmmaker-participant follows the artists. The footage is left unedited, in this case, though it is shaped by the parameters established and the camera angles, frames and, subsequently, subtitles adopted by the artist. In addition to restricting the spectators' views of the city, the work is cut short. The final shot freezes for several seconds on the iconoclastic gesture of one of the artists throwing paint at the piece, suspending the 'story'. In this video, the performers and the surrounding iconic space shift between concealing and revealing and between control and contingency, as well as between artists and participant/s, while questioning the apparent stability of these roles. It focuses, in a contrasting way to Karray's photographic performances, on artists who are paradoxically hidden yet identified. Through a video displayed online, this clandestine intervention becomes public after the event. This work, comparable to the video of El Seed, heightens ambiguity through the artists' performance, but it combines a graffiti style, a time of night and a mode of filming which together indicate the censorship and dangers still faced by artists in Tunisia.

JR's *InsideOut* project ('Part 1 – Tunis') also intervenes at key sites in the Tunisian capital, but during the day and by involving the local public (see www.insideoutproject.net/en/group-actions/tunis-tunisia). The video shows JR and the Tunisian photographers finding and taking photographs of passers-by on the streets of Tunis before enlarging them for display on public walls to replace the ubiquitous image of the former leader. We see ordinary members of the public pasting the images on the wall and, after the event, their responses to the project, including both positive and negative reactions. The multi-layered and extensively edited video by Siddons creates an interface comparable to that of El Madinati's video of El Seed. This video similarly shifts between documentary and artistic modes. Scenes in which the artists plan or discuss the progress of the project in a studio, or they or members of the public are interviewed on the street, are, as in El Seed's work, alternated with often high-speed sequences set to music, which show the project or the wider environment. The video also shifts between shots of the work in process and the finished displays. By contrast, however, with El Seed's use of a distinctive hip hop track which, paired with calligraphy and painted on a mosque, can be connected to secular culture, this video uses a variety of mostly original non-culture-specific music.[58] It also interweaves a sequence, just before the end of the video, showing a fragment of the *InsideOut* project's later journey to Hashma in Japan, incorporating a transversal transnational connection.[59] At the same time, the intervention is similarly anchored in its local context through shots of key sites and via the use of French and Tunisian Arabic by the participants and viewers, or French by the artists. The intended international audience is signalled by the provision of subtitles in English, and the artists often switch between French and English when interviewed. This work also includes a piece of found footage of revolutionary demonstrations in Tunis, which calls to mind Horani's video. In *InsideOut*, 'Part 1 – Tunis' this sequence is one of the first and serves to contextualise the

---

[58] The opening track, 'Patchouli Oil and Karaté', was composed by Max Richter for Ari Folman's film *Waltz with Bachir* (2008). The other tracks are original music by Chapelier Fou.

[59] The transversal connection to Japan emerges explicitly, by contrast with Karray's *Noir*.

project. Yet, closer to the video of El Seed, Siddons's portrayal of this intervention in the streets of Tunis heightens ambivalence around iconic spaces by incorporating contingency through the peripatetic mode and participation. The video of this photographic project, though, reveals alternative forms of engaging – and involving directly – various types of participant, and of filming the project from its preparation to its reception. It conveys tensions particular to Tunisia in the months immediately following the revolution, like Tlili's portrayal of Ahl Al Kahf, but, by contrast, via local responses to the work.

Shots of the completed displays show multiple photographs of ordinary Tunisian people of all generations and communities. The single photograph of the former dictator gives way to plurality and diversity; as one of the photographers, Sophia Baraket, states, 'c'est une sorte de replacement du roi par le peuple' ('it's a kind of replacement of the king by the people'). These images are frequently also unconventional in displaying comical or emotional expressions. Using the genre of the photographic portrait, however, they do not depart radically from the iconic language they replace. This may be one reason for the negative responses of some observers of the images *in situ*: 'Either you put up 10 million Tunisians, or no one', we hear one man say in *Darija* towards the end of the video in a scene showing the photographs being torn down by members of the public. The images, as I mentioned in Chapter 3, seem to have been misinterpreted as elevating a few to a position of superiority. Viewed from below, the photographs pasted at high points might indeed seem to dominate the observer in their placement, large scale and visual clarity; they might appear to fuse with the sites of power they adorn. The video, though, shifts the emphasis from these visual images to the performance and the longer material and dialogical process in which they were produced.

Diverging from the videos of El Seed and Ahl Al Kahf, the images in this video of a photographic project can be seen as records of performances by public participants, taking further the role of chance in the performance of the artwork. The images emerge and evolve in the exchanges between JR and various types of participant, each of whom contributes to shaping the work and becomes – along with JR – a performer in the video: the photographers, the people photographed, those pasting the work on the walls and commenting on the project, and other members of the public who react to the works either verbally or physically. The contingency involved in making the images is conveyed by sequences showing how ordinary people are arbitrarily selected as the photographers drive around Tunis. We see how people choose, to a great extent, how they will be portrayed. The video shows the images to be negotiable and touchable material fragments. We see them emerging from the printer and being handled and rearranged on the ground of a studio by the photographers. We see them moulded onto walls by the glue-covered hands of participants, a gesture which comes to be associated with social and political (revolutionary) activism through one boy's words: 'je voulais rentrer à la maison aujourd'hui bourré de colle, et quand ils vont me poser la question « qu'est-ce que vous étiez en train de faire? » je vais leur répondre « j'étais en train de faire quelque chose pour mon peuple! »' ('I wanted to go home today covered in glue, and when they ask me "what have you been doing?" I'm going to answer "I've been doing something for my people!"'). Close-ups highlight the contingent imperfections in some photographs, as the uneven surface of the wall shows through. Shots of the final stage of the process show strips of the portraits being torn from this surface, while people express their anger at the intervention. This palimpsestic process, in which each kinaesthetic and verbal intervention displays traces of the previous layer or perception of Tunisia, conveys the conflict, contradiction and negotiation involved in 'revolution' and 'democracy'.

The video shows not only a sensorial and social renegotiation of the photographic image but also a reordering of space. Comparable to the mediation of El Seed's graffiti on the Jara mosque, this video situates the work in its wider environment. The spectators of the photographs *in situ* would have been unlikely to view all the interventions, given the distance between them and the absence of framing elements such as a pamphlet or map. The video, though, uses its capacity to compress the space and time of the project to show the various sites and interventions together. On the webpage 'Part 1 – Tunis', moreover, the video is accompanied by a collection of the photographs, which juxtaposes the project's reappropriation of central recognisable embodiments of authority, present and past (on which the video focuses), such as the police station or the Bab Al Bahr, with those covering walls or an ensemble of burnt-out cars on the coastal periphery. It thereby relativises the 'centre' and locus of political power. The video's presentation of the work as a whole, including verbal explanations of the artists' intentions, strengthens the power of the intervention. At the same time, it highlights the complexity of resistance in Tunisia and the tensions that characterised this particular historical moment. The video encourages a rethinking of iconic space not only through this spatio-temporal compression and juxtaposition, but also through the reordering of the art process. The intervention is framed by the negative responses to it, including these as an integral part of the work. At the beginning of the video, following shots of the images being printed and mailed, and piles of destroyed identity documents at the ransacked police station, the video shows traces of the images torn from the walls of Tunis. When the video turns, in the final sequence, to focus on the people who come to tear down the posters, the sites and images accumulate a further layer, which is reflected by differences in language and mode of filming. While English and French (with French or Arabic accents) predominate in the video, there is a noticeable shift, at this point, primarily to Tunisian Arabic. These people convey their views spontaneously, rather than as part of an interview. This shift communicates competing perspectives on what Tunisia should 'look' like (we might recall Mhiri and Jemal Siala's installation), as well as the particular connotations of photographic portraiture in the locality filmed and at this juncture.

The kinaesthetic process displayed in the video of JR's project might also be compared to the traces of opposition to the elements of Jemal Siala and Mhiri's installation that reached the streets of Tunis and Sfax (see Chapter 3). The video of JR's work similarly exemplifies participatory artwork that can be seen as democratic, precisely in including contingent conflicting voices. While some perceived the intervention as unjustly elevating a few to a position of superiority, others, according to photographer Marco Berrebi, saw it as a violation of Islam or simply as unnecessarily provocative; moreover, 'In the flux of Tunisia's political transition, everything is contested after decades of imposed silence.'[60] The video reflects Bishop's and Foster's view that

---

[60] In an interview with Yasmine Ryan, for Al Jazeera, Marco Berrebi, describes how JR and the photographers had to abandon their first attempt to paste the images on a fortress at La Goulette, a suburb north of the capital, after a crowd of locals turned angry. The images had been pasted at night and people had not been consulted. Posters on the Bab Al Bahr (also known as La Porte de France) were also pasted during the night and torn down by 7 a.m. Berrebi cites one of the photographers, Aziz Tnani: 'Some people told us "we saw so many pictures for so many years, we don't want anyone to impose their pictures anymore".' Following this, the project took a more participatory approach in Sfax, Sidi

participatory art is not inherently 'good' and has 'no intrinsic or fixed political affiliation', which I discussed in Chapter 3 (Foster, 2006: 195; Bishop, 2012: 8). Instead, the video records contrasting perspectives, which the project allowed to emerge organically. This video's inclusion of the voices and conflicting responses of the work's local audience contrasts with the video of Ahl Al Kahf's clandestine intervention, which freezes mid-process, and the video of El Seed's work, which conveys a seemingly harmonious intervention and reception. The comments on the video of El Seed's intervention on YouTube do, in fact, include occasional negative, anti-Islamic or pro-Islamic responses.[61] Through the open, public website used for the video of El Seed's work, contingency is heightened and, with this, we might say, the potential for a democratic exchange in a space and time beyond the video. JR's closed project website, by contrast, does not allow for comments. Such democratic exchange does, though, occur through the medium of video and, specifically, via Siddons's use of time, together with JR's use of site and participation. Through this video's extension of the work in time, and its emphasis on the process of production and reception, the former sites of power dominated by Ben Ali's image are not simply reappropriated: they become sites of contestation and dialogue. These sites shape the image, determining its location, scale and surface, while they are also shaped by it. By including hostile responses to the photographs, the video also highlights that the project's medium and method, which was first used in the suburbs of Paris, cannot simply

Bouzid and Le Kram, where they arrived earlier to explain the project and locals helped to create the collages. As Berrebi states: 'Surprise might work with street art projects elsewhere, but the artists quickly realised dialogue is just as crucial to the artistic scene as it is to the political sphere in post-uprising Tunisia.' Many people in Le Kram, though, were still opposed to the photos; this is where they were seen, contrastingly, as a needless provocation or a violation of Islam. See Berrebi, cited in Yasmine Ryan (2011). A blog post by Adeline Chenon Ramlat, regarding the response to the photographs on the Bab Al Bahr, highlights some people's aversion specifically to the use of such a monument as a site for the intervention, while one member of the public she cites attributes this response simply to 'la «dégage attitude»' (Chenon Ramlat, 2011).

[61] One viewer comments: 'youre [sic] also proud to protest and burn U.S. embassies and kill our ambassador over a film speaking the truth for your evil and satanic religion???' A further viewer refers to a comment which had criticised El Seed's use of the Qur'an 'as decorations': 'Somebody disliked this video are you kidding me? Yea, I know were not supposed to use Quran as decorations but maybe this as a reminder yea? [sic]' (the original comment is no longer visible). (Last accessed in 2018.)

be transposed. Indeed, following these interventions in Tunisia, the transnational project encouraged people to choose their own sites and take their own photographs.[62] The dialogical process, in this cultural and historical context, thus shaped not only the site and images but also the art process itself. This video encourages spectators to reassess their views not only of Tunisia but also of the role of art in this context.

'Je danserai malgré tout 3', one of a series of dance videos by Art Solution, converges with those of the diverse street art practices of El Seed, Ahl Al Kahf and JR in focusing on a corporeal performance in such a way that key sites and monuments shift between concealing and revealing, control and contingency (see https://www.youtube.com/watch?v=4OfWQ2GaVHg). This video, though, allows for an alternative perspective on aesthetics of the interface by portraying an intervention that avoids direct physical contact between the body and architecture. This intervention does not leave a mark on the space – either permanent or provisional. The dynamic between control and contingency develops, also, through distinctive means of combining the movements of dancers, participants and cameras.

The idea to produce these videos came to dancer, choreographer and filmmaker Bahri Ben Yahmed, leader of Art Solution, following an incident on 25 March 2012. Ben Yahmed describes, in an interview with *L'Orient-Le Jour*, how artists performing on the Avenue Habib Bourguiba were attacked by Salafist demonstrators and told: 'La rue ne vous appartient plus!' ('The street doesn't belong to you anymore!') (cited by Rania Massoud, 2012). Following this incident, on 28 March the Ministry of the Interior banned all demonstrations on the Avenue Bourguiba (Massoud, 2012). The series of videos – one of which took place outside the Ministry of the Interior – were a means of resisting these practices and affirming that 'La rue nous appartient encore!'; 'Ces vidéos sont l'expression d'un acte de résistance contre l'obscurantisme' ('The street still belongs to us!'; 'These videos are the expression of an

---

[62] For subsequent parts of the project, people have been encouraged to upload their own digital images, which are sent back to them as poster-size prints. This process is shown in the first sequence of Siddons's video, though it was not used for the first part of *InsideOut* in Tunis. The project began before the website was launched and the photographs were archived there (see Ferdman, 2012: 21). The revised method would likely still have provoked the same reactions, recorded by Berrebi and Chenon Ramlat (see above), since these were due to the style and/or site selected.

act of resistance to obscurantism') (Ben Yahmed, cited by Massoud, 2012). The videos were an instant hit, the first – disseminated on YouTube on 8 November – attracting more than 15,000 viewers in a few days; the second receiving 48,000 clicks in just two days (Massoud, 2012). The group appears on the streets 'à la manière d'un flashmob' (Massoud, 2012), surprising passers-by as they suddenly begin to dance. 'Je danserai malgré tout 3' presents the group of dancers in the populated public space in front of the Bab Al Bahr in central Tunis. They move to the mesmerising rhythmic beat of darboukas (Tunisian drums) and encourage passers-by to join them.

This video, by contrast with the videos of graffiti-performance or of the performance surrounding JR's photographs, records a work that was already a performance in its original live form. It does not film the artists or participants in interview, reflecting on the work. This video unfolds simply in real time. Yet, the identifiable Tunisian locality is similarly combined with local, regional and transnational cultural elements. The sounds of darboukas and ululating can be heard amid the shouting, clapping and cheering, while the dancers' movements flow between lyrical dance, breakdance and hip hop, as well as traditional Tunisian and Maghrebi dance.[63] In this video, allusions to various cultural spaces are 'layered' through site, music, corporeal language and, to some extent, verbal language. There is no need for subtitles, though the framing shots display text in French and English. The English name, Art Solution, appears with the French words 'Service de l'UNDERGROUND' in the collective's circular logo in the first shot. Two further preliminary shots reveal an additional title, 'Danseurs citoyens 3', and the words of German-born French diplomat and social activist Stéphane Hessel: 'Créer, c'est Résister. Résister, c'est Créer' ('Creating is Resisting. Resisting is Creating'). This slogan

---

[63] Writing of the series 'Je danserai malgré tout', as a whole, semiologist Mariem Guellouz states that the dances selected by the collective are Western, which might help to explain why some spectators respond with indifference or wariness (Guellouz, 2013). This interview with Guellouz, however, took place before this third video, in which movements reminiscent of traditional Tunisian and wider Maghrebi dance can be seen, and the performance is accompanied by the rhythm of the darboukas. Spectators are presumably still surprised by the incongruity of the dance in the street, the casual clothes of the dancers and the use of Western dance styles, but they are, in this case, visibly enthralled and often amused by the performance, and many participate. Ben Yahmed points to the shift in the series with 'Je danserai malgré tout 3', as I discuss below.

alludes, for those familiar with Hessel, to a further cultural space and connects the ongoing Tunisian revolution to other histories of resistance.[64] The hip hop moves in this intervention can be compared to the visual and auditory references to this genre in the video of El Seed's work. This video similarly also interpolates spectators by juxtaposing an iconic monument and space with the everyday. The dancers wear casual clothes; they and their audience are surrounded by daily scenes of people sitting at cafés or passing by. This video displays a simpler act of resistance to state authoritarianism, more comparable to that of Ahl Al Kahf; the Bab Al Bahr embodies the authority of the former regime, as well as that – post-revolutionary – which attempted to curb freedom of expression in the streets (it was formerly known, moreover, as La Porte de France; see Chapter 3). Yet, converging with the video of Gabès, this video similarly diminishes the power of the iconic through its emphasis on the everyday and corporeal movement: in this case, the everyday, corporeal movement and participation are closely combined.

The title, 'danseurs-citoyens', can be taken to refer not only to the professional dancers but also to the participants. Diverse ordinary people are engaged through encounters in the street, as in JR's project but, in this video, they are drawn in as the performance unfolds. These participants, in this case, perform the same activity as the professional dancers. The established dance group planned and triggered the performance, but they allow it to be shaped by passers-by. These amateur dancers are free to improvise and, when they are dancing face-to-face with the professionals, at times they inspire them spontaneously to take up similar movements. In 'Je danserai malgré tout 3', there is more participation than in the first two videos. Indeed, the moves reminiscent of traditional local and wider regional dance are introduced by the participants, encouraged by the sounds of the darboukas. Ben Yahmed points to the shift in the character of the series with this third video: '*Si les deux premières vidéos visaient à présenter l'idée, dans la troisième nous cherchons à réconcilier les Tunisiens avec l'art de la danse en*

---

[64] Hessel is particularly well known for his political pamphlet *Indignez-vous!* (2010) (Time for Outrage! (2011)). Hessel's name does not appear in this video, though it does appear beside the citation in an opening shot in the first two videos. These additional directions would, therefore, only be apparent to viewers if they had watched one of the first two videos and were familiar with Hessel's work, or if they had read the widely available reviews of the series.

l'associant à la musique traditionnelle' ('If the first two videos aimed to present the idea, in the third we sought to reconcile Tunisians with the art of dance by associating it with traditional music'); he sees dance as a means for Tunisian people to find and express their identity: '*la danse parle au Tunisien qui est en eux.*' ('*dance speaks to the Tunisian in them*') (cited by Khlifi, 2013); italicised in the original). The Bab Al Bahr and this central public space are counterbalanced by uncontrolled, and uncontrollable, corporeal language, which had been banned by Ben Ali's regime and which continued to be censored in 2012. Art historian Tracy Warr has highlighted the inherent instability of corporeal language: '[c]ompared to verbal language or visual symbolism, the "parts of speech" of corporeal language are relatively imprecise. The body as a language is at once inflexible and too flexible. Much can be expressed, whether deliberately or not, through the body's behaviour ... No amount of critical contextualizing or artists' insistence on intention can stabilize the language of the body' (Warr, ed., 2000: 13). At this site and historical moment in Tunisia, dancing is unavoidably an act of resistance. In this case, corporeal instability and uncontrollability are heightened through the contingent involvement of ordinary people and the spontaneous nature of their engagement while going about their daily business. The performance develops amid a crowd of people and everyday activity, while the boundaries between art and life are crossed as some observe from afar, stop to watch, or join the dance. Yet, it is the video of this everyday performance that frames it explicitly, and strengthens it, as an act of resistance and ensures its relative durability and its reach across and beyond Tunisia.

The coupling and interchangeability of creating and resisting, which is signalled by the introductory quotation from Hessel, binds the performance to the political. This relationship is reinforced by the framing of the dance against the backdrop of the Bab Al Bahr and surrounding architecture. The iconic space shifts in and out of view as the cameras follow the dancers. This act of filming while following is comparable to that of Ridha Tlili for his video of Ahl Al Kahf, though in Art Solution's video the performers move within the same area and the viewpoint follows the performers and shifts between cameras, moving around the evolving group. It is the displacements of both that cause the grand imposing monument either to appear in parts in the background or to slip out of the frame entirely. The contrasting final

Digitising Street Encounters 219

sequence, after the dance has ended, is an aerial shot which pans to the right, framing and anchoring the act of resistance in its wider environment and context. The video is, until this moment, tightly focused on the dance and the Bab Al Bahr. The fragmentary and shifting space we see contrasts with the whole, static and apparently timeless 'postcard' view of the Bab Al Bahr that has frequently been circulated. We see the everyday life and the diversity of Tunisian society, which are usually excluded by the frame. The video's display online allows, moreover, for conflicting perspectives on Tunisia.[65]

While this intervention does not leave a trace on the street, the video converges with those of El Seed, Ahl Al Kahf and JR in interpolating diverse spectators by capturing the interaction between ordered public space and disruptive corporeal performance. The artists, in this case, perform in both live and screened versions of the intervention. Yet, their centrality is similarly questioned by the involvement of others. Here, though, participants contribute to the performance in the same way as the artists. The absence of sequences showing artists and members of the public – participants, observers or passers-by – separately, including scenes of the work being planned or artists or others reflecting on the work, contributes to this blurring of boundaries. Dance and daily life evolve and intermingle, moreover, in the same space. The representation of space depends, to a great extent, on the dancers – professional and amateur – who are the focus of the piece. The dancers are allowed largely to determine the shape and pace of the footage, as well as the camera angles and levels of focus adopted. Their 'unstable' movement, identified explicitly with resistance, is heightened through the improvised interactions between dancers, participants and cameramen.

These diverse online videos presenting street art or dance in public spaces in Tunisia converge with studio-based performances in

---

[65] Evidence of the video's reach can be seen in the comments on YouTube. Some reveal their origins: many are from Tunisia; one is from Algeria; one is from Romania. The comments are in English, French, Arabic, *Darija* and/or emojis (or the smile symbol made of a colon and bracket). The responses are reminiscent of those to the video of El Seed's graffiti-performance: most are positive, congratulating the artists or expressing their pride to be Tunisian, while two comments reflect the view that this dance is not representative of Tunisians and 'tounes balad al ISLAM!!!' 'Tunisia country of ISLAM!!!'. The video's display online extends participation to verbal modes and allows democratically for conflicting perspectives on Tunisia, which are not captured within the video.

alternative media and/or contexts in interpolating spectators, but also distancing them. Spectators are similarly drawn in through the corporeal, the haptic, the auditory and the verbal, while they are variously attracted or distanced by a performance that shifts between concealing and revealing and between contrasting local and transnational cultural spaces. Yet, each of these videos of an outdoor intervention extends the performance in time and space to produce a more complex multi-layered interface that disrupts familiar views of iconic sites. The original intervention becomes a performance, if it was not already a performance, but it is shown to be connected to, and shaped by, the artist, the site and the community. The artist/s interacts with participants, from the filmmaker, cameramen or co-photographers to the passers-by who are involved, directly or indirectly, knowingly or unknowingly. In some cases, we see public responses to the work: verbal or corporeal, positive or negative. The intervention, like the iconic sites themselves, emerges and evolves in these dynamic exchanges between moving bodies on and off screen.

Conclusion

These diverse works imaging bodies in photography or video converge in forging an ambivalent corporeal language between essentialising external and internal perceptions of revolution and nation. They each provide an alternative to the 'spectacular' revolutionary body through which they rework specific icons or iconic spaces. They resonate with the words of Meriem Bouderbala and Amelia Jones in attracting yet distancing the spectators, while they develop a shifting, multi-layered interface. They might also be seen to revitalise and re-historicise the practice of concealing and revealing the body.

In each work, the embodied spectators are engaged through the layers that expose or obscure the bodies' contours and surfaces – fabric, writing, or light and shadow – or/and through the performers' looks, expressions, gestures or movements. The intersubjective gap is maintained, at the same time, through framing, composition, multiplication, constrained angles, extreme close-ups, rhythmic editing, a shifting viewpoint or high-speed footage. The body and the icons or sites with which the performer interacts hover or shift between concealment and exposure, and between the times, spaces and media which are alternated, juxtaposed, rearranged or superimposed. The

Conclusion

interface is complicated further by references to particular images, sites, materials, practices, clothing, music, or movements, which will resonate differently with diversely located (and travelled) spectators. The content of the work is also subject to interpretation and evolution due to the use of various languages and accents, which are incorporated through oral narrative or written text and produced during the performance, the after-process or the exhibition of the work in a gallery or online. Icons and sites are frequently reshaped, not only through spontaneously created footage or contributions – including responses to the work – by people other than the artist/s but also via the contingent movements of the body. Such movements, comparable to the contingent encounters I discussed in Chapters 2 and 3, range from the imperceptible shifts that cause henna, fabric or shadows to change shape or shade to the spontaneous or unknowing poses, actions or displacements of the artist/s or participants. Through such shifts, people and spaces avoid objectification; viewers and viewed are connected while opacity is protected.

The trope of concealing and revealing can run the risk of reifying Orientalist or patriarchal images. Yet, it can be used in new and multidirectional ways to explore and question the tendency to polarise religious and secular views, to convey freedom of expression but also censorship or clandestine creation and (different degrees of) danger for the artist, or to include conflicting views and voices. The shifts between stability and instability, in these works, convey a revolution between constraint and liberation, yet also certainty and uncertainty. These shifts can be used to convey women's – and men's – predicament between victimhood and agency, and that of societies between stasis and dynamism, commemoration and hope for the future, censorship and open debate. In combining sensorial, medial and cultural means of interpolating and distancing their diverse internal and external public, such art reworks former icons and sites of power. At the same time, it alerts spectators to the ongoing need for resistance to forms of authoritarianism or to attitudes that divide cultures and communities.

Conclusion
Art and Revolution: Aesthetics and Approaches

A wide-ranging corpus of art exploring revolutions in countries from Tunisia to Syria moves beyond what Jellel Gasteli dubbed 'icons of revolutionary exoticism'. This art forges a way between the essentialising internal and external visions perpetuated by iconic or iconoclastic images, encouraging a more nuanced understanding of the revolutions. It also enables spectators to develop a greater consciousness – mediated through their senses as well as through their intellect – of the meaning of the term 'revolution'. Diverging from the idea of a completed cycle that is implied by this term, 'revolution' comes to signify not simply liberation but also uncertainty and fragility. It accommodates transition and negotiation. By contrast with iconic representations, this art creates a space and a moment in time for reflection on specific local experiences of revolt or on the wider complex phenomenon of the Uprisings. It encourages patience and humility in attempting to understand their diverse and still unfolding trajectories. This art frequently points to the emergence of new or ongoing forms of constraint, as a result of reductive and, at times, extremist visions. At the same time, it resists these visions, creating a space beyond the habitual revolutionary binaries of friend and enemy, or secularism and religion, allowing for diversity and dialogue as it gestures towards the future. This art is resolutely anchored in distinct historical and political contexts. While certain works present a 'reordering' of space and the sensorium in ways that call to mind Rancière's argument regarding the re-'distribution of the sensible' (2004: 12–13 [2000]), this corpus demonstrates an alternative relationship between art and politics. It creates a shifting space between politics and poetics. These works can be situated on a continuum between art and activism, often crossing the languages, practices and spaces of both. They frequently allude to an icon, while exceeding and transforming it. But they do not transform it entirely, replacing one icon with another; these works explore passages between meanings and beyond messages. They shift between stability and instability and involve their diverse audience in this process. Indeed, moving away from the direct and unidirectional communication of the creator's message, which is sought via icons, the relationship between art and activism is shaped and reshaped – in different sites and formats – between the artist/s, the work and its participants.

This art exploring the revolutions evokes different languages, states or identities, while holding them in tension. Apparent polar opposites are questioned and shown to coexist interdependently, in a reciprocal, relational dialogue that allows alternative visions to emerge. These works render perceptible the separation between opposites or between multiple essentialising discourses – or, in some cases, beyond one particular constraining vision. It is the dynamic between stability and *in*stability that creates a space for alternative voices and visions. This dynamic resonates, to some extent, with existing ideas and practices, while it also moves beyond them. It might call to mind, in some works, Duchamp's exploration of the interval or nuance that separates material objects, dimensions, senses, states or concepts. Yet, works exploring the revolutions allude specifically to iconic visions and reductive discourses in contexts of ongoing revolution or/and emerging democracy. The space they create is associated with resistance in the sense that it makes way for alternative, non-essentialising voices, visions and understandings of distinct revolutionary circumstances and stages. These works, moreover, frequently employ or call to mind diverse enduring transnational – including local or regional – practices or materials, which already evoke the passages and shifts that are characteristic of the infra-thin. These practices are similarly anchored and adapted, or new practices are invented, to explore the boundary not only between the specific and the singular, and between metaphor and materiality, but also between the translatable and the untranslatable, politics and poetics. Contingent encounters in art exploring the revolutions similarly resonate with diversely transnational practices – from enduring traditions of weaving, ceramics and calligraphy or chance aesthetics to social practices associated with tourism, voting or internet fora. Yet, this art also invents new combinations or strategies of balancing control and contingency in response to diverse contexts of revolution. It deliberately incorporates contingency, moreover, for the purposes of resistance. It is through the presence of seemingly static, anchoring elements that the dynamic between control and contingency – like that between visibility and invisibility – comes to be associated with resistance. We perceive, in these contingent encounters – as in work that evokes an infra-thin critique – allusions to apparent stability (via diversely recognisable faces, spaces, structures or practices, for example) *together with* unstable, non-discursive, irreducible elements.

The intersubjective gap that this dynamic creates calls to mind Duchamp's note on the infra-thin separation between the work of art and the spectator's gaze. It also resonates with theory and practice surrounding this gap in relation to images of the body or cultural bodily practices. Yet, in these works exploring diverse manifestations of the Arab Uprisings, the body and its movements – like contingent or infra-thin materials or practices – generate instability in relation to markers of stability. This artwork, as we have seen, interpolates spectators via a more complex, multi-layered interface, which involves sensorial, medial and cultural elements. It reveals alternative means and purposes of concealing and revealing the body. At the same time, it can be seen to expand this trope beyond the use of fabric or marks on the skin to encompass the frame or the boundaries surrounding cultures or communities. This interface generates a shifting gap between spectators and not only the bodies they perceive but also the icons or iconic spaces that are destabilised and reshaped by those bodies. Such an interface can, as I suggested at the outset, also be found in the works explored in the first three chapters. This concept can be extended to works that explore and renegotiate an object or space. This art exploring the revolutions involves spectators by immersing them while simultaneously distorting or constraining their view of a potentially iconic body, object or space. Spectators are diversely drawn into these works by familiar faces, spaces, structures, images, practices or languages. At the same time, they are encouraged to consider the revolutions in ways that move beyond the binaries of success and failure. The ideas and practices demonstrated across this corpus are interconnected.

Each work generates an alternative space and an intersubjective gap in shifting between presence and absence, revealing and concealing, control and contingency, the visual and other senses, stasis and movement, inside and outside, and/or meaning (referential or metaphorical) and non-discursive sound, materiality or corporeality. The body, object or scene hovers between appearance and disappearance through the use of white on white, figuration on a transparent surface, light and shadow, evolving organic matter, or shifting fabric – to evoke absence or hide presence. It can be partially hidden or revealed through framing, restrictive camera angles, or the blurring of an image through close-ups or high-speed travelling or filming. The boundary between inside and outside is explored not only via fabric or frame but also through the reflective surfaces of windows, the play of light and shadow or, metaphorically, through role reversals. The potential icon is suspended, alternatively or additionally, in the passage between the visual or verbal and the haptic, the auditory, the olfactory, the kinetic or/and the kinaesthetic. Alternatively, it shifts between different media, formats or sites. The space between the work and the spectators is, at times, created through the coexistence of stillness and movement – of organic materials (from henna to jasmine), kinetic objects, footage, or the performer/s, artist/s or participant/s. It is produced through the juxtaposition of form and formlessness, wholeness and fragmentation, or a linear sequence or process that is reordered, repeated, accelerated, decelerated or superimposed by another image. This shifting space is frequently generated via the dynamic between control and contingency. This occurs not only through stable and unstable substances, parameters and processes, or stasis and the unpredictable movements of the artist's or performer's body, but also via participants' contributions to the work at the stages of its production, exhibition and reception – from conceptual or physical interactions to active and creative additions. Through overlapping means of exploring the dynamic between stability and instability, this art evokes the revolutions while protecting opacity, in a flexible and provisional sense, and encourages spectators to contribute to this process from their diverse locations and perspectives.

Rather than analyse these multisensorial works via postcolonial concepts, which were developed in relation to literature or anthropology, I chose to experiment with these interconnected concepts, inspired by the works themselves. My intention was also to adopt an approach I defined as diversely transnational in drawing inspiration from local, regional or other cross-cultural art practices, artists' statements, and criticism from authors based in and beyond the MENA region (primarily in Tunisia, Europe or the USA, such as Tahar Benjelloun, Mohamed Ben Soltane, Jocelyne Dakhlia, Nouri Gana, Jellel Gasteli, Aurélie Machghoul, Alia Nakhli, Jacques Rancière, Hocine Tlili, and Rachida Triki). Duchamp's notes and practices were, for example, balanced with intentional and ironic engagements with his work and uses of potentially 'infra-thin' materials and practices from Tunisia, the wider Maghreb and its diaspora, Syria, or Brazil. The transnational, as I stated at the outset with reference to Drewal, Jay and Appadurai, is heterogeneous, multidirectional, and evolving. It includes transversal trajectories. These can be metaphorical, as they are in the dialogue between Morocco and Brazil in Erruas's installation. Alternatively, such connections are made literally, as exemplified by the processes involved in creating Hamid's *Mohammad Bouazizi* or the Ouissis' project *Laaroussa* – or in producing Henriot's project, which emerged physically on the border between Syria and Turkey. The transnational, as I have used the term in this book, includes the journeys of works from before the stage of production to beyond that of their exhibition, in alternative ways or formats. My analysis of contingent encounters of resistance engaged with the work of critics such as Umberto Eco, Laura U. Marks, Caroline E. Jones, Claire Bishop and Anna Dezeuze, curators Patricia Triki and Christine Bruckbauer, and artists from Georges Bataille and Guy Debord to Hassan Messaoudy and Mounir Fatmi to Katia Kameli, Yto Barrada and Wassim Ghozlani. In relation to the interface, I drew on the criticism of Amelia Jones and Lev Manovich and the statements and practice of artists including Meriem Bouderbala, Lalla Essaydi, Majida Khattari, Mouna Karray and 'JR'. This multidirectional crossing of theory and practice, of different disciplinary fields and of divergent genres of writing, is, I hope to have shown, particularly appropriate in this context. This approach has allowed a multiplicity of converging, and sometimes conflicting, voices and viewpoints in analysing these emerging aesthetics and their evolving relationships to changing revolutionary contexts.

Considering these works of art in the light of existing concepts and practices highlights the distinctiveness of these works and the contexts they explore. The works of art, in turn, allow for alternative perspectives on ideas that are often associated exclusively with European and North American art. They can be seen to bring to the foreground the tension, in the infra-thin, between metaphor and materiality, specificity and singularity, and to link these apparent poles to the discursive and the non-discursive, to diversely familiar 'readable', culturally locatable signs or sites and sensorial, often contingent elements. They might remind us that the infra-thin can involve, variously, the separation or interval between or beyond entities, or multidirectional outward expansion, while they take this further to evoke diverse and evolving collective identities. Materiality converges, again, with meaning in works that incorporate formless materials or substances. These works exceed Bataille's focus on pure materiality, while they also move beyond Caroline A. Jones's identification of the *informe* with self-expression and existentialism or, through Fautrier's work, its connections with commemoration. Analysing works that use the peripatetic mode in the light of Debord's concept of the *dérive* highlights the specificity of their contingent encounters of resistance. The artist-travellers' journeys are reminiscent of this idea of drifting through urban environments. Yet, through these works, the freedom associated with the peripatetic mode is relativised through deceleration and vertical travel at a specific site and historical moment, as well as related obstacles from demonstrations to checkpoints, or police interrogations which lead to coercive displacement. Chance is, at the same time, heightened in these works, but, paradoxically, by imposing stricter parameters – including extreme limitations on sight.

Works that exceed icons by involving others frequently cross the boundaries conventionally established between definitions of participatory and interactive art, and/or between object and process. They can also be seen to question the critical tendency to separate participatory art from chance aesthetics. Participants' involvement can be direct or indirect, provisional or enduring, knowing or unknowing. Contingent encounters hold in tension various stages of the work, which frequently evolves and shifts between formats and contexts. Participatory art produced in this context reflects the view shared by Claire Bishop and Hal Foster that this mode is not inherently 'good' or reflective of a stable political affiliation (Bishop, ed., 2006; Foster, 2006: 195; Bishop, 2012). In certain projects participation is employed primarily as a means to generate contingency, which can, despite the artist's inclusionary intentions, marginalise participants. Others, though, do allow participants to assume a greater, and acknowledged, role in the conceptualisation and/or production of the work. Some works, moreover, incorporate unexpected hostile reactions to the project, democratically exposing plural and conflicting viewpoints, and allowing them to influence the artist's participatory method. Finally, constructions of a multi-layered and culturally multidirectional interface in works exploring a potentially iconic body, object or landscape question, as I have suggested above, the tendencies either to oppose or to fuse viewer and viewed, which Amelia Jones has associated with European and American art.

Re-evaluating the infra-thin, chance aesthetics, participatory art and corporeal images through these works, these ideas and practices are relativised, anchored (in an evolving and already transcultural locality) and historicised. These works expose the unevenness within transnational flows and demonstrate how, just as art practices are reshaped, so too must critical terms be nuanced in relation to specific contexts. These works can be seen to resist a simplistic definition, and celebratory perception, of the 'transnational', as becomes particularly clear when JR's participatory method meets with hostility in Tunis or when Hamwi's 'dérive' in Damascus is halted. Indeed, at the same time, these works move beyond such ideas and practices. As the artists of these works explore the world through shifting local, regional and other transnational lenses, they continue the process of transformation which modernisms have long tended to involve. This art is not without risks, as we have seen in relation to certain participatory work and certain images of the body. Yet, it develops innovative aesthetics capable of conveying alternative perspectives of the revolutions, and of exploring the wider idea of 'revolution'.

References

25 ans de créativité arabe. (2012). Milan: Silvana Editoriale/Institut du Monde Arabe [2nd ed. (2013): *25 Years of Arab Creativity. The Contemporary Arab Art Scene*. Abu Dhabi Festival/Institut du Monde Arabe]; available at: https://issuu.com/hushia80/docs/web_25years_single_463e08f2847112.

Abassi, A. (2010). Mais qui tourne le dos? PRESENCE DES ARTS: Aïcha Filali expose à la galerie Ammar-Farhat. *La Presse de Tunisie*, 18 March; available at: www.turess.com/fr/lapresse/2513.

Adcock, C. (1987). Duchamp's Eroticism: A Mathematical Analysis. *Dada/Surrealism*, 16, 149–67.

Ades, D., N. Cox and D. Hopkins (1999). *Marcel Duchamp*. London: Thames & Hudson.

Al-Arabi Al-Hor (2012). Ahl al-Kahf: Graffiti (in both Arabic and English), 21 June [Arabic/ English]: www.middleeastdigest.com/pages/index/6058/ahl-al-kahf_graffiti.

Allani, A. (2013). The Post-revolution Tunisian Constituent Assembly: Controversy over Powers and Prerogatives. *The Journal of North African Studies*, 18, 1: 131–40; available at: https://doi.org/10.1080/13629387.2012.713590.

Allenby, J. (2002). Re-inventing Cultural Heritage: Palestinian Traditional Costume and Embroidery since 1948. *Textile Society of America Symposium Proceedings*, 500, 101–11; at DigitalCommons@University of Nebraska – Lincoln: http://digitalcommons.unl.edu/tsaconf/500.

Alley, R. (1981). Catalogue entry for *Large Glass* by Marcel Duchamp. In *Catalogue of the Tate Gallery's Collection of Modern Art Other Than Works by British Artists*. London: Tate Gallery and Sotherby Parke-Bernet, pp. 186–91.

Al-Shami, L. (2016). Emerging from "The Kingdom of Silence". Beyond Institutions in Revolutionary Syria. *Ibraaz*, 010_07 / 9 (December) (series: Future Imperfect); at: www.ibraaz.org/publications/75.

Al-Sumait, F., N. Lenze and M. C. Hudson (2014a). Introduction: Broadening Conversations on the Arab Uprisings. Crossing Disciplines, Approaches, and Geographies. In F. Al-Sumait, N. Lenze and M. C. Hudson, eds., *The Arab Uprisings: Catalysts, Dynamics, and Trajectories*. London: Rowman & Littlefield, pp. 16–36.

eds. (2014b). *The Arab Uprisings: Catalysts, Dynamics, and Trajectories*. London: Rowman & Littlefield.

Appadurai, A. (1996). *Modernity at Large: Cultural Dimensions of Globalization*. Minneapolis and London: University of Minnesota Press.

Aragon, L. (1963). *Le Fou d'Elsa*. Paris: Gallimard.

Asad, A. (2016). This Palestinian Artist Embroiders Images of Syrian Gore and Violence. *Vice* (10 January); at: www.vice.com/en_uk/article/nn9mdd/this-palestinian-artist-stitches-embroideries-of-syrian-gore-and-violence.

Bahnasî, A. (1984). *Al-Khatt al-ʿarabî'usûluhu, nahdhatuhu,'intishâruhu* (« L'Écriture arabe, ses origines, sa renaissance et sa diffusion »). Damascus: Dar Al Fikr.

Bahri, I. (2017). Video interview for 'Instruments' (exhibition at Jeu de Paume, Paris, 2017).

Bailey, D. and G. Tawadros, eds. (2003). *Veil: Veiling, Representation and Contemporary Art*. Cambridge, MA: MIT Press; London: Institute of International Visual Art.

Bank, C. (2016). Calling Things by Their Real Names: Anonymity and Artistic Online Production During the Syrian Uprising. *Fusion Journal*, 9; available at: Calling Things by Their Real Names: Anonymity and artistic online production during the Syrian Uprising @ Fusion Journal (fusion-journal.com).

Barthes, R. (1980). *La Chambre claire: note sur la photographie*, Paris: Gallimard.

Bataille, G. (1970). Le Dictionnaire critique: l'informe. *Documents*, 1. 7: 382. Reprinted in G. Bataille, *Œuvres complètes*, vol. 1. Paris: Gallimard.

Bathurst, M. (2012). The Watchtower of Happiness and Other Landscapes of Occupation. *Designweek*, 21 November: www.designweek.co.uk/whats-on/the-watchtower-of-happiness-and-other-landscapes-of-occupation/3035620.article.

Bayat, A. (2010). *Life As Politics: How Ordinary People Change the Middle East*. Stanford, CA: Stanford University Press.

Belhassine, O. (2010). En souffrances contemporaines. Présence des arts – Exposition: « La Part du Corps ». *La Presse de Tunisie*, 22 May; available at: www.turess.com/fr/lapresse/5822.

Ben Azouz, I. (2018). Interview // Meriem Bouderbala, artiste du vivant. *Ideomagazine*, 7 July; at: www.ideomagazine.com/meriem-bouderbala/.

Ben Jelloun, T. (2011). *L'Étincelle: révoltes dans les pays arabes*. Paris: Gallimard.
Ben Labidi, I. (2019). On Naming Arab Revolutions and Oppositional Media Narratives. *International Journal of Cultural Studies*, 22 (3; May): 450–64.
Ben Mhenni, L. (2011). *Tunisian girl: blogueuse pour un printemps arabe* [title, and original text (blog), in Arabic/English/French]. Montpellier: Indigène.
Ben Rejeb, L. (2013). United States Policy towards Tunisia. What New Engagement after an Expendable "Friendship"? In N. Gana, ed., *The Making of the Tunisian Revolution: Contexts, Architects, Prospects*. Edinburgh. Edinburgh University Press, pp. 81–102.
Ben Soltane, M. (2011). Souffle de liberté / Tunisie. Exposition virtuelle. *Nafas Art Magazine* (September); at: https://universes.art/en/nafas/articles/2011/breath-of-freedom/img.
— (2012). Élan et espoir: perspectives de développement des arts visuels en Tunisie après la "révolution". In B. Barsch and C. Bruckbauer, eds., *Connect: Rosige Zukunft: Aktuelle Kunst aus Tunesien* [French/German/English], translations by A. Baatsch et al. Bielefeld and Berlin: Kerber Verlag, pp. 217–31.
Ben Yakoub, J. (2017). Coloring outside the Lines of the Nation. An Iconological Analysis of the Tunisian Revolution. *Middle East: Topics & Arguments*, 8: 31–44.
Bhabha, H. (1994). *The Location of Culture*. London and New York: Routledge.
Binder, P. and G. Haupt. (2010). Tunisia's Art Scene. Interview with Curator and Philosopher Rachida Triki on the Current Developments in Tunisia. *Nafas Art Magazine* (June); at: http://universes-in-universe.org/eng/nafas/articles/2010/tunisia_art_scene.
Bishop, C. (2012). *Artificial Hells: Participatory Art and the Politics of Spectatorship*. London and New York: Verso.
— ed. (2006). *Participation*. London: Whitechapel.
Bois, Y-A. and R. Krauss (1996). *L'Informe: mode d'emploi*. Paris: Centre Georges Pompidou.
Bordier, D. (2013). Le Mouton noir porte la voix des femmes syriennes. *La Nouvelle République* (2 February); at: www.lanouvellerepublique.fr/poitiers/le-mouton-noir-porte-la-voix-des-femmes-syriennes.
Bouderbala, M. (2012). Meriem Bouderbala, Exotisme Partagé. *ArteEast. The Global Platform for Middle East Arts* (Winter 2013; artist's statement dated 2012); at: https://arteeast.org/quarterly/meriem-bouderbala-exotisme-partage/?issues_season=winter&issues_year=2013.
Boudjelal, B. (2009). *Jours intranquilles [Disquiet Days]*, ed. T. O'Mara. London: Autograph ABP.

Bourriaud, N. (1998). *Esthétique relationnelle*. Dijon: Les Presses du réel.
Bowcock, S. (2016). Performing for the Camera. *HarpersBazaarArabia.com* (summer), 46–47.
Bredoux, L. and M. Magnaudeix (2012). *Tunis connexion: enquête sur les réseaux franco-tunisiens sous Ben Ali*. Paris: Seuil.
Brownlee, J., T. Masoud and A. Reynolds (2015). Introduction: The Third Arab Spring. In *The Arab Spring: Pathways of Repression and Reform*. Oxford: Oxford Scholarship Online, pp. 1–14.
Bruckbauer, C. and P. K. Triki (2012). Un avenir en rose. Un passé mauve, un présent parsemé d'obstacles noirs. Expériences personnelles des commissaires et remarques sur les objectifs de ce projet. In B. Barsch and C. Bruckbauer, eds., *Connect: Rosige Zukunft: Aktuelle Kunst aus Tunesien* [French/German/English], translations by A. Baatsch et al. Bielefeld and Berlin: Kerber Verlag, pp. 25–31.
Bruckbauer, C. and P. K. Triki (2016). *The Turn. Socially Engaged Art Practices in Tunisia. Ibraaz*, 010_02 (21 June); at: www.ibraaz.org/essays/158/.
Cage, J. (1961). *Silence*. Middletown, CT: Wesleyan University Press.
Calle, S. (1998). *A Suivre*, Doubles-jeux, livre 4. Arles: Actes Sud.
Charrad, M. M. and A. Zarrugh (2014). Equal or Complementary? Women in the New Tunisian Constitution after the Arab Spring. *The Journal of North African Studies*, 19, 2, 230–43; available at: https://doi.org/10.1080/13629387.2013.857276.
Chebbi, A. Al-K. (1966). *Aghani Al-Hayat* [Songs of Life]. Tunis: Al-Dar al-tunisiya li-l-Nashar.
Chenon Ramlat, A. (2011). La Rue tunisienne, le photographe et JR ... (21 March); at: http://blogs.mediapart.fr/blog/adeline-chenon-ramlat.
Clifford, J. (1997). *Routes: Travel and Translation in the Late Twentieth Century*. Cambridge, MA, and London: Harvard University Press.
Cohen Hadria, M. (2013). *Trois artistes tunisiennes: Nicène Kossentini, Mouna Karray et Moufida Fedhila* (London: KT Press)
Collet, B. (2009). Statement on Safaa Erruas. www.safaaerruas.com/en/pdfs/texte.pdf (December); translation R. Stella.
  (2013). Mouna Karray. In *Ici, ailleurs. Une Exposition d'art contemporain*. Paris (printed Padua): SkiraFlammarion, pp. 122–23.
Cosmic Vinegar (n.d.). Interview with Majd Abdel Hamid. [no author name provided]; at: https://cosmicvinegar.wordpress.com/interviews/interview-with-majd-abdel-hamid/
Crinson, M. (2006). Fragments of Collapsing Space: Postcolonial Theory and Contemporary Art. In A. Jones, ed., *A Companion to Contemporary Art since 1945*. Oxford: Blackwell, pp. 450–69.
Cronin, M. (2000). *Across the Lines: Travel, Language, Translation*. Cork: Cork University Press.

Cros, C. (2006). *Marcel Duchamp*, trans. V. Rehberg. London: Reaktion.
Dagher, C. (1990). *Al-hurûfiyya al-'arabiyya: fann wa huwiyya (Le lettrisme arabe: art et identité)*. Beirut: All Prints Distributors & Publishers.
Dakhlia, J. (2011). *Tunisie: le pays sans bruit*. Paris: Actes Sud.
Davila, T. (2010). *De l'inframince: brève histoire de l'imperceptible*. Paris: Editions du Regard.
Davis, M. E. (2007). *Erik Satie*. London: Reaktion.
Debord, G. (1956). Théorie de la dérive. Translated by K. Knabb, at: www.cddc.vt.edu/sionline/si/theory.html.
de Certeau, M. (1990). *L'Invention du quotidien, vol. 1: Arts de faire*. Paris: Gallimard. [First published 1980.]
Dedman, R. (2013). Emerging Syrian Artists at P21 in London. *Culture and Conflict: Investigating Contemporary Art in Response to International War and Conflict* (review, 11 August); at: www.cultureandconflic.org.uk/news/emerging-syrian-artists-at-p21-in-london/.
  (2016). Unravelled [press release]; at: racheldedman.com/Unravelled-at-Beirut-Art-Center.
Dempsey, A. (2000). Jean Fautrier: Head of a Hostage, 1943–4. *Tate.org* (January); at www.tate.org.uk/art/artworks/fautrier-head-of-a-hostage-t07300.
Depardon, R. (2004). *Errance*. Paris: Editions du Seuil.
Dezeuze, A., ed. (2010). *The 'Do-It-Yourself' Artwork: Participation from Fluxus to New Media*. Manchester: Manchester University Press.
Dirié, C. (2013). Lara Favaretto. In *Ici, ailleurs. Une exposition d'art contemporain*. Paris (printed Padua): SkiraFlammarion, 106–7.
Downey, A. (2014a). For the Common Good? Artistic Practices and Civil Society in Tunisia. In A. Downey, ed., *Uncommon Grounds: New Media and Critical Practices in North Africa and the Middle East*. London: I.B. Tauris, pp. 53–69.
  ed. (2014b). *Uncommon Grounds: New Media and Critical Practices in North Africa and the Middle East*. London: I.B. Tauris.
Dream City 2013 (2013). COLLECTIF WANDA (TUNISIE). Le Ciel est par-dessus le toit Architecture. *DREAM CITY 2013 – VOYAGE A L'ESTAQUE*'; at: dreamcity2013.wordpress.com.
Drewal, H. J. (2013). Local Transformations, Global Inspirations. The Visual Histories and Cultures of Mama Wata Arts in Africa. In G. Salami and M. Blackmun Visonà (eds.), *A Companion to Modern African Art*. Chichester: Wiley & Sons, Inc., pp. 23–49.
Duchamp, M. (1969). *Notes and Projects for the Large Glass*, introduction by A. Schwartz; trans. G. H. Hamilton, C. Gray and A. Schwarz. London: Thames and Hudson.
  (1999). *Notes*, introduction by P. Matisse; preface by P. Hulten. Paris: Flammarion, pp. 19–36. [First published in *View*, March 1945.]

Dunoyer, B., La Luna, A. Machghoul, S. and S. Ouissi, C. Thullier, S. Ben Ayed and A. Blaiech (2011). *Z.A.T Penser la Ville Artistiquement*, 3 (Special issue on the project *Laaroussa*) (August; French/Arabic).
Durand, R. (2010). Kader Attia in Conversation with Régis Durand. *NKA Journal of Contemporary African Art*, 26 (Spring), 70–79.
Eco, U. (2006). The Poetics of the Open Work. In C. Bishop, ed. *Participation*, pp. 20–40. [First published 1962.]
El Madinati (2012). Calligraffiti on Jara Mosque, Gabès – El Seed. Video available at: www.youtube.com/watch?v=NKNTkG5dr4A [Arabic; uploaded 7 September 2012. Also uploaded to Vimeo 6 September 2012].
El Seed (2011). El Seed. With an introduction by P. Zoghbi and D. Karl. In P. Zoghbi and D. Karl, eds., *Arabic Graffiti*. Berlin: From Here to Fame, pp. 101–9.
Eluard, P. (1942). Liberté. In P. Eluard, *Poésie et Vérité*. Paris: Editions de la main à la plume.
Entelis, J. P. (2011). Algeria: Democracy Denied, and Revived? *The Journal of North African Studies*, 16, 4 (Special Issue: North Africa's Arab Spring, ed. G. Joffé), 653–78. doi: 10.1080/13629387.2011.630878.
Enwezor. O. and C. Okeke-Agulu (2009). *Contemporary African Artists since 1980*. Bologne: Damiani.
Erruas, S. (2012). Catalogue entry. In *25 ans de créativité arabe*. Milan: Silvana Editoriale, p. 80.
Esman, A. (2013). Where Sacred Law and Pleasure Collide: The Photographs of Lalla Essaydi. *BlouinArtInfo* (8 December); at: allaessaydi.com/news/PDFS/interviews/BlouinArtInfo_Dec_2013.pdf.
Ferdman, B. (2012). Urban Dramaturgy: The Global Art Project of JR. *PAJ: A Journal of Performance Art*, 34, 3 (September), 12–26. doi: 10.1162/PAJJ_a_00107.
Fisher, J. (2005). The Syncretic Turn. Cross-cultural Practices in the Age of Multiculturalism. In Z. Kocur and S. Leung, eds., *Theory in Contemporary Art since 1985*. Malden, MA, and Oxford: Blackwell [first published 1996], pp. 233–41.
Flaubert, G. (1863 [1862]). *Salammbô*. Paris: Michel Lévy frères.
Forde, K. (2001). You Have Just Entered Room "010101 Round Table". *Open: The Magazine of SFMOMA*, 4 (Winter/Spring), 35.
Foster, H. (2006 [2004]). Chat Rooms. In C. Bishop, ed., *Participation*. London: Whitechapel, pp. 190–95. [First published as Arty Party. *London Review of Books* (4 December 2004), pp. 21–22.]
Gabsi, W. (2012). After the Storm. Michket Krifa in Conversation with Wafa Gabsi. *Ibraaz*, 003, 2 May; at: www.ibraaz.org/interviews/26.
Gafaïti, H., ed. (1999). *Rachid Boudjedra. Une poétique de la subversion: I. Autobiographie et histoire*. Paris: L'Harmattan.

Gana, N. (2013a). Introduction: Collaborative Revolutionism. In N. Gana, ed., *The Making of the Tunisian Revolution: Contexts, Architects, Prospects*. Edinburgh. Edinburgh University Press, pp. 1–31.

(2013b). Visions of Dissent, Voices of Discontent: Postcolonial Tunisian Film and Song. In N. Gana, ed., *The Making of the Tunisian Revolution: Contexts, Architects, Prospects*. Edinburgh. Edinburgh University Press. pp. 181–203.

(2013c). *The Making of the Tunisian Revolution: Contexts, Architects, Prospects*. Edinburgh. Edinburgh University Press.

George, S. (1998). Fast Castes. In J. Miller and M. Schwarz, eds., *Speed: Visions of an Accelerated Age*. London: Photographers' Gallery; Whitechapel Art Gallery, pp. 115–18.

Georgeon, D. (2012). Revolutionary Graffiti: Street Art and Revolution in Tunisia. *Wasafiri*, 72: 70–75.

Glissant, E. (1990). *Poétique de la relation*. Paris: Gallimard, pp. 203–09.

Goldberg, R. (1979). *Performance: Live Art, 1909 to the Present*. London: Thames and Hudson.

Graham, B. (2010). What Kind of Participative System? Critical Vocabularies from New Media Art. In A. Dezeuze, ed., *The 'Do-It-Yourself' Artwork: Participation from Fluxus to New Media*. Manchester: Manchester University Press, pp. 281–305.

Grenier, C. and C. Boltanski. (2007). *La Vie possible de Christian Boltanski*. Paris: Seuil.

Gruber, C., ed. (2018). Special Issue: Creative Dissent: Visual Arts of the Arab World Uprisings. *Middle East Journal of Culture and Communication*, 11, 2. doi : 10.1163/18739865-01102002.

Guellouz, M. (2013). L'Interview #3: créer, résister – « Je danserai malgré tout » (10 January); at: www.semiozine.com/linterview-3-creer-resister-je-danserai-malgre-tout.

Hafez, S. (2014). The Revolution Shall Not Pass through Women's Bodies: Egypt, Uprising and Gender Politics. *The Journal of North African Studies*, 19, 2 (Special Issue: Women, Gender and the Arab Spring, ed. A. Khalil), 172–85. doi: 10.1080/13629387.2013.879710.

Halasa, M. (2012). Syrian Art Comes of Age, *Ibraaz*, 004 / 21 (November); at: www.ibraaz.org/news/42.

Halasa, M., Z. Omareen and N. Mahfoud, eds. (2014). *Syria Speaks: Art and Culture from the Frontline* [Arabic/English]. London: Saqi Books.

Hall, D. and S. J. Fifer (1990). Introduction: Complexities of an Art Form. In D. Hall and S. J. Fifer, eds., *Illuminating Video: An Essential Guide to Video Art*. New York: Aperture in association with the Bay Area Video Coalition; London: distributed by Hale, pp. 13–30.

Hall, S. (1990). Cultural Identity and Diaspora. In J. Rutherford, ed., *Identity: Community, Culture, Difference*. London: Lawrence and Wishart.

Hallward, P. (2001). *Absolutely Postcolonial: Writing between the Singular and the Specific*. Manchester: Manchester University Press.

Hamid, M. A. (2015a). Storytelling with Majd Abdel Hamid. Part 1. *Ashyaa* (14 December; no author's name provided); at: http://ashyaa-things.tumblr.com/post/135196824676/storytelling1.

(2015b). Storytelling with Majd Abdel Hamid. Part 2. *Ashyaa* (16 December; no author's name provided); at: http://ashyaa-things.tumblr.com/post/135324591416/storytelling2.

(2016). Bouazizi (2012). https://majdabdelhamid.com/ (30 June).

Hariman, R. and J. L. Lucaites. (2007). *No Caption Needed: Iconic Photographs, Public Culture, and Liberal Democracy*. Chicago and London: University of Chicago Press.

Hashemi, N. and D. Postel (2013a). Introduction. Why Syria Matters. In N. Hashemi and D. Postel (eds.), *The Syria Dilemma*. Cambridge, MA, and London: MIT Press, pp. 1–14.

eds. (2013b). *The Syria Dilemma*. Cambridge, MA, and London: MIT Press.

Hashim, A. (2011). What's in a Flag? *Al Jazeera* (24 February); at: www.aljazeera.com/indepth/spotlight/libya/2011/02/2011224123588553.html.

Inda, J. X. and R. Rosaldo (2008). Tracking Global Flows. In J. X. Inda and R. Rosaldo, eds., *The Anthropology of Globalization: A Reader*. Malden, MA, and Oxford: Blackwell, pp. 3–46.

Iskandar, A. (2014). Free? Not So Fast! The Fourth Estate Flourishes and Falters with the Arab Uprisings. In F. Al-Sumait, N. Lenze and M. C. Hudson, eds., *The Arab Uprisings: Catalysts, Dynamics, and Trajectories*. London: Rowman & Littlefield, pp. 133–47.

Ismaël (2012). La Cité du spectacle: à propos de Dream City à Sfax. *Nafas Art Magazine*; available at: https://universes.art/en/nafas/articles/2012/dream-city-sfax/francais.

Jaouad, H. (2011). From the Streets of Tunisia to Wall Street. *Huffpost* (21 December); available at: www.huffpost.com/entry/tunisia-elections_b_1025803.

Jay, P. (2011). *Global Matters: The Transnational Turn in Literary Studies*. Ithaca, NY, and London: Cornell University Press.

Jdey, A. (2017). "Instruments" d'Ismaïl Bahri: délicatesses vidéographiques [copyright: *Nawaat*]; available at: www.selmaferiani.com/instruments-dismail-bahri-delicatesses-videographiques-fr/.

Joffé, G., ed. (2013). *North Africa's Arab Spring*. London: Routledge.

Jones, A. (1994). *Postmodernism and the En-gendering of Marcel Duchamp*. Cambridge [Eng.]. New York: Cambridge University Press.

(1998). The "Pollockian Performative" and the Revision of the Modernist Subject. In A. Jones, *Body Art: Performing the Subject*. Minneapolis: University of Minnesota Press, pp. 53–102.

(2013). The Body and/in Representation. In N. Mirzoeff, ed., *The Visual Culture Reader*, 3rd ed. London and New York: Routledge, pp. 363–83. [First published 2006.]

Jones, C. A. (2006). Form and Formless. In A. Jones, ed. *A Companion to Contemporary Art since 1945*. Malden, MA: Blackwell, 127–43.

Kaabi-Linke, T. (2013). On Revolution and Rubbish. What Has Changed in Tunisia since 2011. *Ibraaz*, 004, 29 January; at: www.ibraaz.org/essays/54.

Kahlaoui, T. (2013). The Powers of Social Media. In N. Gana, ed., *The Making of the Tunisian Revolution: Contexts, Architects, Prospects*. Edinburgh. Edinburgh University Press, pp. 147–58.

Kallel, S. (2012). Sonia Kallel. In B. Barsch and C. Bruckbauer, eds., *Connect: Rosige Zukunft: Aktuelle Kunst aus Tunesien* [French/German/English], translations by A. Baatsch et al. Bielefeld and Berlin: Kerber Verlag, 90–95.

Karoui, S. (2012). Art et politique en Tunisie de 1957 à 2012. In B. Barsch and C. Bruckbauer, eds., *Connect: Rosige Zukunft: Aktuelle Kunst aus Tunesien* [French/German/English], translations by A. Baatsch et al. Bielefeld and Berlin: Kerber Verlag, pp. 203–15.

Katchka, K. (2013). Creative Diffusion. African Intersections in the Biennale Network. In G. Salami and M. Blackmun Visonà (eds.), *A Companion to Modern African Art*. Chichester: Wiley & Sons, Inc., pp. 489–506.

Kester, G. (2004). *Conversation Pieces: Community and Communication in Modern Art*. Berkeley, CA, and London: University of California Press.

(2011). *The One and the Many: Contemporary Collaborative Art in a Global Context*. Durham, NC: Duke University Press.

Khalil, A. (2011). Tunisia's Women: Partners in Revolution. *The Journal of North African Studies*, 19, 2 (Special Issue: Women, Gender and the Arab Spring, ed. A. Khalil), 186–99. doi: 10.1080/13629387.2013.870424.

Khatib, L. (2013). *Image Politics in the Middle East: The Role of the Visual in Political Struggle*. London: I.B. Tauris.

Khatibi, A. (1983). *Maghreb pluriel*. Paris: Denoël.

Khlifi, R. (2013). Indignation. Vu de Tunisie – Je danserai malgré tout. *Courrier International* (6 March 2013); available at: www.courrierinternational.com/article/2013/03/07/vu-de-tunisie-je-danserai-malgre-tout [last accessed October 2020] [original article Tunisian Dancers Take Back the Streets, tunisia-live.net (15 January 2013)].

Khouri, R. G. (2014). Foreword. The Long View of the Arab Uprisings. In Al-Sumait, F., N. Lenze and M. C. Hudson, eds., *The Arab Uprisings: Catalysts, Dynamics, and Trajectories*. London: Rowman & Littlefield, pp. 6–14.

Kilani, M. (2002). *L'Universalisme américain et les banlieues de l'humanité*. Lausanne: Payot.

Kippelen, V. (2017). A Conversation with Lalla Essaydi about 'Bullets,' the Arab Spring and Violence against Women. *Artsatl* (17 February); at: www.artsatl.org/conversation-lalla-essaydi-bullets-arab-spring-violence-women/.

Kraidy, M. (2016). *The Naked Blogger of Cairo: Creative Insurgency in the Arab World*. Cambridge, MA: Harvard University Press.

Kravagna, C. (2010). Working on the Community: Models of Participatory Practice. In A. Dezeuze, ed., *The 'Do-It-Yourself' Artwork: Participation from Fluxus to New Media*. Manchester: Manchester University Press, pp. 240–56.

Labidi, L. (2014a). Political, Aesthetic, and Ethical Positions of Tunisian Women Artists, 2011–13. *The Journal of North African Studies*, 19, 2 (Special Issue: Women, Gender and the Arab Spring, ed. A. Khalil), 157–71. doi: 10.1080/13629387.2014.880826.

(2014b). The Arab Uprisings in Tunisia: Parity, Elections, and the Struggle for Women's Rights. In F. Al-Sumait, N. Lenze and M. C. Hudson, eds., *The Arab Uprisings: Catalysts, Dynamics, and Trajectories*. London: Rowman & Littlefield, pp. 148–70.

Lachman, C. (1992). "The Image Made by Chance" in China and the West: Ink Wang Meets *Jackson Pollock's Mother*. *The Art Bulletin*, 74, 3, 499–510.

Laggoune-Aklouche, N., F-Z. Lakrissa, R. Moumni and P. Sénéchal (2017). La Place institutionnelle de la discipline « l'histoire de l'art » au Maghreb: un état des lieux. *Perspective: Actualité en Histoire de l'Art*, 2; at: https://journals.openedition.org/perspective/7378, 31–48.

Latiri, D. (2013). *Un amour de tn: Carnet photographique d'un retour au pays natal après la Révolution*. Tunis: Editions Elyzad.

Le Bars, S. (2012). Un artiste marocain se résout à retirer une œuvre jugée blasphématoire. *Le Monde*, 6 October; available at www.lemonde.fr/societe/article/2012/10/06/un-artiste-marocain-se-resout-a-retirer-une-uvre-jugee-blasphematoire_1771154_3224.html.

Lionnet, F. (2011). Counterpoint and Double Critique in Edward Said and Abdelkebir Khatibi: A Transcolonial Comparison. In A. Behdad and D. Thomas, eds., *A Companion to Comparative Literature*. Malden, MA, and Oxford: Blackwell, pp. 387–407.

Lionnet, F. and Shu-Mei Shih, eds. (2005). *Minor Transnationalism*. Durham, NC: Duke University Press.

Lloyd, F. (1999). *Dialogues of the Present: Women Artists of the Arab World*. London: Women's Art Library.

ed. (1999). *Contemporary Arab Women's Art: Dialogues of the Present*. London: Women's Art Library/I.B. Tauris.

ed. (2001). *Displacement and Difference: Contemporary Arab Visual Culture in the Diaspora*. London: Saffron Books.

L'Orient-Le Jour/Agences (2012). Dégagements... La Tunisie un an après. *L'Orient-Le Jour*, 18 February [no author named]; at: www.lorientlejour.com/article/745696/%2522Degagements..._la_Tunisie_un_an_apres%2522.html.

Lyons, J. D. (2014). The French Aesthetics of Contingency. *SpazioFilosofico*, 12 (October), 417–37.

Machghoul. A. (2012a). Enfin libres! L'espace public en Tunisie est-il aujourd'hui vraiment public? In B. Barsch and C. Bruckbauer, eds., *Connect: Rosige Zukunft: Aktuelle Kunst aus Tunesien* [French/German/English], translations by A. Baatsch et al. Bielefeld and Berlin: Kerber Verlag, pp. 131–49.

(2012b). « Tisser la médina » de Sonia Kallel, une œuvre en hommage aux tisserands. (27 September); available at: www.mille-et-une-tunisie.com/accueil/magazine/3729-l-tisser-la-medina-r-de-sonia-kallel-une-uvre-en-hommage-aux-tisserants-.html.

(2013). Tunisie: l'art en espace public, révélateur des enjeux d'une société. *Archivio Antropologico Mediterraneo*, XVI 15, 1, 29–44; at: www.archivioantropologicomediterraneo.it/riviste/estratti_15-1/05.pdf.

Maghraoui, D. (2011). Constitutional Reforms in Morocco: Between Consensus and Subaltern Politics. *The Journal of North African Studies*, 16, 4 (Special Issue: North Africa's Arab Spring, ed. G. Joffé), 679–99. doi: 10.1080/13629387.2011.630879.

Malivel, G. (2013). Ici, ailleurs. Trajectoires méditerranéennes. *ART ABSOLUMENT* (March–April), 60–63. Extract on Mouna Karray's *Noir* available at mounakarray.com.

Malone, M., ed. (2009). *Chance Aesthetics*. St. Louis, MO: Mildred Lane Kempner Art Museum.

Manovich, L. (2001). *The Language of New Media*. Cambridge, MA, and London: MIT Press.

Marboeuf, O. (2013a). "De magie à possession". *Journal Phantom*, 3; at: www.khiasma.net/magazine/bahri-ismail-magie-possession/.

(2013b). « Filmer à blanc ». *Journal Phantom*, 5; at: www.khiasma.net/magazine/filmer_a_blanc/.

(2013c). Dialogue between Ismaïl Bahri and Olivier Marboeuf, Marseille, FID Marseille International Cinema Festival (July); at www.ismailbahri.lautre.net/index/php?/textes/; original text at: www.phantom-productions.org/blog/entretien-avec-ismail-bahri-2/.

Marks, L. U. (1999). *The Skin of the Film: Intercultural Cinema, Embodiment and the Senses*. Durham, NC: Duke University Press.

(2014). Arab Glitch. In A. Downey, ed., *Uncommon Grounds: New Media and Critical Practices in North Africa and the Middle East*. London: I.B. Tauris, pp. 257–71.

Marzouki, N. (2013). From Resistance to Governance: The Category of Civility in the Political Theory of Tunisian Islamists. In N. Gana, ed., *The Making of the Tunisian Revolution: Contexts, Architects, Prospects*. Edinburgh. Edinburgh University Press, pp. 207–23.

Massoud, R. (2012). Je danserai malgré tout … dans les rues de Tunis. *L'Orient-Le Jour* (12 December); at: www.lorientlejour.com/article/791895/Je_danserai_malgre_tout..._dans_les_rues_de_Tunis.html.

Meador, D. (2012). Arab Spring Meets Warhol in Ramallah Show. *The Electronic Intifada* (4 December); at: http://electronicintifada.net/content/arab-spring-meets-warhol-ramallah-show/11967.

Mercer, K., ed. (2008). *Exiles, Diasporas and Strangers*. Cambridge, MA: MIT Press; London: Institute of International Visual Art.

Mercier, J. (2014). Portfolio. Mouna Karray. Noir. *L'Œil de la photographie* (5 June); at: www.mounakarray.com/texts/jeanne-mercier-noir-oeil-de-la-photographie.html.

Merone, F. and F. Cavatorta (2013). The Rise of Salafism and the Future of Democratization. In N. Gana, ed., *The Making of the Tunisian Revolution: Contexts, Architects, Prospects*. Edinburgh. Edinburgh University Press, pp. 252–69.

Messoudy, H. (2011). 'Two Daughters of the Same Parents'. In P. Zoghbi and D. Karl, eds., *Arabic Graffiti*. Berlin: From Here to Fame, pp. 31–32.

Mignolo, W. (2011). *The Darker Side of Western Modernity: Global Futures, Decolonial Options*. Durham, NC: Duke University Press.

Mirzoeff. N., ed. (2000). *Diaspora Visual Culture: Representing Africans and Jews*. London: Routledge.

Moma.org. (n.d.). Gold Marilyn Monroe. Andy Warhol (American, 1928–1987); at: www.moma.org/learn/moma_learning/andy-warhol-gold-marilyn-monroe-1962/.

Morgan, H. (2016). A Single Body, Suppressed. Museum, 4 (March); at: www.mounakarray.com/texts/KARRAY-Mouna-2016-03-00-Museum.pdf.

Mondomix (2012). Festival Libertés à l'ICI – Majida Khattari. Available at: www.youtube.com/watch?v=pMeG22ENW8o (posted 19 July 2012).

Morineau, C. (2006). De l'imprégnation à l'empreinte, de l'artiste au modèle, de la couleur à son incarnation. In C. Morineau (ed.), *Yves Klein: corps, couleur, immatériel*. Paris: Centre Pompidou, pp. 120–29.

Morris, N. and D. J. Rothman, eds. (1995). *The Oxford History of the Prison*. Oxford: Oxford University Press.

Morton, P. (2000). *Hybrid Modernities: Architecture and Representation at the 1931 Colonial Exposition, Paris.* Cambridge, MA, and London: The MIT Press.

Mosaic Initiative. (2012). #withoutwords Artist Profile: Hazar Bakbachi-Henriot [no named author]; at: https://mosaicinitiative.org.uk/without words-hazar-bakbachi-henriot-artist-profile/ [last accessed October 2020].

Murphy, E. C. (2013). Under the Emperor's Neoliberal Clothes! Why the International Financial Institutions Got It Wrong in Tunisia. In N. Gana, ed., *The Making of the Tunisian Revolution: Contexts, Architects, Prospects.* Edinburgh. Edinburgh University Press, pp. 35–57.

Musée du Louvre. (n.d.). La Liberté guidant le peuple. Dossier Documentaire'; *at:* www.louvre.fr/sites/default/files/medias_fichiers/fich iers/pdf/louvre-la-liberte-guidant-le-peuple-dossier-documentaire.pdf.

Naef, S. (1992). *L'Art de l'écriture arabe: passé et présent.* Geneva: Slatkine.

Nakhli, A. (2017). L'Écrit dans les arts visuels en Tunisie (1960–2015). *Perspective: Actualité en Histoire de l'Art*, 2; at: https://journals .openedition.org/perspective/7378, 221–28.

Nasser-Khadivi, D. and Rafif, A. C., eds. (2015). *Lalla Essaydi. Crossing Boundaries. Bridging Cultures.* Courbevoie (Paris): ACR Edition.

Naumann, F. M. (1999). *Marcel Duchamp: The Art of Making Art in the Age of Mechanical Reproduction.* New York and London: Harry N. Abrams.

Nochlin, L. (1991). The Imaginary Orient. In L. Nochlin, *The Politics of Vision: Essays on Nineteenth-Century Art and Society.* Oxford and New York: Routledge, pp. 33–59.

O'Brien, D. J. and Prochaska, D. (2004). *Beyond East and West: Seven Transnational Artists.* Krannert Art Museum.

Olcèse, R. (2013). Exposer la lumière, *A bras le corps* (December); at: www .abraslecorps.com/pages/magazine.php?id_mag=104.

Ouissi, S. and Ouissi, S. (2007). Dream City – Edition 2007; at: www.lartrue.com/.

Ounaina, H. (2012). De la censure artistique en Tunisie: lecture sociohistorique. In B. Barsch and C. Bruckbauer, eds., *Connect: Rosige Zukunft: Aktuelle Kunst aus Tunesien* [French/German/English], translations by A. Baatsch et al. Bielefeld and Berlin: Kerber Verlag, pp. 183–201.

Pigeat, A. (2013). Introducing Ismaïl Bahri. *Art Press*, 406 (December; translated by C. Penwarden), 47–49.

Piot, O. (2011). *La Révolution tunisienne: dix jours qui ébranlèrent le monde arabe.* Paris: Les Petits Matins.

Pratt, M. L. (1992). *Imperial Eyes: Travel Writing and Transculturation.* London: Routledge.

Rahn, J. (2002). *Painting without Permission: Hip-Hop Graffiti Subculture*. Westport, CT, and London: Bergin & Garvey.

Rancière, J. (2004). *The Politics of Aesthetics: The Distribution of the Sensible*, translation and introduction by G. Rockhill. London and New York: Continuum. [First published 2000.]

Reigeluth, S., ed. (2013). Q&A: Ismaïl Bahri and Black Ink, *Revolve* (2 November); at: www.revolve-magazine.com/home/2013/11/02/qa-ismail-bahri-and-black-ink/ [no author named; first published in Revolve's Tunisia Report 2013, ed. S. Reigeluth].

Rothberg, M. (2009). *Multidirectional Memory: Remembering the Holocaust in the Age of Decolonisation*. Stanford, CA: Stanford University Press.

Roy, O. (2012). The New Islamists: How the Most Extreme Adherents of Radical Islam are Getting with the Times. *Foreign Policy* (16 April); at: www.foreignpolicy.com/articles/2012/04/16/the_new_islamists?page=0,2.

Ryan, Y. (2011). Art Challenges Tunisian Revolutionaries. *Al Jazeera* (26 March); at: www.aljazeera.com/indepth/features/2011/03/201132223217876176.html.

Saadeh, R. (2013). In Conversation with Raeda Saadeh. *A Room of My Own*; at: http://aroomofmyown.net/2013/02/26/in-conversation-with-raeda-saadeh/ [no author named; first published at The International Museum of Women (February)].

Safadi, R. and Neaime, S. (2016). Syria: The Painful Transition towards Democracy. In I. Elbadawi and S. Madkisi (eds.), *Democratic Transitions in the Arab World*. Cambridge: Cambridge University Press, pp. 184–208.

Said, E. (1994). *Culture and Imperialism*. London: Vintage. [First published 1993.]

(1995). *Orientalism: Western Conceptions of the Orient*. Harmondsworth: Penguin. [First published 1978.]

Salah-Omri, M. (2012). A Revolution of Dignity and Poetry. *Boundary 2*, 39, 1, 137–65; at: www.researchgate.net/publication/259926758_A_Revolution_of_Dignity_and_Poetry.

(2013). Writing African Modernism into Art History. In G. Salami. and M. Blackmun Visonà (eds.), *A Companion to Modern African Art*. Chichester: Wiley & Sons, Inc., pp. 3–19.

Salami. G. and M. Blackmun Visonà, eds. (2013). *A Companion to Modern African Art*. Chichester: Wiley & Sons, Inc.

Shilton, S. (2013a). *Transcultural Encounters: Gender and Genre in Franco-Maghrebi Art*. Manchester: Manchester University Press.

(2013b). Art and the Arab Spring: Aesthetics of Revolution in Contemporary Tunisia. *French Cultural Studies*, 24, 129–45; at: https://doi.org/10.1177/0957155812464166.

(2016). Digital Art and the Tunisian Revolution. *Wasafiri: The Magazine of International Contemporary Literature*, 31, 4 (Special issue: Print Activism Twenty-First Century Africa, guest edited by Ruth Bush and Madhu Krishnan), 69–75; at: http://dx.doi.org/10.1080/02690055.2016.1218114.

(2018). Identity and 'Difference' in French Art: El Seed's Calligraffiti from Street to Web. In K. Kleppinger and L. Reeck, eds., *Post-Migratory Cultures in Postcolonial France*. Liverpool: Liverpool University Press, pp. 239–56.

Shohat, E. and R. Stam (1994). *Unthinking Eurocentrism: Multiculturalism and the Media*. London: Routledge.

Spivak, G. (1988). Can the Subaltern Speak?. In C. Nelson and L. Grossberg, eds., *Marxism and the Interpretation of Culture*. Basingstoke: Macmillan Education, pp. 271–313.

Stirner, M. (1899). *L'Unique et sa propriété*. Paris: P. V. Stock, Editeur; trans. Robert L. Reclaire. [First published 1845.]

Stonock, L. (2016). Mapping the Possible: Syrian Organizations, Movements and Platforms. *Ibraaz*, 010_07 / 9 (December); at: http://dx.doi.org/10.17613/M6TZ6H.

Swartz, A. (1997). Accession II: Eva Hesse's Response to Minimalism. *Bulletin of the Detroit Institute of Arts*, 71, 1/2, pp. 36–47; at: http://dx.doi.org/10.17613/M6TZ6H.

Tate Modern. (2014). Mira Schendal, 01 March – 24 June 2014, Tate Modern, London and Pinacoteca do Estado de Sao Paulo; at: www.serralves.pt/documentos/Roteiros/MiraSchendel_Eng.pdf. [Exhibition document; no author's name provided.]

Tate.org. (n.d. a). 'Suprematism'; at: www.tate.org.uk/art/art-terms/s/suprematism.

(n.d. b). 'What Was Andy Warhol Thinking?'; at: www.tate.org.uk/art/artists/andy-warhol-2121/what-was-andy-warhol-thinking.

Teather, D. (2009). Recession and Debt Dissolve Dubai's Mirage in the Desert. *The Guardian* (*The Observer*, 29 November), at: www.guardian.co.uk/business/2009/nov/29/dubai-financial-crisis.

The Museum of Modern Art. (2004). *MoMA Highlights*. New York: The Museum of Modern Art. [First published 1999.]

Tlili, H. (2012). Entre Orient et Occident: l'évolution de l'art plastique en Tunisie. In B. Barsch and C. Bruckbauer, eds., *Connect: Rosige Zukunft: Aktuelle Kunst aus Tunesien* [French/German/English], translations by A. Baatsch et al. Bielefeld and Berlin: Kerber Verlag, pp. 161–81.

Tn News. (2012). Chkoun Ahna: Exploring Tunisian Identity through Art. *Tn News*; *at*: http://tn-news.com/v4_portal/article/view/2223299.

Triki, R. (2009). Art et résistance transculturelle. *Museum International*, no. 244, 61, 4, 54–62.

(2012a). Tunisia: A Dynamic and Vigilant Art Scene. *Nafas Art Magazine* (February); at: http://universes-in-universe.org/eng/nafas/articles/2012/tunisia_art_scene.

(2012b). Une scène artistique résistante. In B. Barsch and C. Bruckbauer, eds., *Connect: Rosige Zukunft: Aktuelle Kunst aus Tunesien* [French/German/English], translations by A. Baatsch et al. Bielefeld and Berlin: Kerber Verlag, 35–49.

(2013). Enjeux sociopolitiques des arts contemporains en Tunisie. *Archivio Antropologico Mediterraneo*, XVI 15, 1, 25–28; at: www.archivioantropologicomediterraneo.it/riviste/estratti_15-1/04.pdf.

(2017). L'Art au Maghreb: de l'appropriation à la réécriture. *Perspective: Actualité en Histoire de l'Art*, 2; at: https://journals.openedition.org/perspective/7378, 9–13.

Tripp, C. (2013). *The Power and the People: Paths of Resistance in the Middle East*. Cambridge: Cambridge University Press.

Verlaine, P. (1942). *Sagesse*. Cambridge: Cambridge University Press. [First published 1880.]

Warhol, A. and P. Hackett (1980). *POPism: The Warhol '60s*. San Diego, NY, and London: Harcourt Brace Jovanovich.

Warr, T., ed. (2000). *The Artist's Body*. London: Phaidon Press.

Westgeest, H. (1996). *Zen in the Fifties: Interaction in Art between East and West*. Zwolle: Waanders.

Whiting, C. (1987). Andy Warhol: The Public Star and the Private Self. *Oxford Art Journal*, 10, 2, 58–75.

Wiley, G. (2013). REVIEWED: Lalla Essaydi: Beyond Beauty. *ArtworldNow: Contemporary Art around the Globe* (29 November); at: lallaessaydi.com/news/PDFS/Reviews/Artworldnow_Nov_2013.pdf.

Wooster, A. S. (1990). Reach Out and Touch Someone: the Romance of Interactivity. In D. Hall and S. J. Fifer, eds., *Illuminating Video: An Essential Guide to Video Art*. New York: Aperture in association with the Bay Area Video Coalition; London: distributed by Hale.

Young Artist of the Year Award 2012 Brochure (in English and Arabic); available at: https://issuu.com/qattan.foundation/docs/yaya_2012_brochure.

Index

Abassi, Asma, 64
Adcock, Craig, 48
Adnen, 203
Ahl Al Kahf, 15, 35, 172, 202, 207–11, 214–15, 217–19
Al Mahdy, Aliaa, 10, 166–67
Al-Arabi Al-Hor, 202
Allani, Alaya, 56, 150
Allenby, Jeni, 127
Alley, Ronald, 63
Al-Messadi, Mahmoud, 4
Al-Shami, Leïla, 20
Al-Sumait, Fahed, et al., 2, 6, 43, 53
Ammar, Hela, 202
Appadurai, Arjun, 25–26
Arab Spring, 1–7
Arab Uprisings, 2–3, 6–7
Aragon, Louis, 185
Aranda, Samuel, 34, 166, 178, 180, 185
Arebi, Naziha, 35, 171, 191–97, 200–1, 209
Arp, Jean, 76
Art Solution, 14–15, 35, 172, 202–3, 215–19
Asad, Amira, 127–28, 130
Attia, Kader, 27, 71, 97
Ayédadjou, Tobi, 134

Bahnasi, Afif, 23
Bahri, Ismaïl, 33, 81, 98, 100, 103–12, 114–15, 144, 146, 206
Bailey, David, 22
Bakbachi-Henriot, Hazar, 157–58, 226
Bank, Charlotte, 196
Banksy, 207
Barakat, Sophia, 202
Barrada, Yto, 99–100, 113, 115
Barthes, Roland, 103
Bataille, Georges, 28, 79, 97, 227

Batal, Dia, 160
Bathurst, Matilda, 155
Bayat, Asef, 6, 64
Belhassine, Olfa, 57
Belkadhi, Mohamed Ali, 5, 8
Ben Azouz, Inès, 87–88
Ben Jelloun, Tahar, 44, 49
Ben Labidi, Imed, 2, 4
Ben Mhenni, Lina, 23
Ben Rejeb, Lofti, 9, 52
Ben Salah, Saloua, 135
Ben Slama, Mohamed, 5
Ben Soltane, Mohamed, 5–6, 24–25, 46, 64, 76, 103, 123
Ben Yahmed, Bahri, 203, 215–17
Ben Yakoub, Joachim, 11
Benaïssa, Khaled, 114
Benyahia, Samta, 71
Berrebi, Marco, 213, 215
Bhabha, Homi, 22, 41
Bishop, Claire, 29, 78, 121–22, 126, 213, 227
Blackmun Visonà, Monica, 28, 40
Bois, Yves-Alain, 79
Boltanski, Christian, 69
Bordier, Dominique, 158
Bouanani, Medhi, 5
Bouderbala, Meriem, 30, 32, 60, 81–82, 87–91, 93–94, 96, 105, 168–69, 175, 179, 186, 190–91, 220
Boudjelal, Bruno, 100
Bourriaud, Nicolas, 29, 121
Bouzid, Nouri, 4
Bowcock, Simon, 189
Bredoux, Lenaig, 9
Breton, André, 76
Brownlee, Jason, et al., 2–4
Bruckbauer, Christine, 5, 19, 29, 77, 86, 122

245

Cage, John, 76–77, 109
Calle, Sophie, 80
Charrad, Mounira, 56, 150
Chebbi, Abou Al-Kasem, 4–5, 20
Chenon Ramlat, Adeline, 214–15
Cheu, Chouaib, 203
Clifford, James, 17
Cohen Hadria, Michèle, 5
Collectif La Luna, 134
Collectif Wanda, 15–16, 34, 117, 124, 137, 142, 149, 157, 161
Collet, Bernard, 55, 188
Constant, Benjamin, 177
contingent encounters of resistance, 28–29, 32, 74–165, 227
Crinson, Mark, 22
Cronin, Michael, 111

Dada, Ghada, 203
Dagher, Charbel, 23
Dakhlia, Jocelyne, 1, 9, 43, 49, 85, 90, 152
Dargueche, Wissal, 202
David, Jacques-Louis, 177–78
Davila, Thierry, 40, 95
Davis, Mary E., 187
de Certeau, Michel, 102, 105, 140
Debarrah, Hamid, 71
Debord, Guy, 28, 80, 99, 112, 227
Dedman, Rachel, 128–29, 159
Delacroix, Eugène, 8, 168, 173, 180, 183–85, 199
Dempsey, Amy, 80
Depardon, Raymond, 80
Dezeuze, Anna, 78, 120–21
Dirié, Clément, 93
Dou Di, Nahed, 203
Dourai, Rania, 202
Downey, Anthony, 10, 20
Dream City, 5, 16, 19, 60, 78, 122, 124, 136–37, 141–43, 145, 149, 190
Drewal, Henry John, 25–26, 28, 40, 226
Driss, Hichem, 202
Duchamp, Marcel, 12, 27, 32, 38, 40–44, 46–50, 54, 59, 63, 65–66, 68–69, 72, 76, 95–96, 146, 223–24
Dunoyer, Béatrice, 131, 134

Dunoyer, Béatrice, et al., 131
Durand, Régis, 97

Echakhch, Latifa, 93
Eco, Umberto, 76, 78
El Fani, Nadia, 20
El Général, 5, 20
El Madinati, 202–3, 208–10
El Seed, 35, 172, 202–9, 211–12, 214–15, 217, 219
Eluard, Paul, 180
Ennahda, 3, 81, 85, 88, 187
Entelis, John P., 113
Enwezor, Okwui, 22
Erruas, Safaa, 15, 32, 36, 42, 53–57, 59, 61, 69–70, 82, 90, 128, 147, 188, 193, 226
Essaydi, Lalla, 34, 170, 172–79, 181–85, 187, 189–90, 193, 200–1

Fatmi, Mounir, 15, 25, 27, 32, 36, 42, 50–54, 70, 97, 112, 146
Fautrier, Jean, 79–80, 97, 227
Favaretto, Lara, 33, 81–82, 93–94, 97, 112, 161
Febrik, 18, 34, 124, 143, 153–57, 161, 199
Fedhila, Moufida, 78, 143, 152
Ferdman, Bertie, 215
Ferhani, Hassen, 114
Fifer, Sally-Jo, 103
Filali, Aïcha, 5, 15, 32, 36, 42, 53, 61, 63–68, 70–71, 81–86, 92, 94, 99, 113, 130, 147, 150, 161, 180, 190
Fisher, Jean, 23, 41
Flaubert, Gustave, 187
Foster, Hal, 30, 122, 126, 213, 227

Gafaïti, Hafid, 23
Gana, Nouri, 4–7, 15, 20, 43, 64, 92, 96, 101
Gasteli, Jellel, 7, 9, 87, 222
George, Saadeh, 71
George, Susan, 102
Georgeon, Dounia, 10
Ghozlani, Wassim, 5, 99, 113, 130, 146
Glissant, Edouard, 31, 50
Goldberg, RoseLee, 96
Gorani, Joude, 113
Graham, Beryl, 119, 126, 162–63

Index

Grenier, Catherine, 69
Gruber, Christiane, 10
Guellouz, Mariem, 216

Hafez, Khaled, 159
Hafez, Sherine, 10–11, 167, 174
Halasa, Malu, 15, 20
Halasa, Malu, et al., 20
Hall, Douglas, 103
Hall, Stuart, 112
Hallward, Peter, 41
Hamid, Majd Abdel, 13, 15, 23, 33, 74, 117, 123–32, 134–35, 137, 141–42, 157–59, 187, 226
Hamwi, Azza, 19, 33, 113, 228
Hariman, Robert, 8, 11, 167
Hashemi, Nader, 43, 62
Hashim, Asad, 192
Hatoum, Mona, 175
Hesse, Eva, 60
Hessel, Stéphane, 216–18
Holbein the Younger, Hans, 178
Horani, Philip, 15, 19, 35, 171–72, 191, 196–201, 203, 206, 210

Inda, Jonathan Xavier, 23, 26
infra-thin critique, 27, 31, 36–73, 226
Iskandar, Adel, 7, 130
Ismaël, 141

Jaou, 19
Jaouad, Hedi, 4
Jay, Paul, 17, 25–26, 226
Jdey, Adnen, 103
Jemal Siala, Mouna, 13, 15–16, 34, 59, 117, 124, 143, 148–53, 155, 157, 161, 187, 190, 213
Jones, Amelia, 30, 169–70, 179, 186, 198, 203, 206, 220, 228
Jones, Caroline A., 79, 227
JR, 35, 65, 78, 143, 152, 172, 202, 210–17, 219, 228

Kaabi-Linke, Nadia, 33, 74, 81–82, 91–95, 112
Kaabi-Linke, Timo, 91, 94
Kahlaoui, Tarek, 4

Kallel, Sonia, 15–16, 34, 36, 42, 53–54, 56–61, 64, 70–71, 123, 130–31, 134–42, 147, 149–50, 157, 159, 161–63
Kameli, Katia, 99, 113–14, 195, 209
Karabibene, Halim, 5, 159
Karoui, Selima, 29, 123
Karray, Mouna, 13, 33, 35, 61, 74, 81, 98, 100–5, 109, 112, 114, 140, 144, 159, 171–72, 188–91, 199–201, 204, 206, 209–10
Katchka, Kinsey, 79
Kester, Grant, 29, 121, 128, 137
Khalil, Andrea, 1, 85
Khatib, Lina, 9–11
Khatibi, Abdelkebir, 22, 56
Khattari, Majida, 34, 61, 171–72, 175, 179–87, 189–90, 200–1
Khayata, Mohammed, 162–63
Khiari, Nadia, 20
Khlifi, Roua, 218
Khouri, Rami G., 2–4, 6–7, 41, 85, 152, 181
Khrayyif, Bashir, 4
Kilani, Mondher, 25, 76, 92
Klein, Yves, 27, 68, 96
Klimt, Gustav, 175, 178
Kossentini, Nicène, 5, 12, 15, 18, 32, 36, 42, 44–50, 52–53, 56, 66, 68, 70, 82, 85, 94, 146, 161
Kraidy, Marwan, 10–11, 63, 165–68
Krauss, Rosalind, 79
Kravagna, Christian, 117, 120, 126, 140
Krifa, Michket, 7, 87

Labidi, Lilia, 10, 56, 150
Lachman, Charles, 77
Laggoune-Aklouche, Nadia, et al., 17
Lamine, Hela, 12, 15, 32, 74, 81–82, 86–87, 93–96, 102–3, 186
Laroussi el-Metoui, Mohamed, 4
Latiri, Dora, 23
Le Bars, Stéphanie, 38
Lionnet, Françoise, 22, 26
Lloyd, Fran, 22, 71
Lucaites, John, 8, 11, 167
Lyons, John D., 76

Machghoul, Aurélie, 5, 78, 122, 137, 152
Maghraoui, Driss, 113
Magnaudeix, Mathieu, 9
Malevich, Kasimir, 54–55
Malivel, Garance, 188, 191
Malone, Meredith, 76
Man Ray, 95
Manovich, Lev, 169
Marboeuf, Olivier, 112
Marks, Laura U., 77, 109, 169
Marzouki, Nadia, 1, 85
Massi, Souad, 197–98, 200
Massoud, Rania, 215
Maz, Bahri, 203
Meador, Daryl, 67
Mercer, Kobena, 22
Mercier, Jeanne, 189
Merone, Fabio, 92
Messoudy, Hassan, 77
Mhiri, Wadi, 13, 15–16, 34, 117, 124, 143, 148–53, 155, 157, 161, 213
Michelangelo, 54, 166, 178, 180, 185–86
Mignolo, Walter, 17, 25, 76, 92
minor transnational, 23
Mirzoeff, Nicholas, 23
modernism, 28
Monet, Claude, 87–89
Morineau, Camille, 68
Morris, Norval, 144
Morton, Patricia, 10
multidirectional, 22
multi-layered interface, 30–31, 34–35, 166–221, 224–25, 227

Naef, Silvia, 23
Nakhli, Alia, 23, 46
Neaime, Simon, 43, 62
Neshat, Shirin, 175
Nochlin, Linda, 206

O'Brien, David J., 22
Okeke-Agulu, Chika, 22
Ondak, Roman, 27
opacity, 31
Ouissi, Selma and Sofiane, 5, 13, 15, 19, 33, 78, 117, 122–23, 130–37, 142, 157, 159, 226
Ounaina, Hamdi, 5, 123

Pigeat, Anaël, 106
Piot, Olivier, 10
Pollock, Jackson, 76, 198, 206
Postel, Danny, 43, 62
Pratt, Mary Louise, 28
Prochaska, David, 22

Rafif, Ahmed-Chaouki and Dina Nasser-Khadivi et al., 177
Rahn, Janice, 202
Rancière, Jacques, 20, 222
Reigeluth, Stuart, 110
revolution, 7
Rieffel, Véronique, 180
Rosaldo, Renato, 23, 26
Rothberg, Michael, 22
Rothman, David J., 144
Roy, Olivier, 10, 84

Saadeh, Raeda, 161
Safadi, Raed, 43, 62
Safadi, Shada, 15, 32, 36, 42, 53, 61–62, 67–70, 160–61
Said, Edward, 22, 206
Salah-Omri, Mohamed, 5
Salami, Gitti, 28, 40
Salih Al-Jabiri, Muhammad, 4
Sboui, Amina, 10–11, 166–67
Schendel, Mira, 55
Sedira, Zineb, 71
Shih, Shu-Mei, 23, 26
Shohat, Ella, 22
Siddons, Alastair, 202, 210–15
Spivak, Gayatri, 22
Stam, Robert, 22
Stella, Frank, 139
Stirner, Max, 76
Stonock, Lois, 20
Swartz, Anne, 60

Tawadros, Gilane, 22
Teather, David, 52
Tlatli, Moufida, 4
Tlili, Hocine, 25, 46, 65
Tlili, Ridha, 202, 207–11, 218
Tnani, Aziz, 202
transcultural, 28
    résistance transculturelle, 24

Index

transnational, 24–27
Triki, Patricia, 5, 19, 29, 77, 86, 122
Triki, Rachida, 17, 19, 24–25, 46, 57–58, 123, 208
Tripp, Charles, 10
Troudi, Oussema, 98, 146, 159, 162
Tuma, Tarek, 70
Tzara, Tristan, 96

Verlaine, 144–45, 147

Warhol, Andy, 125, 127, 130
Warr, Tracy, 218
Westgeest, Helen, 77
Whiting, Cécile, 127
Wiley, Gloria, 175, 178
Wooster, Ann Sargent, 120

Zarouar, Hocine, 178
Zran, Mohamed, 4

Printed in the USA
CPSIA information can be obtained
at www.ICGtesting.com
CBHW070329240824
13631CB00005B/433